MARLBOROUGH'S BATTLEFIELDS

JAMES FALKNER'S

GUIDE TO

MARLBOROUGH'S
BATTLEFIELDS

by

James Falkner

Pen & Sword
MILITARY

First published in Great Britain in 2008 by
Pen & Sword Military
an imprint of
Pen & Sword Books Ltd
47 Church Street
Barnsley
South Yorkshire
S70 2AS

ISBN: 978-1-84415-632-0

A CIP catalogue record for this book is
available from the British Library.

Typeset in 9.5/11.5 Palatino by
Concept, Huddersfield.

Printed and bound in England by
CPI UK.

Pen & Sword Books Ltd incorporates the imprints of Pen & Sword
Aviation, Pen & Sword Maritime, Pen & Sword Military, Wharncliffe
Local History, Pen and Sword Select, Pen and Sword Military Classics
and Leo Cooper.

For a complete list of Pen & Sword titles please contact
PEN & SWORD BOOKS LIMITED
47 Church Street, Barnsley, South Yorkshire, S70 2AS, England
E-mail: enquiries@pen-and-sword.co.uk
Website: www.pen-and-sword.co.uk

CONTENTS

LIST OF MAPS

LIST OF COLOUR PLATES

A kneeling British Grenadier gathers captured French colours. (*From the Blenheim Tapestry. By kind permission of His Grace the Duke of Marlborough*)

The Schellenberg Tapestry. (*By kind permission of his Grace the Duke of Marlborough*)

The 1st English Foot Guards wade the Nebel stream to attack Blindheim village.

Houses in Blindheim village, contemporary with the battle in 1704.

A plan of the famous victory at Blenheim obtained by his Grace the Duke of Marlborough over the Elector of Bavaria and Marshals Tallard and Marsin, the 13th August 1704.

The Duke of Marlborough on the field of Blenheim. (*From the Blenheim Tapestry. By kind permission of his Grace the Duke of Marlborough*)

Ramillies. Marlborough's horse stumbles, and the Duke is thrown to the ground.

Ramillies. Marlborough and his staff oversee the cavalry battle. (*Courtesy of the Marquess of Anglesey*)

Walled farmhouse in Offuz, scene of Earl Orkney's infantry attack, 23 May 1706.

The great cavalry pursuit after Ramillies. (*Courtesy of the Marquess of Anglesey*)

18th century map of the Oudenarde battlefield. (*Courtesy of Erik Wauters*)

The Oudenarde Tapestry at Blenheim Palace. (*By kind permission of his Grace the Duke of Marlborough*)

The Allied and French infantry struggle for possession of the Bois de Sars Triangle at Malplaquet.

Prince Eugene of Savoy, Marlborough's comrade and close friend. A contemporary cartoon portrait. (*Author's collection*)

THE NETHERLANDS
Campaigns of 1702–13

- - - Boundary of Spanish Netherlands
✕ Marlborough's battles

0 10 20 30 40
⌐————————————————⌐ Miles

N

HOLLAND

ENGLAND

Str. of Dover

THE HAGUE RYSWICK
ROTTERDAM
R. Rhine
R. Waal
R. Maas

ZEELAND
WALCHEREN
FLUSHING
BERGEN-OP-ZOOM

ECKEREN
ANTWERP
DOVER
OSTEND BRUGES
NIEUPORT WYNENDAEL
DUNKIRK
CALAIS
GHENT
DENDERMONDE
R. Ysel
Lines of Brabant
R. Dyle
R. Demer
BOULOGNE
YPRES
COURTRAI
ALOST
LOUVAIN
MENIN
OUDENARDE
R. Ysche BRUSSELS
R. Gheete
ELIXHEIM
AIRE ST VENANT
R. Scheldt
SP. NETHERLANDS
RAMILLIES
BETHUNE LILLE TOURNAI ATH
R. Dyle
NAMUR
MORTAGNE
Flanders
ST GHISLAIN MONS CHARLEROI
R. Sambre R. Meuse
R. Deule
Lines of Non Plus Ultra
DOUAI VALENCIENNES
MALPLAQUET
ARRAS ARLEUX BOUCHAIN MAUBERGE
R. Scheldt
ABBEVILLE
CAMBRAI LE CATEAU

R. Somme
AMIENS ST QUENTIN R. Oise
SEDAN

FRANCE

PREFACE

Between 1704 and 1709, during the War of the Spanish Succession, John Churchill, 1st Duke of Marlborough, led the armies of the Grand Alliance to win four major victories over the renowned French armies of the Sun King, Louis XIV. The astonishing achievement by Queen Anne's Captain-General effectively limited the martial power of France for a generation and more. Not until the ambitious career of Napoleon would that nation again be able, albeit for a relatively short period, to dominate much of western Europe as Louis XIV had done for so many years in the latter part of the seventeenth century.

The Marshals of France whom Marlborough defeated were the most distinguished soldiers of their time; they had acquired a tradition of victory. England, by contrast, started the war as a relatively insignificant power militarily, and Marlborough's own reputation as an army commander was so far rather slim. With the victories at Blenheim, Ramillies and Oudenarde all this changed. By the time of the more qualified success at Malplaquet in 1709 Marlborough had become the acknowledged foremost Captain of his generation, and professional soldiers from all over Europe hurried to join his armies and take part of the glory that he won. By contrast, Louis XIV was in despair at the repeated failures of his commanders and the fact that northern France had been invaded, much of it laid to waste on Marlborough's orders. The King acknowledged his defeat and would offer much for peace, almost at any price. Only short-sighted fumbling by the parties to the Grand Alliance allowed him, and his armies, to recover much of what had been lost by the untidy close of the war in 1713.

The eventual failure of the Grand Alliance to bring France to its knees or to secure the Spanish throne for an Austrian prince (neither of which was a war aim for the Allies at the beginning) does not diminish Marlborough's military achievements. On two occasions, at Blenheim in 1704 and Ramillies in 1706, his dynamic tactics, irresistibly dictating the pace of the battle, brought utter defeat to French armies. These victories were the wonder of the age. Two years after Ramillies, Marlborough overtook the French army while on the march near to Oudenarde, and, in a dazzling display of almost off-hand tactical confidence, he crossed the wide river Scheldt under the very noses of the French commanders and smashed the right Wing of their army. Rarely has intuitive tactical skill been so well demonstrated. Despair and defeat faced France, and the great city and fortress of Lille was lost, but the Grand Alliance bungled the negotiations for peace, and in the autumn of 1709 the sombre battle at Malplaquet was fought. Once again Marlborough was successful, forcing the

French army from a massively strong defensive position, but the cost was very heavy, and the Duke's critics were given powerful ammunition with which they would bring him down before long. It is interesting that the French tend to regard Malplaquet as a victory, on the overly simple basis that their losses were less than those suffered by Marlborough's army. They are wrong. Marshal Villars only fought at Malplaquet in order to save the nearby fortress of Mons and in this key task he failed – the place fell to the Duke's army a few weeks after the battle, while the tired French army looked on.

Three hundred years or so after these exciting events, it is pleasant to be able to say that the battlefields on which Marlborough achieved his resounding victories are relatively unspoiled by modern development. Blindheim (Blenheim) village still sits amidst wide Bavarian cornfields, and Ramillies in Belgium is hardly touched. Even at Oudenarde, where the modern town sits close alongside the battlefield, the fields, gardens and streams where most of the infantry fighting took place are fairly untouched, and it is easy to visualise the desperate events that took place there. The dark woods near to the village of Malplaquet on the French–Belgian border are still in place, pretty well where they were in Marlborough's time, enabling the visitor to trace the bloody events of the battle without too great a leap in imagination.

Notes on old and new styles of dating

In the early eighteenth century the Julian Calendar (Old Style or OS) was still in use in the British Isles, whereas on the Continent the Gregorian Calendar (New Style or NS) was used. This new system was ten days ahead of the old up to 1700 and eleven days ahead thereafter. As Britain adopted the Gregorian Calendar later in the eighteenth century, and almost all the narrative in this book takes place on the Continent, the New Style has been used throughout, unless indicated otherwise. Care has to be taken with contemporary accounts as at this time the New Year was reckoned to start from 25 March (Lady Day). Therefore an account written in the period might refer to 10 March as being in 1708 but we would now put it in 1709. The valuable journal left by John Deane of the 1st English Foot Guards is in this form, for example, so it is as well to be on the watch.

Spelling and grammar

I have not altered the original, often rather idiosyncratic, spelling found in many of the contemporary accounts which are quoted in this book. Where others have already put the grammar into modern form, however, no attempt has been made to change it back to what might have been the original.

British, Dutch and German troops, and others

In the early eighteenth century the English, Scots and Irish each had their own separate establishments and budgets; many Welsh soldiers also served of course, but there was no separate Welsh establishment. Contemporary accounts often refer to these troops as being 'English' but I have used the more precise term where appropriate, as in 'a Scottish battalion'. Although the term 'British' was not really in wide use until after the Act of Union in 1707, I have occasionally referred to Queen Anne's soldiers en bloc as being 'British' to avoid unduly lengthy phrases such as 'English, Scots, Welsh and Irish troops'. To add complication, the Dutch also recruited Scottish troops into their service, and these are referred to as being 'Scots-Dutch'. They also recruited large numbers of Protestant German and Swiss troops; these are often referred to simply as 'Dutch'. Many German troops were provided by princely states owing allegiance to the Emperor in Vienna, and they are often described as 'Imperial' troops, even though they were not Austrian. Excellent use was also made of the Danish troops provided for service with the Alliance, due, in part, to the influence of Prince George of Denmark, Queen Anne's often under-rated husband and consort.

France also obtained substantial numbers of foreign troops for service. The Swiss and émigré Irish regiments were well known and enjoyed a fine reputation. German troops in French service, from regions such as Alsace, were usually clad in blue coats, and were at times mistaken for Bavarian troops who were clothed in a similar way. The elite French Gens d'Armes wore long, laced red coats – this colour was by no means the exclusive preserve of Queen Anne's troops. The soldiers recruited from the Spanish Netherlands, whether in the service of the French or the Austrian claimant to the throne in Madrid, were widely described as 'Spanish' troops, even though we would know them today as Belgians; few soldiers were to come from the Iberian pensinsula for service in northern Europe. Professional troops from many other countries volunteered to serve in the opposing armies, making their choice according to their religious leanings.

Loyalties could be a little mixed in the complex political and dynastic arena of western Europe at this turbulent time. The Comte de Merode-Westerloo, a Walloon officer who left drily amusing memoirs, began the war in the service of Philip V, the French claimant, but resigned his commission, and subsequently campaigned for Charles (Carlos) III, the Austrian claimant. There was nothing irregular about this; it was all above board. Louis-Guillaume, the Margrave of Baden, commanded Imperial forces on the upper Rhine until his death in 1707, and yet he was the godson of Louis XIV. The Elector of Bavaria, who allied himself to the French, was the son-in-law of the Austrian Emperor

Leopold, while the heir to the throne of France, the Duc de Bourgogne, was married to Princess Adelaide of Savoy, whose own father was at war with Louis XIV, having abandoned his alliance with France. Perhaps most famously of all, James FitzJames, the Duke of Berwick, one of the most accomplished and dangerous Marshals of France, was the nephew of the Duke of Marlborough by his older sister and King James II, when the latter was Duke of York; uncle and nephew eyed each other across a potential battlefield on more than one occasion, apparently never with rancour or animosity, and frequently exchanging polite letters..

WHO WAS WHO ON MARLBOROUGH'S BATTLEFIELDS

Albemarle, Arnold Joost van Keppel, Earl (1669–1718). Accomplished Dutch cavalry officer. A favourite of William III, he was one of Marlborough's closest colleagues. Fought at Ramillies and Malplaquet. Beaten by Villars at Denain (1712).

Albergotti, Lieutenant-General François-Zénoble-Philippe, Comte de (1654–1717). Italian-born officer in the French service. Injured at Malplaquet. Subsequently became a distinguished diplomat.

Alegre, Yves, Marquis d' (1653–1733). French cavalry commander, taken prisoner at Elixheim. Marshal of France (1724).

Anhalt-Dessau Leopold, Prince of (1676–1747). Prussian officer commanding Eugene's infantry at Blenheim and German infantry at Oudenarde and Malplaquet. 'The Old Dessauer' of Frederick the Great's wars.

Anjou, Philippe, Duc de (1683–1746). Youngest grandson of Louis XIV. The French contender for the Spanish throne who became Philip V of Spain in 1700.

Argyll, John Campbell, 2nd Duke of (1678–1743). Known to the troops as 'Red John', he fought as an infantry commander at Ramillies, Oudenarde and Malplaquet. An increasingly sharp critic of Marlborough, Argyll was influential in the negotiations that led to the Union of England and Scotland. Commanded Allied forces in Spain in the later campaigns. Field-Marshal (1736).

Armstrong, Major-General John (1674–1742). Marlborough's Chief of Engineers (1704). Wounded at Malplaquet. Surveyor-General of the Ordnance (1723).

Auvergne, François Egon de la Tour, Prince d' (younger brother of the Duc de Bouillon). Lieutenant-General of Cavalry in the Dutch service. Led the main Allied cavalry advance at Malplaquet.

Baden, Louis-Guillaume, Margrave of (1655–1707). Godson of Louis XIV. Known as 'Turken Louis' for his valiant exploits in the campaigns leading to the siege of Vienna. Imperial field commander at the Schellenberg where he was wounded. Died, possibly from gangrene in the leg, two years later.

Berwick, James FitzJames, Duke of (1670–1734). Marshal of France (1706). Natural son of James II (when Duke of York) and Marlborough's older sister Arabella. One of Louis XIV's best field commanders, he was killed by a roundshot at the siege of Philipsburg.

Biron, Charles Armand de Goutant, Marquis de (1663–1746). Commanded French flank guard at Oudenarde; failed to drive in the Allied bridgehead and was taken prisoner.

Blood, Brigadier-General Holcroft (1668–1707). Commanded Marlborough's artillery at the Schellenberg and Blenheim. His father had tried to steal the Crown Jewels from the Tower of London.

Boufflers Louis-François, Marquis and Duc de (1644–1711). Marshal of France (1693). Outmanoeuvred by Marlborough in 1702 and 1703, but skilfully defended Lille in 1708, and took over command of French army at Malplaquet after Villars was wounded.

Bourgogne (Burgundy), Louis, Duc de (1682–1712). Grandson of Louis XIV and, as Dauphin, became heir to throne of France. Nominally in command of the French army in the Low Countries 1700–03 and also in 1708. Died of measles, as did his wife, Adelaide of Savoy.

Cadogan, Lieutenant-General William, 1st Earl (1665–1726). Marlborough's Quartermaster-General and 'Chief of Staff'. Present at all the Duke's major battles, he commanded the Allied advanced guard at Oudenarde. Became Master-General of the Ordnance on Marlborough's death.

Churchill, Lieutenant-General Charles (1656–1714). Marlborough's younger brother and General of infantry. Fought at the Schellenberg, Blenheim and Ramillies.

Clerambault, Philippe de Pallneau, Marquis de (d.1704). French commander in Blindheim village. Reputedly drowned in the Danube while trying to escape.

Cutts, John, Major-General, 1st Baron of Gowran (1661–1707). 'The Salamander'. Commanded British infantry at Blenheim. Died in Ireland in relative poverty.

d'Arco, Jean, Comte. Piedmontese officer in the Bavarian service. Commanded the Bavarians and French against Marlborough at the Schellenberg, and led the Bavarian infantry at Blenheim.

d'Artagnan, Pierre, Comte, Marquis d'Montesquiou (1709). Marshal of France. Commanded French right flank at Malplaquet, and the French army during Villars's convalescence in 1710.

Davies, Christian, also known as Christian Welsh/Walsh or Mother Ross (died 1739). Female soldier, serving in the guise of a male, who fought at the Schellenberg, Blenheim and Ramillies, where she was wounded. Recounted lively, and occasionally rather improbable, reminiscences in old age as a Chelsea Pensioner.

de la Colonie, Colonel Jean-Martin. French officer seconded to the Bavarian service. Fought at the Schellenberg, Ramillies, Oudenarde and Malplaquet. Author of informative memoirs.

de la Motte, Louis-Jacques de Fosse, Comte. French Major-General. Commander of the Greder Suisse Régiment at Ramillies. Seized Bruges in the summer of 1708, before the battle of Oudenarde.

Dopff, Daniel Wolf, Baron (1665–1718). Dutch Quartermaster-General. Beaten at Eckeren (1703), he fought at Ramillies, Oudenarde and Malplaquet.

Drake, Captain Peter. Irish 'soldier of fortune' who served in both French and Allied armies. Fought at Ramillies, Oudenarde and Malplaquet. Left informative memoirs of his service.

Eugene, François-Eugene de Savoy (1663–1736). Imperial commander, and close friend of Marlborough. Fought at Blenheim, Oudenarde and Malplaquet. Victor at Turin (1706). He was outmanoeuvred by Villars at Denain (1712).

Fagel, Francis Nicholas, Baron (1655–1718). Dutch Lieutenant-General. Present at Ramillies and Malplaquet.

Goor, Major-General Johan Wigand van (1647–1704). Talented Dutch engineer officer, and good friend of Marlborough. Killed leading the assault at the Schellenberg.

Goslinga, Sicco van (1644–1731). Brave but argumentative Dutch field deputy, an arch-critic of Marlborough. Present at Elixheim, Ramillies, Oudenarde and Malplaquet.

Grimaldi, Honoré, Marquis de (1675–1712). Commanded French left Wing cavalry at Oudenarde. He was gravely wounded at the siege of Mons and retired from active service.

Hompesch, Graf Reynard Vincent van (1660–1733). Accomplished Dutch cavalry commander. Fought in all Marlborough's major battles.

Lottum, Philip Karl, Count (1650–1719). Prussian Lieutenant-General. Commanded Hanoverian and Prussian infantry at Oudenarde, and the German and British infantry in the Bois de Sars at Malplaquet. Field Marshal (1713) and commander of the Prussian army.

Lumley, Major-General Henry (1660–1722). British cavalry commander, present at all Marlborough's major battles.

Luxembourg, Christian-Louis de Montmorency, Chevalier and Duc de (1675–1746). Marshal of France (Montmorency, 1734). Son of the famous Marshal Luxembourg. Commanded French reserve cavalry at Malplaquet.

Maffei, Alessandro, Marquis de (1662–1730). Italian Lieutenant-General in the Bavarian service. Fought at the Schellenberg, and led an infantry brigade in Ramillies village where he was taken prisoner.

Marsin, Ferdinand, Comte de (1656–1706). Marshal of France. Commanded French left Wing at Blenheim. Killed at Turin (1706) soon after receiving a premonition of his own death.

Merode-Westerloo, Eugene-Jean-Philippe, Comte de (1674–1732). Walloon officer serving with the French until 1706, and then with the Allies after Ramillies. Author of highly entertaining and caustic memoirs.

Murray, Lieutenant-General Robert, (d.1719). Veteran of the Williamite wars. Commanded the Swiss Brigade at Ramillies which sheltered Marlborough. Governor of Tournai (1716).

Natzmer, Dubislaw (1654–1739). Prussian Major-General and cavalry commander. Defeated at Höchstädt (1703), captured at Blenheim, present at Oudenarde and Malplaquet.

Orange, John Friso, Prince of Orange and Nassau-Dientz (drowned 1711). Dutch commander at Malplaquet.

Orkney, George Hamilton, 1st Earl of (1666–1737). Pugnacious British infantry commander. Fought at the Schellenberg, Blenheim, Ramillies and Malplaquet. Governor of Virginia (1715). First British Field Marshal (1736).

Overkirk, Henry van Nassau, Count (1640–1708). Dutch Veldt-Marshal and close colleague of Marlborough. Commanded Dutch troops at Ramillies and Oudenarde. Died of strain during the siege of Lille.

Oxenstiern, Count (d.1709). Swedish officer in the Dutch service. Fought at Oudenarde and was killed at Malplaquet.

Parke, 'Colonel' Daniel (killed in a riot in 1713). Virginian rake and volunteer in Marlborough's Danube campaign. Took Marlborough's dispatch to London after Blenheim.

Puységur, Jacques François de Chastenet, Marquis de (1655–1743). Marshal of France. Present at Oudenarde and Malplaquet. Influential author on military tactics and thought.

Rantzau, Major-General Jorgen (1652–1733). Commanded Hanoverian cavalry at Oudenarde, and an infantry brigade at Malplaquet.

Sabine, Major-General Joseph (1662–1739). Fought at the Schellenberg, Blenheim and Ramillies. Commanded a brigade in Cadogan's advanced guard at Oudenarde. Led the pursuit of the Jacobite rebels in 1715 Rising.

St Hilaire, Armand de Marmes, Marquis de (b.1651). Skilled French artillery officer. An exponent of aggressive tactics, he developed a theory of artillery-led assault.

Schulemburg, Matthias-Johan, Count (1661–1743). Hanoverian commander of Saxon troops in Allied service. Fought at Ramillies, Oudenarde and Malplaquet.

Tallard, Camille d'Hostun, Comte de (1652–1728). Marshal of France (1703). French commander of right Wing at Blenheim. Held prisoner in Nottingham for eight years, but eventually restored to royal favour.

Tilly, Claude-Frederick de Tserclaes, Count (d.1723). Commander of the Danish cavalry in the turning movement at Oudenarde, and at Malplaquet.

Vendôme, Louis-Joseph de Bourbon, Duc de (1654–1712). Illegitimate grandson of Henry IV of France. Commanded French army at Oudenarde. Died of food poisoning in Spain.

Villars, Claude-Louis-Hector, Duc de (1653–1734). Marshal of France. Commanded French army at Malplaquet and was gravely wounded. Victor at Denain (1712). Became Marshal General (1733).

Villeroi, François de Neufville, Duc de (1644–1730). Marshal of France. Commanded the French army in the Low Countries 1702–03, and was defeated at Ramillies (1706).

Webb, Major-General John Richmond (1667–1724). Present at Ramillies and the victor at Wynendael (1708). Wounded at Malplaquet.

Withers, Lieutenant-General Henry (d.1729). Fought at all Marlborough's major battles. Commanded the detached column at Maplaquet.

Wittelsbach, Maximilien-Emmanuel, Elector of Bavaria (1679–1736). Governor–General of the Spanish Netherlands. Defeated at Blenheim and Ramillies, and tried to seize Brussels (1708). Restored to his estates in 1714.

Württemberg, Karl-Alexander, Duke of (1661–1741). Commanded Danish troops in Allied service through all Marlborough's campaigns.

Zurlauben, Beat-Jacques de la Tour Chatillon, Comte de von (killed 1704). Swiss-born commander of French cavalry of the right Wing at Blenheim.

The War of the Spanish Succession

On 1 November 1700 the invalid and feeble-minded King Carlos II of Spain died in Madrid. He had been described, rather unkindly, as more a medical curiosity than a man and was nicknamed 'the Sufferer'. He was twice married, but had no children. Carlos had for some time been susceptible to French influence at his court. Despite carefully crafted international treaties on the matter of the succession, in particular the Second Partition Treaty of June 1699, in his will he left the throne of Spain to Philippe, Duc d'Anjou, the youngest grandson of Louis XIV of France, the Sun King.

The news of the death of the King of Spain, and the offer of the throne to Anjou, came to the French court at Fontainebleau on 9 November 1700. Despite the understandable excitement this caused, Louis XIV was reluctant at first to allow his grandson to accept the offer. The intention to bestow the crown on the French prince had been known for some time, but now it was a fact, the likely implications had to be faced. Two partition treaties, negotiated in the late 1690s, had brought to a tired end the seemingly interminable French–Dutch wars of the latter part of the century, and their terms set out, among other things,

King Carlos II of Spain. His death in 1700 resulted in the offer of the Spanish throne to a French prince.

1

that the crowns of France and Spain should always be kept separate. The new inheritance, with a French prince soon to be on the Spanish throne, put this important provision in some doubt. Catholic France was not only the single most populous country in western Europe; it was also militarily the most powerful. Louis XIV had a long record of aggressive territorial expansion at the expense of his near neighbours, and to ally the military might of France to the vast Spanish empire in the Mediterranean and the Americas would alarm every Protestant prince in Europe. Renewed war might be the result. The French King had achieved much, pushing France's geographical borders more or less to those of today, but with his treasury in a sorry state another expensive war was not what he wished for.

Despite the obvious concern at the likely reaction of neighbouring states to the offer, Louis XIV was also aware that if he refused his consent the Spanish throne would immediately be offered to Archduke Charles, the young son of the Austrian Emperor. The King was also quite sure that England and Holland would not go to war again just to enforce a partition of the Spanish empire for the benefit of a French prince. Whoever succeeded to the Spanish throne, the partition treaty terms would be void. With some reluctance he gave his consent, and Anjou, now made Philip V of Spain, was introduced to the Spanish Ambassador, Castel del Rey, on 16 November 1700. The Duc de St Simon, who witnessed the spectacle, wrote:

Contrary to all precedent, the King caused the double doors of his cabinet [private suite] to be thrown open and ordered all the crowd assembled without to enter. Then, glancing majestically over the numerous company 'Gentlemen' said he, indicating the Duc d'Anjou 'this is the King of Spain.'

Soon afterwards, Anjou and a huge entourage left for Madrid. Louis XIV moved quickly to avert conflict, and messages were sent to the Emperor Leopold I in Vienna, King William III in London and the States-General at The Hague giving assurances that the French and Spanish thrones would always be kept separate and that the interest of those states would not be put at risk by this inheritance. French diplomatic activity was intense, and all might have been well: no one wanted renewed war, and important territorial concessions in northern Italy were offered to Austria, while England

Archduke Charles of Austria, the Habsburg claimant to the throne in Madrid.

and Holland were inclined to accept Philip on the throne in Madrid as a fait accompli. Louis XIV, usually so astute, now unexpectedly and clumsily fumbled the diplomatic scene.

In February 1701, using the rather thin excuse that he was merely protecting his grandson's inheritance in the Spanish Netherlands (today's Belgium), Louis XIV sent his troops to occupy a string of strategically important towns (Luxembourg, Namur, Mons, Oudenarde, Charleroi, Ath and Nieuport). These places provided a cherished barrier for the Dutch against any renewed French aggression, but the Governor-General in the Spanish Netherlands, Maximilien-Emmanuel Wittelsbach (the Elector of Bavaria), unwisely connived at the French operation and the Dutch were caught off guard. Their garrisons were humiliatingly interned by Marshal Boufflers, the French army commander, and only Maastricht, whose governor robustly refused the French summons to submit, remained in Dutch hands. The Duc de Tallard, the French ambassador in London, had actually advised William III (who was also the Dutch Stadtholder) of

Philippe, Duc d'Anjou. Philip V of Spain. Grandson of Louis XIV. The French claimant to the throne in Madrid.

the impending operation, but he kept the information to himself. The States-General understandably took alarm, and offence, at the loss of the towns so recently guaranteed to them by treaty. Matters were made worse when, in September 1701, Louis XIV went to St Germaine and stood at the deathbed of James II, exiled King of England. He acknowledged to his dying friend that James's son, the Chevalier de St George, was considered by France to be the rightful heir to the throne in London. This was a dreadful diplomatic gaffe; it too broke the partition treaties, and gave great offence in London when it became known. Tallard was promptly expelled from England (this was an error, as his calm influence had been of great value both to William III and Louis XIV).

The threat France posed to its neighbours appeared to grow ever more acute, and earnest negotiations took place between William III, the States-General

Queen Anne. Stubborn and loyal, her friendship with Marlborough was a great asset, while it lasted.

and the Austrian Emperor to form a fresh alliance aimed at limiting the seemingly intolerable power of Louis XIV. A Treaty of Grand Alliance was concluded on 7 September 1701, aimed in the main at securing a division of the Spanish empire between the French and Austrian interests (not necessarily, at this point, requiring that Anjou should relinquish the throne in Madrid). William III did not live to fight another war. He died on 18 March 1702 from the effects of a fall from his horse a couple of weeks earlier. His sister-in-law, the Princess Anne, youngest daughter of James II, ascended the English throne. Despite this change in London, the Dutch were reassured that she was just as resolute as the deceased King. War was declared on France and Spain at the gates of St James's Palace in London on 15 May 1702 and simultaneously in The Hague and Vienna. On hearing the not altogether unexpected news, Louis XIV drily remarked, 'I must be getting old, if ladies are now declaring war on me.'

The French King had not been idle during the preceding months: he had raised 100 new regiments (some units were of doubtful quality, such was the haste to augment the army's strength). The immediate French strategy was to mount a campaign to isolate and overwhelm the Dutch in the north; two armies were available in the Spanish Netherlands for this purpose, both under the nominal command of the King's grandson and heir, the Duc de Bourgogne. The Marquis de Bedmar commanded the 'Spanish' Walloon and Flemish troops covering Brussels, Ghent and Bruges, while Marshal Boufflers had a 60,000-strong French army in Brabant to the east, ready to advance against Dutch-held Maastricht and the fortresses on the lower Rhine, Maas (Meuse) and along the southern borders of Holland. His opponent was Godert Rede van Ginkel, Earl Athlone. The latter was brave and energetic enough, but his army (mostly Dutch, and those in Dutch pay, but also with the British troops so far assembled for the campaign) was soon outmanoeuvred and pinned against the lower Maas river at Nijmegen. Had Boufflers not over-extended his lines of supply and communication from Brabant, the French campaign might have been successful and the Dutch driven out of the war before things really started. That would have ended the Grand Alliance neatly, and Philip V would have been King of Spain, and of an undivided Spanish empire, without further ado.

The Allied forces in the Low Countries were gathering steadily. They were nearly 60,000 strong when John Churchill, the 52-year-old 1st Earl of Marlborough, was appointed the field commander of the Anglo-Dutch armies when on campaign. Delayed by diplomatic business in London and The Hague, he arrived to take command early in June 1702. Athlone was inclined to resent his appointment and be uncooperative, but Marlborough took a firm grip on operations, using to excellent advantage the pause in the pace of the French campaign brought about by the temporary lack of supplies. On 26 July, this 'superb commander', as Athlone would grudgingly, but admiringly, describe the Earl, marched his army south and westwards towards Liège. The sudden move threatened the already extended French lines of supply and communication, and forced Boufflers to pull back into Brabant. Marlborough could have mauled the disordered French army

King Louis XIV of France. Ambitions for his grandson brought war back to Europe.

as it hurried across the heaths of Peer had the Dutch been inclined to involve their troops in a battle there, but they thought it too risky. The Earl had to watch his opponents hurry past 'in the greatest disorder imaginable' and out of his reach.

The Dutch were cautious, but they had much to lose – their borders were nearby and exposed. Their way of campaigning did not suit Marlborough, who was always eager to bring his opponents to battle in the open. This set the pattern for campaigns over the next eighteen months: Marlborough (soon made a duke by Queen Anne in recognition of his successes in the Low Countries) would seize fortresses and confront the French armies only to find that the cautious Dutch field deputies, who accompanied the army but had little military experience, would decide that the conditions were not right and refuse permission for their troops to engage in a pitched battle. The Dutch attitude is understandable, for a major defeat by the French would lay their border open to fresh invasion while England was sheltered by the Channel; the States-General had become wearily used to being invaded by French armies.

On the one occasion in the summer of 1703 that the Dutch were inclined to be active, during operations to seize Antwerp, they were surprised in their camp at Eckeren by Marshal Boufflers, and only a solid defence by their outnumbered infantry prevented a complete catastrophe before Marlborough could arrive with reinforcements. The Duke's hopes of a decisive victory, with the French army broken and in flight, were repeatedly frustrated by his allies, and he began to look around for fresh opportunities, where he would not have to get the permission of the Dutch to fight.

John Churchill, 1st Duke of Marlborough (1650–1722)
by kind permission of His Grace The Duke of Marlborough

John Churchill, 1st Duke of Marlborough, was born in Devon in 1650 into a family impoverished by the English Civil War. His father's connections secured the young man a place at the court of King Charles II at the Restoration. Having entered the army, Churchill served in Tangier, and on attachment to the French army, in one of the English regiments loaned to King Louis XIV during the wars with the Dutch. He acquired a reputation for gallantry, and was introduced to the King while on campaign. He also met many of the French officers he would fight and defeat in later years.

Churchill commanded the royal infantry at the battle of Sedgemoor in 1685, where the Monmouth Rebellion came to grief, but he defected from James II's service to join William of Orange in 1688. Despite this, the Dutch King did not trust him, and Churchill spent some time in the Tower of London on flimsy charges of treason before being restored to royal favour. His influence steadily grew, and he helped William III negotiate the Treaty of Grand Alliance with the States-General of Holland and Imperial Austria. When Queen Anne came to the throne in 1702, Earl Marlborough, as he had become, and his wife Sarah were her best and most loved friends. Appointed Captain-General of Land Forces, Marlborough campaigned with success in the Low Countries, and was made a duke for his services before taking his army to the Danube in the campaign that led to Blenheim in August 1704. This wholly unexpected triumph marked the Duke as the greatest Captain of his age.

The following summer, Marlborough led his army to a small but stunning victory at Elixheim to the south-east of Brussels, and in 1706 he destroyed Villeroi's army at Ramillies, going onto occupy the whole of the Spanish Netherlands. To these successes were added Oudenarde (1708), the capture of Lille later that year, and the controversial battle at Malplaquet (1709), where the Allied casualties were almost twice those of the French. This contributed to the flagging of Marlborough's influence as the War of the Spanish Succession dragged on, and he was dismissed from all his posts in December 1711. Concerned at politically motivated charges of corruption and embezzlement of public funds, Marlborough went to live abroad, but returned with the accession of George I, who reinstated him in his appointments. The Duke suffered increasing ill-health and was victim to several strokes, the first in 1716. He died at Windsor Lodge in June 1722.

Part 1

Blenheim, 13 August 1704

Introduction

On 13 August 1704, John Churchill, 1st Duke of Marlborough, led his troops to a great victory over a larger French and Bavarian army on the plain of Höchstädt beside the banks of the river Danube. The Duke's army was drawn from Britain, Holland, the Protestant German states, Denmark and Imperial Austria, and the battle was at Blenheim on the northern borders of Bavaria.

England (Great Britain from 1707 onwards) became a world power that day, with an extraordinary extension of reach and influence. The battle beside the Danube was the acknowledged wonder of the age, and men wrote afterwards that the news from southern Germany was so exciting that it was impossible to sleep. The Virginian rake Colonel Dan Parke had ridden into London a week or so after the battle with a scrap of paper in his hand, announcing to Queen Anne the triumph over France and its ally, the Elector of Bavaria. Not until the arrival of the Waterloo Dispatch in 1815 would such wild scenes be witnessed again in the capital's streets. Marlborough was acclaimed as the foremost Captain of his generation, and a grateful monarch and nation endowed him with enough money to build a great palace at Woodstock in Oxfordshire, suitable and fit for such a hero. Appropriately enough, that place was to be known as Blenheim Palace. It is now the home of His Grace the 11th Duke of Marlborough.

All the war aims of King Louis XIV of France were ruined that August day in 1704. The previous fifty years had witnessed a series of aggressive campaigns waged upon his unfortunate neighbours, and French territorial expansion into southern Flanders, Artois, Picardy, Languedoc, Lorraine and Alsace had carried that nation to its present-day borders, more or less. Louis XIV was an accomplished soldier, and had enjoyed being on campaign when a young man.

8

However, the success of French arms was largely the result of the labours of the great Marshals of France – Condé, Turenne, Vauban, Luxembourg and others; over the years, the French had acquired a tradition of victory. At Blenheim, Marlborough led his soldiers to a triumph over an entire French army – thousands of prisoners and horses, scores of senior officers, regimental colours, cavalry standards and guns all fell into his hands. A French Marshal sat captive, sipping chocolate in the Duke's own coach. The destruction in the field of an entire French army was a thing unknown in the memories of living men; the shock and disbelief it produced across Europe, the effect on carefully crafted alliances, and the adulation that it brought to Marlborough as the victor cannot be overstated. That the Duke's campaign was of the most daring kind, and the successful result finely balanced, adds to the fascination of the story.

The great contest at Blenheim took place on a battlefield that stretches for nearly 4 miles northwards from the Danube to the Swabian Jura hills. The battle is named after Blindheim village, but is often referred to in France and Germany, and in contemporary accounts, as Höchstädt, 1704 (not the lesser fight there in 1703 that the French won). There has been little intrusive modern development of the area, and the wide Bavarian cornfields, the small copses of trees and the heavily wooded hills to the north are all very attractive. So, too, are the small villages in and around which brutal battles were fought in 1704 – Blindheim, Unterglau, Oberglau and Lutzingen, each with its own distinctive church tower. The general feel of the battlefield has not changed greatly, and the visitor to this beautiful area today can visualise the dramatic contest without too great an effort of imagination.

A Stolen Army: The March to the Danube

The Duke of Marlborough's difficulties with the Dutch persisted through 1703, although he did succeed in capturing more French-held fortresses along the lower Rhine and Meuse. The States-General minted a medal in the Duke's honour, inscribed 'Victorious without Slaughter', but Marlborough could see that this was no way to win the war while the French were doing rather well in campaigns elsewhere, particularly in Spain. Eager to be free from the restraining hands of the Dutch field deputies, who could effectively veto his plans if they seemed to entail too much risk, the Duke devised a plan with the Imperial Austrian Ambassador in London, Count Wratislaw, to take his army to southern Germany. The Elector of Bavaria, although nominally owing allegiance to the Emperor Leopold, had concluded an alliance with Louis XIV, partly to safeguard his appointment as Governor-General of the Spanish

Emperor Leopold I of Austria.

Netherlands but also to take advantage of Vienna's present weakness: the Imperial armies, having to contend with rebellion in Hungary and campaigns on the upper Rhine, in the Tyrol and in northern Italy, were losing their war with the French and their Bavarian allies. Vienna was coming under threat, and if the city fell, even for a short time, then so too would the Grand Alliance, so great would be the shock and loss of prestige for the Empire.

In March 1704 Queen Anne gave Marlborough an order to go to the aid of Vienna 'if he saw fit', and on 19 April the Duke crossed from Harwich to Holland. He wrote from The Hague to a friend in London on 29 April:

My intentions are to march with all the English [troops in Queen Anne's pay] to Coblenz and to declare that I intend to campaign on the Moselle; but when I come there, to write to the [Dutch] States that I think it absolutely necessary for the saving of the Empire to march with the troops under my command and to join with those that are in Germany in order to take measures with Prince Louis of Baden [the Imperial field commander] for the speedy reduction of the Elector of Bavaria.

The Dutch, whose main worry remained the security of their southern borders, were reluctant to see the Captain-General, on whom they placed such reliance, march away. They even planned to recall some troops in their pay who had been serving on the upper Rhine under Johan Vigand van Goor. However, they were persuaded to agree to the new campaign after Marlborough made it plain that he intended to march southwards with or without their blessing and convinced the States-General that his intention really was to campaign against the Marquis de Bedmar in the Moselle valley. During discussions at The Hague in early May, the Duke also assured the Dutch that he would return in good time if the French commander in the Spanish Netherlands, Marshal Villeroi, mounted an attack on the troops remaining to guard Holland. In fact, Marlborough had calculated that, as he marched south, taking the course of the Rhine, the French commander would be drawn after him, forced to march south also to avoid being outflanked; he would have no time to attack the

Dutch. With fine calculation of strategic imperatives, Marlborough could see that by marching away he would draw the French army with him.

Such a huge project could not be prepared for, or undertaken, in secret, but Marlborough let it be known quite widely that the Moselle valley was his preferred choice for the summer campaign. To the French this seemed perfectly logical if he could persuade the Dutch to let him go, which they doubted; they had garrisoned the valley with good troops, just in case. On 4 May 1704, the British garrison in Breda began moving to the concentration area ordered by Marlborough. Other garrisons joined the march, and Marlborough's younger brother, Charles Churchill, took command of the troops on 8 May. The river Meuse was crossed at Ruremond five days later to reach the concentration area at Bedburg near to Cologne. After a grand review of the army, on 19 May, Marlborough's troops began their march southwards. The route, which at first was along the west bank of the Rhine, was clear for use only because of the Duke's successes over the previous two years in removing French garrisons from the towns past which the troops now marched. The pace that was set was not severe – exhausted men would be of no use when the time came to fight – and the arrangements to supply the army were excellent, so that the soldiers made good time.

The Dutch troops had been left to guard their southern border, under command of Veldt-Marshal Henry of Nassau, Count Overkirk. Increased French activity in response to Marlborough's march alarmed him, and an urgent appeal was sent after the Duke, begging that the move to the Moselle be suspended. Marlborough sent Overkirk an encouraging message but refused to halt his army for, just as anticipated, as he marched southwards the strategic emphasis of the war inexorably moved with him. The French were having to respond to his actions, not he to theirs.

While Marlborough had been preparing for his great march, the French were striving to maintain Marshal Ferdinand Marsin with his army in Bavaria. The Marshal had been operating with the Elector of Bavaria against the Imperial commander, Louis-Guillaume, Margrave of Baden. Despite some local successes, Marsin was now rather isolated, and his lines of supply and communication with France lay through

Louis-Guillaume, Margrave of Baden. Imperial Commander at the Schellenberg.

the rocky passes of the Black Forest. On 12 May 1704, Marshal Tallard began to take a convoy of supplies, money and troop reinforcements from the Rhine to support Marsin. With considerable skill, he brought the huge, vulnerable convoy through the difficult country, neatly outmanoeuvring Baron Thungen, the Imperial general on the Rhine who sought to block his path. Marsin marched westwards to meet Tallard; he received 8,000 fresh troops, a great quantity of supplies and munitions, and over 1 million louis d'or in cash to sustain the French army in Bavaria. Tallard then returned with his own troops to the Rhine, once again side-stepping Thungen's efforts to intercept him. This whole vast operation was an outstanding military achievement and it remains greatly to Tallard's credit.

In the Low Countries, Marshal Villeroi watched the red-coated soldiers march away with some puzzlement. If they went south, then it seemed that he must follow or be outflanked, and the Dutch borders, as a result, would remain untroubled. Yet, the chance now arose, surely, to attack the Dutch while Marlborough's attention was elsewhere. Villeroi's appeal to Louis XIV for advice met with the dry response, 'If the Duke marches, then so too must you march', and so the French troops were soon also on the roads leading southwards. The Dutch saw this and knew Marlborough's prediction of the French reaction to his moves was quite correct. Their fears were calmed. Captain Robert Parker, who tramped up the Rhine with the Royal Irish Regiment, summed things up nicely when he wrote late in May that:

> *Villeroi by this time had arrived at Treves [Trier on the Moselle] with the greater part of his army from the Netherlands, to oppose the Duke in this quarter. This made the Dutch easy, for they were apprehensive, that on the Duke's marching from them, the French would over-run their whole country.*

So secure did the States-General now feel that van Goor, whose Dutch corps had been operating on the upper Rhine with the Imperial army, was informed that he was now under Marlborough's orders, should the Duke wish to use him and his troops in this new, far-off campaign. As an indication of the faith the Dutch had come to put in the Duke's plans and abilities, this was very significant. Meanwhile, Marlborough's army marched onwards in the fine weather, and was reinforced at regular intervals by contingents of Hessian, Prussian and Hanoverian troops, which the Duke had arranged should rendezvous with him as he moved towards the south. Sombre news came in, however: on 23 May, Marlborough learned of Tallard's success in reinforcing and replenishing Marsin's army. Such an operation, while undoubtedly a drag on French strategic resources, could well be attempted again, and the next time Tallard and his own army might well remain in Bavaria to confront the Duke with superior numbers.

On 26 May, Marlborough's troops reached Coblenz, where the Rhine and Moselle meet, and where huge amounts of stores for the coming campaign had been gathered in advance. If the Duke was going to attack Isidore Bedmar, he must now turn to the west into the Moselle valley. Instead, the next day the army crossed over a bridge of pontoon boats to the eastern bank of the Rhine. Captain Blackad(d)er, one of Marlborough's marching captains, wrote rather glumly that, 'This is likely to be a campaign of great fatigue and trouble. I know not where they are heading us.' John Deane, serving with the 1st English Foot Guards, wrote in his journal, 'On the 15th [OS] marched and incampt by Coblenz. Here my Lord Duke left us and tooke the horse with him before us into Germany.' Meanwhile, Marshal Villeroi was writing to Louis XIV, 'There will be no campaign on the Moselle, the English have all gone up into Germany.' Not the Moselle, certainly, but the Duke could still strike at Alsace, for he had his engineers construct another pontoon bridge across the Rhine at Philipsburgh, as if for that very purpose. Meanwhile, Marlborough's army marched steadily onwards and the river Neckar at Heidelberg was reached without incident.

The most careful preparations had been made for the march up the Rhine; the availability of supplies depending upon hard cash, and the ability of the English commissaries to pay in gold, ensured that frequent stockpiles of food, fodder, boots and clothes awaited the marching soldiers. Local farmers, assured that they would be well paid for their produce, brought their wares to the roadside to sell to the quartermasters as the army passed. As Robert Parker remembered approvingly, 'Surely never was such a march carried on with more order or regularity and with less fatigue both to man and horse.' Marlborough's chaplain Dr Francis Hare wrote that, 'His Grace was not unmindful to provide money and order regular payments for everything that was brought into the camp, a thing unknown hitherto in Germany.' Not all went well though, as the weather became unseasonably bad and rain turned the roads heavy with mud, slowing the pace of the march.

The French armies had been drawn away from the vulnerable Dutch border, but Marlborough's army was in turn exposed while on the move. If Bedmar in the Moselle valley, or Tallard in Alsace, spotted Marlborough's plan soon enough, they could quickly move to fall on the flank of the marching columns and cumbersome trains. With Villeroi's army closing up behind, Marlborough would face two enemy forces and disaster might result, with the troops a long way from their bases, out of position and outnumbered. Such a danger depended entirely upon the French realising the Duke's intentions, and this they failed to do. The Duke's march to the Danube was too daring a project, too imaginative for the French Marshals to credit, for they were too accustomed to turn to Versailles for advice on operational matters. Puzzled and perplexed,

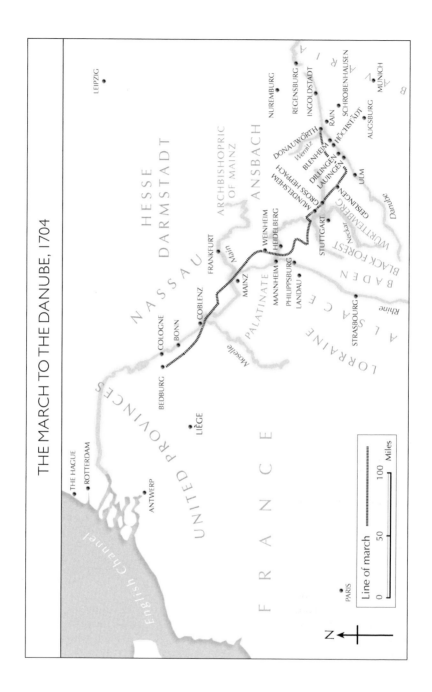

THE MARCH TO THE DANUBE, 1704

English Channel

THE HAGUE
ROTTERDAM

ANTWERP

LIÈGE

BEDBURG

COLOGNE
BONN

COBLENZ

UNITED PROVINCES

FRANCE

PARIS

Moselle

Line of march

0   50   100   Miles

N

LEIPZIG

NASSAU

HESSE
DARMSTADT

ARCHBISHOPRIC
OF MAINZ

FRANKFURT

Main

MAINZ

WEINHEIM
HEIDELBERG

MANNHEIM
PHILIPSBURG
LANDAU

PALATINATE

Neckar

STUTTGART

WÜRTTEMBERG

BLACK FOREST

BADEN

ALSACE

STRASBOURG

LORRAINE

Rhine

ANSBACH

NUREMBURG

REGENSBURG

INGOLDSTADT

SCHROBENHAUSEN

MUNICH

RAIN
EICHSTÄDT
AUGSBURG

DONAUWÖRTH
Wernitz
BLENHEIM
GROSS HEPPACH
DILLINGEN
LAUINGEN

MÜNDELSHEIM
GIESLINGEN

ULM

Danube

BAVARIA

they watched Marlborough march past and away from their grasp. Eventually, Villeroi and Tallard met in Alsace, and they again appealed to Louis XIV for instructions: 'You, who understand the ways of war so much better than we.' The King sent an order that Tallard should take his army to reinforce Marshal Marsin, who was already in Bavaria. Villeroi was to remain and hold Alsace secure; he was also to prevent the Imperial German and Dutch troops on the upper Rhine from going with Marlborough over the mountains of the Swabian Jura to the Danube valley.

After passing Heidelberg, Marlborough's army turned eastwards at Wiesloch, heading through pleasant farmland towards Württemberg. Spirits lifted among the marching troops, who even found time to notice how very pretty the German girls were. The Neckar was crossed near to Heilbronn, and on 10 June 1704, at the small village of Mundleheim, Marlborough for the first time met the President of the Imperial War Council, Prince Eugene of Savoy, who came to the Duke's camp with Count Wratislaw. The two commanders immediately struck up a close and valuable friendship. The next day Eugene inspected Marlborough's cavalry and dragoons, and he complimented the Duke on their quality and good condition after their long march. On 13 June, the Imperial field commander, the Margrave of Baden, joined them at the Inn of the Golden Fleece in Gross Heppach. Baden, unlike Eugene, was not an easy colleague to work with; he was proud and obstinate, and had learned his trade as a soldier in a more sedate school than either Marlborough or Eugene. He was brave enough, as events would prove, but given the choice he would march and countermarch to try and catch an enemy at a disadvantage, then sit down to besiege towns rather than actually engage in a battle in open field. This sedate manner of war, not unlike that favoured by many Dutch generals, was less risky to reputations and, perhaps, less expensive in highly trained troops than Marlborough's way. The two men could not easily agree how best to proceed with the campaign. However, Eugene had built a formidable reputation as a bruising fighter against the Turks and his way of war was much more akin to that of Marlborough. The Prince also had some doubts about Baden's reliability, for he was a close friend of the renegade Elector of Bavaria – they had shared many a campaign against the Turks together in the past – and it was suspected that Baden was even now corresponding with the Elector in an indiscreet way. This concern was such that Eugene had the authority to remove the Margrave from his post if he saw fit and send him to Vienna in disgrace, but in the end it did not prove necessary.

The plan for the coming campaign that the Margrave now outlined to his two colleagues was quite sound, as far as it went, with he and Marlborough each operating independently in an encirclement of the Elector's army. This would both offer the prospect of overwhelming the French and Bavarians before reinforcements could arrive from beyond the Rhine, and permit each commander to exercise authority over his own troops unhampered by the presence of the other. It had already been agreed that Eugene would go to command the Imperial and Dutch forces on the upper Rhine at the Lines of Stollhofen, and prevent further support being sent to Marsin and the Elector. However, the first part of the plan could not proceed, as the Danish contingent under the Duke of Württemberg was making slow time in marching to join the Allied army. Until they arrived, Marlborough did not have the strength to operate independently in Bavaria, and for the time being he had to make the best of working with Baden. However, as an indication of the high trust he enjoyed at the political level, Marlborough now received plenipotentiary authority from London and The Hague to negotiate a treaty with the Elector of Bavaria, on whatever terms he saw fit, if the opportunity arose.

On 14 June, Eugene left for the Rhine, and Marlborough wrote the next day to a friend from his camp at Ebersbach:

> *Prince Eugene went post for the Rhine, where he was to arrive this morning, and Prince Louis [Baden] is to be at the same time with his army on the Danube. I followed our troops hither, intending to join him in a few days, it being agreed that we act in conjunction for ten or twelve days till the next of the troops come up. We propose to march directly to the Elector, who, it is thought will either retire over the Danube or march to his strong camp at Dillingen and Lavingen.*

To complicate matters, the States-General now asked again for the return to the Low Countries of their troops, but Marlborough turned a deaf ear. He wrote to his close friend Anthonius Hiensius, the Grand Pensionary of Holland, 'I beg you will take care that I receive no orders from the States that may put me out of a condition of reducing the Elector, for that would be of all mischiefs the greatest.'

One obstacle that had to be crossed before the campaign could proceed was the steep Geislingen pass in the Jura hills. The weather continued to be bad and the roads were in a dreadful condition. John Deane wrote:

> *It hath rayned thirty-two days together more or less and miserable marches we have had for deep and miry roads and through tedious woods and wildernesses and over vast high rocks and mountains, that it may be easily judged what our little army endured and what unusuall hardship they went through.*

Marlborough's army would be vulnerable to attack as they threaded their way through the Geislingen pass because the Elector of Bavaria might move to block the route, and if the rearguard and baggage train of the Allied army were threatened by the French, the main body could hardly turn about in their tracks to support them.

As it turned out, the Elector chose not to take the initiative, and news was soon received in the Allied camp that his army had fallen back. 'We have advice that the Elector has re-passed the Danube with all his troops,' the Duke wrote to London. A message came in from the Margrave of Baden that his Imperial troops had moved to secure the head of the pass, and so Marlborough's army plunged in and came through safely. On 22 June 1704, the marching troops met those of the Margrave at Launsheim on the northern approaches to Bavaria. Their combined armies comprised 60,000 men, and the Duke now had a superiority in numbers against any of the French columns ponderously manoeuvring against him. The major strategic shift in the Allied effort, from the Low Countries in the north to the valley of the Danube in the south, had been accomplished, and France had lost the initiative in the war.

With the Allied armies now combined, the Elector and Marsin, conscious of their weakness in numbers until French reinforcements arrived, put their 40,000-strong army into an entrenched camp at Dillingen on the north bank of the Danube. Marlborough had not been able to bring the big guns of his siege train from the Low Countries, and Baden failed to provide any, despite giving assurances that he would do so. The Duke could not attack the Elector in his camp, and had to manoeuvre to cross the Danube at another point, hoping to force the French and Bavarians out into the open where they could be brought to battle. The lines of supply and communication for his army were now established into Franconia and central Germany; these were fairly secure from French interference, but the Duke's forward base at Nordlingen was too far north to be convenient once the line of the Danube was crossed. Marlborough had to look around for an alternative: his eye fell on Donauwörth at the confluence of the Danube and Wörnitz rivers. This small town offered a good river crossing place and would be a secure forward base, but it was overlooked by the 'Hill of the Bell', the Schellenberg.

As Marlborough's army drew near to Donauwörth, he received interesting information regarding the measures the Elector of Bavaria was taking to repulse him. The Duke's chaplain Francis Hare wrote:

Some 13,000 of the enemy were encamped upon the Schellenberg and they were very busy in fortifying and entrenching themselves. His Grace sent out the Quartermaster-General [William Cadogan] with a party of 400 horse to gain more particular intelligence.

Comte Jean d'Arco, a Piedmontese officer in Bavarian service, had been sent from the Elector's camp at Dillingen with about 12,000 men to hold the grassy hill and walled town. He had sixteen Bavarian and seven French infantry battalions, six squadrons of French and three squadrons of Bavarian dragoons

The Schellenberg. Donauwörth seen from the slopes of the Schellenberg.

and sixteen guns. This was a well-balanced and potent force; the troops were of good quality, led by veteran officers. In addition, Donauwörth was held by a regular French infantry battalion and two battalions of Bavarian militia. However, the old defensive position on the hill, a fort built by the Swedish warrior king Gustavus Adolphus during the Thirty Years' War, was neglected and broken down. The walls of the town were second-rate and dilapidated, with little modern sophistication to ward off a determined attack. Getting his men in place on 30 June 1704, d'Arco set them to improve the breastworks on the Schellenberg, and conscripted peasants to help with the labouring task. Several of the locals who fled to avoid the impressments came to the Allied camp with useful news of the preparations on the hill.

John Deane would be among those who went into action on the Schellenberg, and he wrote:

> *The enemy was incampt upon the hill called Schellinburgh neare to the toune of Danuwert, being the strongest pass in all Germany and they made it stronger than ordinary this yeare by reason they heard of the English army coming to make them a visitte.*

The Margrave of Baden protested when he learned that Marlborough had plans for an outright assault, arguing that casualties were sure to be severe. However, despite the obvious need for cooperation, Marlborough had the most authority as the representative of Queen Anne who was by now virtually the paymaster of the Imperial armies. The Duke was aware that every day which passed allowed the Elector to strengthen the defences on the hill, as the movement towards the river crossings at Donauwörth could not be hidden. On 30 June, the Allied army was marching eastwards to Amerdingen, just 15 miles short of Donauwörth. Matters became more urgent on 1 July, when a messenger arrived from Prince Eugene with the unwelcome news that Tallard had eluded him on the Rhine, and was now marching with another French army through the Black Forest to reinforce Marsin and the Elector. If Marlborough did not force the line of the Danube quickly, and carry the war into Bavaria now, he might never do so.

The Schellenberg was to be subject to a direct storm, as Marlborough did not have time to manoeuvre d'Arco out of position. The Duke had 130 men selected from each of the forty-five battalions of the Allied army, forming a body of 5,850 in total. These were the grenadiers and other volunteers for the dangerous task of being stormers. A 'Forlorn Hope' of eighty men was picked from the 1st English Foot Guards, commanded by Lord John Mordaunt and Colonel Richard Munden, and would spearhead the attack. Marlborough could not spare the time for the main body of the Allied army to close up, but he formed a second echelon for the attack, which comprised two 'divisions', each of eight battalions (British, Dutch, Hanoverian and Hessian), under command of Lieutenant-General Withers and Count Horn. Backing them would be thirty-five squadrons of British and Dutch cavalry and dragoons, led by Henry Lumley and Graf Reynard van Hompesch. Lastly, Baden, whose Wing of the army was behind Marlborough's on the line of march, would hold a brigade of Imperial grenadiers ready for action when the opportunity arose, as there was not sufficient frontage to allow them to deploy fully at first. Colonel Holcroft Blood would bring a battery of guns into action near to the hamlet of Berg, just to the north of Donauwörth, to support the attack, and the Margrave would also provide a battery for this task. In all, Marlborough was able to deploy about 22,000 troops in this bold and brutally direct operation. Given the narrow frontage on which the Allies could operate, this was probably the maximum practical number of men to deploy, at least until the leading echelons had moved forward to the attack, but the numerical advantage over the defenders was quite slim, with every chance that the attack might not succeed.

The Allied army left camp on the march to battle in the early hours of 2 July. The roads were muddy and progress was slower than expected. Despite this, the fast-flowing Wörnitz river was crossed at Ebermorgen by mid-afternoon, using an old stone bridge, and pontoons laid on the adjacent meadows. The troops' approach had been detected during the morning by d'Arco's outposts, and Marlborough was fired on briefly while carrying out his own reconnaissance of the defensive preparations on the Schellenberg. However, he was able to see that the ground beyond the Danube was being prepared for a camp –

tent lines were being marked out, ready for the arrival of substantial numbers of troops; it was evident that d'Arco expected to be reinforced, probably on the following day. As if in response, the Duke ordered Cadogan to begin to mark out a camp well short of the Wörnitz, giving the impression that the army would spend the night there rather than mount an attack immediately. Time seemed to be on the side of the defenders as the afternoon wore on; d'Arco expected to be joined by the Elector and his main force the next day, and was quite relaxed at news of the Allied approach. Leaving the supervision of the still incomplete defences on the hill to his subordinates, he went off to have lunch with the French commander in Donauwörth, Colonel DuBordet.

As the marching columns poured across the Wörnitz and drew near the dark hill, the Bavarian outposts set fire to the hamlet of Berg and hurried off to give the alarm. D'Arco, rudely interrupted from his comfortable lunch, took to his horse and hurried up the slopes, calling to his labouring soldiers to drop shovels, take up their muskets and fall into their ranks. Colonel Jean-Martin de la Colonie, a French officer who fought that day in the Bavarian service, wrote that:

> *The Schellenberg height is oval in plan, with a gentle slope on the southern side, which affords very easy communications with Donauwert; whilst on the northern [side] the country is covered with very thick woods and undergrowth reaching close up to the old entrenchments.*

These thick woods and undergrowth limited Marlborough's freedom of action, and he had to throw his stormers into the battle on a very narrow front. Among the marching Allied soldiers nearing the hill was a female dragoon, Christian Davies, and she remembered:

> *Our vanguard did not come into sight on the enemy entrenchments til the afternoon; however, not to give the Bavarians time to make themselves yet stronger, the duke ordered the Dutch General Goor, who commanded the right Wing, comprised of English and Dutch with some auxiliary troops, to attack, as soon as possible.*

The attack went in just after 6pm, the soldiers tramping across the small but boggy Kaiback stream to get to the foot of the hill. Blood's gunners pounded the defenders from a battery position near to Berg, and caused havoc among the French infantry exposed on the higher ground above the breastwork, which was manned by the Bavarians. De la Colonie wrote that he was drenched in the blood and brains of one of his officers, the Comte de la Bastide, with almost the first roundshot: 'The enemy's battery opened fire on us, and raked us through and through.'

The Wings of an Army

In the early eighteenth century it was common practice for armies in the field to comprise two Wings, which functioned in a similar manner to modern army corps (except that, unlike the present-day formations, they were not self-sufficient and would rarely operate independently). Each Wing would be commanded by a general officer of broadly equal rank who, in turn, would report to the army commander.

In August 1704, the Allied army fought at Blenheim with Prince Eugene's Wing on the right and Marlborough's Wing on the left. Eugene deferred to Marlborough as the commanding general in the planning and execution of the battle, and threw his smaller Wing into expensive attacks to fix their opponents and prevent effective cooperation between the different parts of the French and Bavarian army. This overall plan worked very well, despite the strains of that long summer afternoon, because of the trust and friendship which existed between the two men. The Elector of Bavaria, Marshal Tallard and Marshal Marsin, by comparison, operated very differently. The Elector, by virtue of his rank, was the more senior commander, but his own depleted army was just a fraction of the size of the French forces present. Tallard and Marsin paid lip-service to deferring to the Elector, but there was little cooperation between them. Marsin refused to move to Tallard's support later in the day, and the two Wings of the French and Bavarian army fought their own independent battles, almost entirely separately, as if they were two distinct armies, neither of which had an interest or stake in the success of the other.

Care should be taken when reading accounts of battles at this time, not to confuse the movements of the two Wings. The terms 'right' and 'left' are for identification only and do not relate to their actual deployment. The right Wing might well be holding ground on the left flank, while the left Wing prepares to attack on the right!

The Allied stormers had each been handed a bundle of fascines (sticks) with which to bridge any ditch obstacles. The soldiers wastefully threw these away into a dry gully or cart-track that they had to cross as they toiled up the lower slope, which was heavy going despite de la Colonie's assertion that the gradient was gentle. The French and Bavarian defenders watched their approach in silence, the only sound being the tapping of a French side-drummer trying to mask the intimidating shouts and hurrahs of the advancing stormers. As the range closed, the leading ranks of panting Allied soldiers came into view, and they were suddenly swept with heavy volleys of well-directed musketry and canister fire from above. John Deane described the opening phase of the assault:

> *No sooner did our Forlorne Hope appear but the enemy did throw in their volleys of canon balls and small shott among them and made a brave defence and a bold resistance against us as brave loyall hearted gentlemen souldiers ought to for there prince and country.*

Scores of the leading attackers were tumbled down in the blast, and the confusion was made worse by handfuls of fizzing hand grenades which were showered easily down the slope into their toiling ranks. With admirable discipline, though, the gaps in the ranks were closed up and the attackers pressed forward towards the defences, where a savage contest with bayonet and musket butt began wherever the soldiers could reach each other. The ditch running across the front of the breastwork caused great difficulty, as the attackers now had no fascines with which to bridge the obstacle. The general officer leading the assault, van Goor, was killed, and many of the regimental officers, conspicuous in their laced coats, were shot down. Colonel Munden, who went in with the Forlorn Hope of English Foot Guards, remembered that his hat was all shot to pieces by musket balls, but he came through the day unhurt.

With their ranks torn with canister and musketry, the stormers fell back down the slope, away from the tormenting fire of the defenders. Exultantly, scores of Bavarian grenadiers came pouring over the breastworks in pursuit to drive their opponents to ruin and defeat at the foot of the hill. They were too rash, for the second echelon of Allied infantry, under Henry Withers, was now moving into position to support the attack. Orkney's Regiment and the 1st English Foot Guards met the counter-attack with solid volleys, and the slopes of the Schellenberg were now strewn with Bavarian dead and wounded too. The grenadiers scrambled back into cover as Marlborough's renewed assault went in, but once again the fire of the defenders broke up the Allied ranks. Count von Styrum dismounted and went forward on foot to encourage the soldiers, but he too was killed. The attackers fell back a second time to recover their order. The ground in front of the breastworks was grotesquely covered with the groaning, shrieking wreckage of their assault.

Marlborough was close by, anxiously watching the progress of the attack. He now ordered his squadrons of cavalry and dragoons to close up to the foot of the hill, along the line of the Kaiback stream. As Francis Hare put it, 'The Horse and Dragoons stood so close and animated the Foot so much that they rallied and went in again.' This move made it difficult for any waverers among the assault squads to make off to a place of greater safety, but Marlborough's chaplain was too delicate to say so. Thus encouraged, the Allied attack was pressed forward through a concentrated and vicious volume of musketry the like of which, it was afterwards said, had never been seen on a battlefield before. Despite the gallantry of the Allied soldiers, many of whom now had no officers to command them, the defence was as sturdy as ever, the casualties were appalling, and a dangerous stalemate seemed to have been reached on the hill.

At this time, Marlborough learned that the line of gabions linking the walls of the town with the breastworks on the Schellenberg was quite unoccupied. The French troops stationed there by d'Arco, the Nectancourt Régiment, had apparently been drawn into the desperate fighting on the slopes above and the left flank of his position was laid bare. The Duke sent an officer to find Baden and bring him forward with his Imperial troops, now approaching Berg in increasing numbers. The Margrave needed no urging and was already hurrying his grenadiers along the Kaiback stream, little troubled by some scattered firing from the garrison in the town. The Imperial troops formed up at the foot of the hill, staring upwards at the raw open flank of d'Arco's position.

Despite other pressing demands on his attention, the approach of Baden's troops along the small stream had not gone unnoticed by d'Arco. He hurried to the rear of the hill to bring forward the dismounted dragoons, held in reserve there, to counter the new threat. This soon proved to be an error: as the dragoons advanced against the flank of the Imperial troops climbing the slope, they were thrown back by the volleys of three companies of Baden's grenadiers, who turned half-right to meet them. The shaken dragoons were reluctant to try again, although Colonel DuBordet tried a sortie from the garrison in Donauwörth to support them. D'Arco found himself out of position and out of contact with his main body of troops fighting for their lives on the crest of the hill.

At the breastwork the deadly struggle continued, and Count Alessandro Maffei, now the senior Bavarian commander in the defences, saw the grey-coated Imperial infantry steadily climbing the slopes from the direction of town. In the dust and smoke of the battle recognition was difficult, and some officers called out to those around them not to fire as these men must surely be reinforcements from the garrison in Donauwörth. Almost immediately, the error was realised, as Baden's troops began to form their line of battle in the rear of the French and Bavarian position. Their musketry volleys swept through the ranks of the defenders, many of whom, taken entirely by surprise, were suddenly called on by their officers to change front and face to the left to

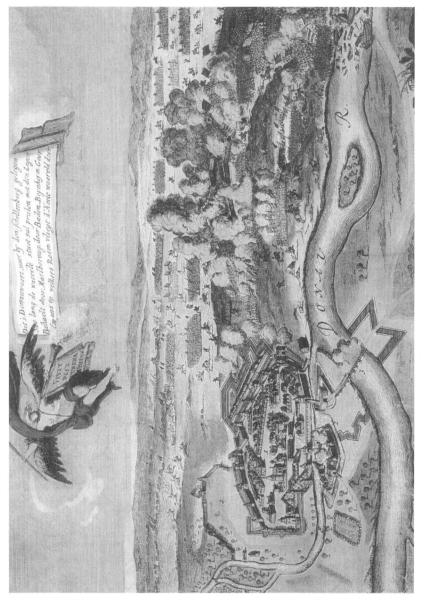

The Schellenberg. 18th century depiction of Marlborough's great attack, 2 July 1704.

meet the new and unexpected threat. Confusion resulted as Marlborough's stormers, reinforced by dismounted dragoons sent in by the Duke, scrambled over the now weakly held breastwork and pressed forward, crowding the defenders back towards the crown of the hill. De la Colonie wrote:

> They [Baden's troops] arrived within gunshot of our flank at about 7.30 in the evening, without our being aware of the possibility of such a thing, so occupied were we in the defence of our own particular post and the confidence we had as to the safety of the rest of our position. ... My men had no sooner got clear of the entrenchments than they found that the slope was in their favour, and they fairly broke and took to flight, in order to reach the plain that lay before them before the enemy's cavalry could get upon their track.

The defenders, after a gallant fight but outflanked and outnumbered, were running for safety. Baden had been wounded in the foot, but Marlborough anticipated the collapse and his squadrons of cavalry were well closed up. These horsemen were now sent in ruthless pursuit, chasing and cutting down the fugitives without mercy, and the dragoons were also remounted to take part in the bloody work. Comte d'Arco, with his army broken and in flight, hurried to the sanctuary of the walls of Donauwörth, as did Maffei, but they had to hammer on the gates before the nervous garrison could be induced to admit them. On the hill, the Bavarian gunners, professional to the last, sacrificed themselves to spike their guns before the victors laid hands on them. While light lasted the pursuit was pressed onwards, and many of d'Arco's soldiers attempting to cross the Danube were drowned when a pontoon bridge collapsed. Rain had begun to fall, adding to the misery of the hundreds of wounded of both armies who lay littered across the Schellenberg.

Not only were all the guns on the Schellenberg captured by the victorious Allies, so too were the French and Bavarian regimental colours, except those of de la Colonie's regiment, the Grenadiers Rouge (Boismarel's Grenadiers), who managed to keep together, more or less. The valuable Bavarian engineer pontoon train was left at the water's edge for Marlborough to seize. So devastating was the defeat that, of the 12,000 troops deployed in the defence on the hill, no more than about 3,000 men ever rallied to the colours. The precise number of Bavarians and French killed that day is not known, but over 2,000 unwounded prisoners were taken by the Allies. These soldiers were the best that the Elector had, and the destruction of d'Arco's corps in this way had a distinct effect on the ability of Marlborough's opponents to face him in the coming campaign. Bavaria had become a limping ally for the French.

Marlborough's army had paid a severe price for their victory. Of the 22,000 troops engaged in the storm, some 1,400 were killed and over 4,000 wounded

(1,500 of the casualties were British, every third man in the line that day). Only seventeen of Mordaunt's eighty-strong Forlorn Hope survived the day. The hospitals that the Duke had set up in Nordlingen were overwhelmed with the wounded, and the 'widows' of the army were instructed to report there to tend the stricken soldiers (at least one of whom was also a woman). Among the fallen were several general officers, and fine soldiers like van Goor and von Styrum would be sorely missed in the weeks to come. Still, Donauwörth was abandoned by Colonel DuBordet that night. Marlborough now had his forward base for the coming operations and the vital crossing point over the Danube. Congratulations on the daring success came to his camp from many quarters, although some expressed consternation at the scale of the losses, and one critic sarcastically asked whether there 'were not many such hills in Germany, and must a battle be fought for each one?' Perhaps the most expressive tribute was that from Emperor Leopold, whose capital of Vienna was no longer under threat. The victory on the Schellenberg was, he wrote, due to the 'wonderful ardour and constancy of the troops under your command.'

So Truly Great

Getting across the Danube was one thing, but forcing peace on the Elector of Bavaria was quite another. Shocked at the destruction of d'Arco's corps on the Schellenberg, which he had viewed from the other side of the river, the Elector knew that his position at Dillingen was no longer tenable. He abandoned the line of the Danube, drew his garrisons out of Nieuberg and Ratisbon, and fell back southwards, coming to rest behind the shelter of the river Lech, near to Augsburg. In the wake of the defeat, the Elector sent envoys to discuss peace terms with Marlborough, but it turned out that he was just playing for time, hoping to blunt the Allied campaign while Marshal Tallard and his French army drew nearer. The Electress, more pragmatic than her volatile husband, begged him to negotiate seriously with Marlborough, but the Elector put his faith in the French.

Reinforcements were daily joining the Allied army – the Danish cavalry arrived on 6 July – and the town of Nieuburg had been abandoned by the Bavarians, which further freed Marlborough's lines of supply and communication northwards. His advanced detachments crossed the Lech on pontoon bridges at Gunderkingen on 9 July, feeling out the strength of opposition. However, the lack of a proper siege train hampered operations, and the reduction of the small town of Rain was a tedious and time-consuming business. The Duke wrote to London on 13 July, 'We have been waiting for the arrival of the great guns from Nuremberg, in order to attack Rain, where there is a garrison of about a thousand men, which is not thought advisable to leave behind us.' The town fell to Marlborough three days later, and he marched his troops towards Munich and sowed alarm throughout Bavaria.

The Duke then turned aside to face the Elector and Marsin at Augsburg, and on 18 July his army closed up to the Lech at Friedberg. He had won the strategic prize of placing his numerically stronger army between the French and Bavarians and the city of Vienna. However, on 26 July, exasperated at the prevarication of the Elector's envoys, Marlborough, having swept the country-side along the Lech clear of provisions, let loose his cavalry and dragoons on a campaign of devastation across the rich lands south of the Danube. This had two aims: firstly, to put pressure on the Elector to make peace; and secondly, to ruin Bavaria as a base from which the French and Bavarians could either attack Vienna or pursue the Duke into Franconia if he had to withdraw northwards. Time was not on Marlborough's side: autumn was approaching and if he could not force a decision in the Danube valley before winter, he must take his army into central Germany to provision and find billets. The Dutch would almost certainly demand the return of their own troops, and the Duke's whole plan would be in ruins.

For miles around, Bavarian villages and hamlets were put to the torch after cattle and crops were seized for the commissaries of the Allied army: 'With fire and sword the country round, was wasted far and wide, and many a nursing mother then and suckling baby died.' The Margrave of Baden protested to Marlborough at the supposed barbarity of the campaign, so the Duke directed him to use his own Imperial cavalry on later operations. The Duke was sensitive to adverse comments, and wrote to his wife that the English cavalry had no part in the devastation. This was irrelevant (and not true), as Marlborough gave the orders for the operation no matter which troops were involved. The responsibility was his and the troops thought none the worse of him for it. Christian Davies, serving still with Hay's Dragoons despite wounds suffered at the Schellenberg, wrote of the conduct of the Allied soldiery in the Danube campaign:

> The allies sent parties on every hand to ravage the country, who pillaged above fifty villages, burnt the houses of peasants and gentlemen, and forced the inhabitants, with what few cattle had escaped the insatiable enemy, to seek refuge in the woods. ... I had left the hospital time enough to contribute to their misery and to have a share in the plunder.

The burning of Bavaria was a ruthless act of war, but some observers felt that the scale of the devastation was exaggerated for propaganda purposes. Colonel Jean-Martin de la Colonie remembered, 'I followed a route through several villages said to have been reduced to cinders, and although I certainly found a few burnt houses, still the damage was as nothing as compared with the reports current through the country.' Samuel Noyes, however, wrote that, 'In this last march particularly we entirely burnt a mighty pretty village with a noble church and cloister.' The destruction, on whatever scale, was justified militarily, for the Elector was obliged to disperse much of his small army to protect his own estates. With no richly stocked countryside left to supply the voracious demands of the French and Bavarian troops, the Elector's ability to campaign was, at best, foundering, and he now had to trust that time would run out for his opponent.

All this while, the French army under Marshal Tallard was struggling through the passes of the Black Forest. He had eluded Prince Eugene's vigilance on the Rhine, but the predatory foraging customs by which the French troops fed themselves earned the hatred of the peasantry of the unfortunate regions through which they marched. Their advanced guards fought a battle to clear the roads of bands of desperate villagers, while partisans and brigands closed around their rearguard to murder couriers, harry foragers and pick off stragglers. To add to their troubles, the French cavalry found their horses falling prey to glanders (known as the 'German sickness') and they were not in top condition on arrival in Bavaria as a result. The veteran Swiss regiments of infantry in French service had exercised their right under the terms of their enlistment not to campaign beyond the Rhine frontier, and Louis XIV decided that they should not be coerced. Accordingly, a number of inexperienced French infantry battalions were sent to replace them and to march with Tallard to Bavaria.

After wasting several days laying siege to Villingen, Tallard drew off on learning of Eugene's approach; the Prince had brought only 20,000 men, as the Lines of Stollhofen could not be left unguarded. Making as good time as his enormous supply train allowed, the Marshal delivered his wagons to the depots in Ülm. He then combined his 34,000-strong army with that of Marsin and the Elector on 6 August 1704 at Biberbach. Tallard was not impressed to find that, as he had suspected, not only were the depots and magazines in Bavaria inadequate to provision his army for very long without further re-supply from beyond the Rhine, but the Elector had also dispersed his army in response to Marlborough's campaign of ravaging the region. He wrote to the French Minister of War, Michel de Chamillart, of the Elector's attitude at this critical time:

There was the total ignorance of the enemy's strength, and M. de Baviere [the Elector] having all his troops, except five battalions and about twenty-seven squadrons, spread out about the country to protect his salt-works, a gentleman's private estate in fact, instead of what they should have guarded – his frontiers.

Marsin was just as scathing in his reports: 'The Elector has thirty-five good battalions and forty-three squadrons of good troops, of which since the entry of the enemy into Bavaria he has had [only] twenty-three squadrons and five battalions with the army.'

Eugene had hovered around Tallard's flank during the passage through the Black Forest, but with his lack of numbers could not do much to disrupt the march seriously. The same day that the French and Bavarian armies met near Augsburg, the Prince encamped his small force on the plain of Höchstädt on the north bank of the Danube. The evening of 6 August, he rode over to confer with Marlborough at Schrobenhausen just south of Donauwörth, accompanied only by a single trooper as escort. In an intriguing twist to the campaign, the Margrave of Baden had suggested that he should take his own Imperial troops to besiege the Bavarian-held fortress of Ingolstadt on the Danube, some miles below Donauwörth. This was a plan discussed earlier in the campaign, but shelved at the time. Now, happy to have the possibly unreliable Imperial general out of the way, Marlborough quickly agreed to the operation. After conferring with his colleagues over the following two days, Baden marched off eastwards with a corps of over 12,000 infantry and 3,700 cavalry on the evening of 9 August. The Duke allowed Baden to go, and took a considerable risk in the process, for in doing so, he gave up a precious numerical advantage. Now, 56,000 French and Bavarian troops were facing 52,000 British, Dutch, Danish, German and Imperial soldiers. Marlborough plainly felt the price worth the paying; he and Eugene were about to embark on a campaign of the most daring and dangerous kind, and it had little hope of success while the obstinate Margrave was on the scene.

Although they were not yet aware that Baden had gone, Tallard, Marsin and the Elector now felt confident enough to challenge their opponents while the two Wings of the Allied army were still apart – Marlborough at Rain to the south of the Danube, and Eugene about twenty miles away at Höchstädt on the north bank. If either could be caught while separated from the other in this way, the French and Bavarians should be able to overwhelm their less numerous opponents, and the whole Allied campaign on the Danube would be over. Eugene, with the smaller force, seemed the more vulnerable, but Marlborough could not move to combine with him until he was sure that his opponents had crossed to the north bank of the Danube. To do so prematurely might risk Baden's detachment at Ingolstadt becoming prey to a French and Bavarian raid (if nothing worse) mounted south of the river. Timing was everything.

Tallard would have preferred to wait, replenish his supplies and allow Marlborough's Danube campaign to wither away in the cold weeks of autumn. The region was unfamiliar to him, and there was some doubt as to the actual strength of the Allied army. To wait seemed to be the prudent course. Meanwhile, further reinforcements and supplies could be summoned from the Rhine – the remaining Imperial troops at the Lines of Stolhoffen had not the strength to prevent them. However, Marsin was an ambitious man in a hurry; newly created a Marshal of France, he had a reputation to make. The Elector was also anxious to push the pace of the campaign, for it was on his lands that the Allied cavalry were exercising their undoubted talent for barn-burning. He and Tallard had sharp words over whether to wait or to advance, the Marshal replying to the Elector's scoffing at his caution, 'I should imagine that you wished to gamble with the King's forces, without having any of your own, to see at no risk what would happen' – an obvious allusion to the continued dispersion of the Bavarian troops on secondary guard duties. At last it was agreed to strike at Eugene, and on 9 August, as Baden marched off to Ingolstadt, their army began crossing the Danube on pontoon bridges to the now derelict camp at Dillingen, a few miles to the west of Höchstädt.

Eugene was in a very exposed position so far forward. He wrote to Marlborough on 10 August 1704:

> The enemy have marched. It is almost certain that the whole army is passing the Danube at Lauingen. They have pushed a Lieutenant-Colonel who I sent to reconnoitre back to Hochstadt. The Plain of Dillingen is crowded with troops. I have held on all day here; but with eighteen battalions I dare not risk staying the night. I quit however with much regret being good, and if he [Tallard] takes it, it will cost us much to get it back. Everything, milord, consists in speed and that you put yourself in movement to join me tomorrow. While I was writing sure news has reached me that the whole army has crossed.

The Prince prudently drew his troops eastwards along the course of the Danube towards Donauwörth, and sent pioneers on ahead to prepare fresh defences on the Schellenberg in case they should be needed. In moving away he subtly, but certainly, pulled the French and Bavarians forward from their river crossing places and into a position to be the target for an attack. Marlborough had learned from his own scouts that his opponents had crossed to the north bank of the Danube. He at once detached twenty-seven cavalry squadrons, commanded by the Duke of Württemberg, to support Eugene, and a strong detachment of twenty battalions of infantry, under his younger brother, Charles Churchill, followed. Marlborough and Eugene met at Münster, on the Kessel stream just to the west of Donauwörth, and the junction of their armies

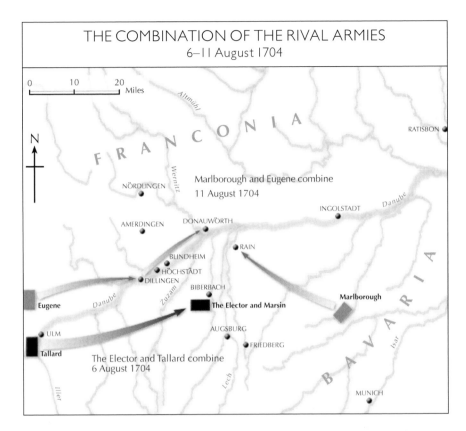

THE COMBINATION OF THE RIVAL ARMIES
6–11 August 1704

0   10   20
Miles

Altmühl

FRANCONIA

N

RATISBON

NÖRDLINGEN

Wernitz

Marlborough and Eugene combine
11 August 1704

INGOLSTADT

Danube

AMERDINGEN   DONAUWÖRTH

RAIN

BLINDHEIM
HÖCHSTÄDT
DILLINGEN
BIBERBACH

Marlborough

Eugene   *Danube*   *Zuzam*   The Elector and Marsin

BAVARIA

ULM   AUGSBURG

FRIEDBERG

Isar

Tallard   The Elector and Tallard combine
6 August 1704

Iller   *Lech*

MUNICH

was safely achieved in the afternoon of 11 August. In many ways, the most perilous part of the Allied campaign had passed.

News that Baden had been detached to Ingolstadt was rumoured in the French and Bavarian camp that very evening. If this proved to be so, the Allied forces, even when combined, were quite correctly thought to be fewer in numbers and guns than the army which their opponents could deploy on the plain of Höchstädt. It seemed clear to the Elector and the two Marshals that Marlborough had fumbled his campaign. He had not prevented them from combining their own armies and had then allowed Baden to go off with a powerful corps on what was plainly a secondary operation. So, it appeared that the initiative now lay firmly with them. This was a comforting thought, but the French and Bavarian commanders were becoming careless, and this was dangerous in the presence of such opponents as Marlborough and Eugene; the price for carelessness would be heavy.

During 11 August, Tallard and his colleagues pushed their troops forward from Dillingen, past the marshy ground along the Pulver and Brunnen streams near Höchstädt, to encamp their 56,000 troops and 90 guns amid the comparatively dry and lush cornfields between the villages of Lutzingen, Oberglau and Blindheim. In doing so they overran some of Eugene's small forward detachments. The site they now occupied enjoyed the open, level plain stretching for 4 miles from the banks of the Danube to the wooded hills of the Swabian Jura to the north. This was a good place to make a camp, with fresh water nearby and forage for horses plentiful in the neighbourhood. It might also be a good place to fight, provided that preparations were made in good time. The plain of Höchstädt was certainly well suited for mounted operations, and this would please the French, with their numerous cavalry, very well. As an added comfort, the Nebel stream ran straight across the plain and shielded the French and Bavarian camp from sudden attack. So, there the army stayed, comfortably setting up their massed lines of tents on 12 August.

Tallard wanted to dam the Nebel stream to increase the extent of the water obstacle, and also to erect an earthen redoubt in the centre of his camp and equip it with artillery. The Elector asked him to do neither, wishing to protect the still-unharvested crops of his own farmers. Thinking it of no importance, the Marshal agreed, and the ground remained undisturbed. The Comte de Merode-Westerloo, a wittily observant Walloon officer who served with Tallard's army, described the area occupied by the French and Bavarians:

> *Our right Wing was on the left bank of the River Danube with the village of Blindheim [Blenheim] some two hundred paces to its front. All the generals of the right Wing had quarters there. In the front of this village ran a small stream [the Nebel], running from its source a mile away to the left. . . . The Elector and his men held a position reaching as far as the village of Lutzingen, which contained his headquarters, with the woods stretching away to Nordlingen to his front. Before this position was an area of marshy ground, a few hamlets and one or two mills along the little stream. Blenheim village itself was surrounded by hedges; fences and other obstacles enclosed gardens and meadows. All in all this position was pretty fair, but had we advanced a mere 800 or 1,000 paces farther to our front we would have held a far more compact position, with our right still on the Danube and our left protected by woods.*

The Comte, although speaking with the valuable benefit of hindsight, was absolutely right in this last comment. A more serious omission by the French and Bavarian commanders is hard to imagine than apparently to give no thought to holding the village of Schwenningen, lying about a half-mile in advance of their encampment. Here the wooded hills and the Danube were no more than a mile apart, instead of the 4 miles that had to be covered on the plain, and, at the very least, the place should have been held by a strong forward detachment.

While the French and Bavarians settled into their seemingly safe camp, Marlborough and Eugene, with 52,000 men and 60 guns, were marching steadily towards them, shielded by the outcropping wooded hills, through the villages of Münster and Tapfheim. In the afternoon of 12 August, the two commanders ascended the church tower at Tapfheim to view their opponents' camp, and then went to a small hill near to the hamlet of Wolperstetten for a closer look. To their delight they could plainly see the tent lines that were being laid out a few miles away on the firm ground of the plain of Höchstädt rather than in the less comfortable, but more secure, marshy ground near that town itself. Captain Robert Parker wrote afterwards that, 'Here was a fine plain without a hedge or ditch for the cavalry on both sides to show their bravery.' Although Parker seemed to overlook the presence of the Nebel stream, he was right in that the open plain beyond that obstacle was excellent cavalry country.

The whole of 12 August was alive with alarms and skirmishes as the outposts and scouts of the two armies brushed against each other. The Duc d'Humières, one of Tallard's cavalry commanders, was sufficiently concerned to send forward the Marquis de Silly with a detachment of forty squadrons to find out what the Allies were doing. These were driven off by Archibald Rowe's brigade of British infantry, who were deployed to cover the pioneers of the advancing

Blenheim. The plain of Höchstädt, looking from the French position towards the Nebel stream.

33

army, labouring to bridge the streams in the area and improve the crude forest tracks leading westwards to Höchstädt. Marlborough wrote, 'Intelligence was brought that the enemy's squadrons had attempted to fall on our workmen, but had been repulsed by the guard which covered them.' It was not quite that simple: the 1st English Foot Guards had to go to Rowe's assistance before the unwelcome French attention was dealt with. Marlborough then moved quickly to secure the narrow strip of land between the marshy Danube and the wooded Fuchsberg hill, at the Schwenningen defile. Rowe's brigade, together with the 1st English Foot Guards and Wilkes's Hessian brigade, occupied the village that evening as dusk fell.

The seizure of this important tactical ground without any real fighting was a significant achievement for Marlborough. Had Tallard manned the village of Schwenningen, the Duke would have had to fight on a very narrow frontage compared with that on the plain of Höchstädt. The simple reason for this oversight was that neither the French nor the Bavarian commander expected to have to fight here at all. Numerically superior, and with the certain knowledge that time was against their opponents, they appeared to be mesmerised by the prospect that Marlborough would lamely abandon his campaign and take the prudent course – to withdraw along his lines of supply into Franconia. Prisoners taken by de Silly's cavalry in the fighting that afternoon, when questioned, supposed that their army was about to withdraw. In the meantime, the French and Bavarians could occupy their comfortable camp, with flanks secured by the Danube on the one hand and the hills of the Jura on the other, while awaiting developments and watching for a chance to strike at any clumsy move their opponents might make.

That night, Marlborough's army lay in the woods near to Schwenningen, just across the Fuchsberg hill from the plain of Höchstädt. The soldiers slept for a few hours in the open, under brilliant stars, while in the opposing camp the troops relaxed in their tents, entirely ignorant of the calamity that was to befall them the following day. Merode-Westerloo, who had tried to take part in the skirmishing that day, remembered:

> *I rode out beyond Blindheim village into the corn-filled plain – taking good care not to get too far away from any escort, which I might well have needed. When I saw our troops falling back I also returned to the camp, and sat down to a good plate of soup in Blindheim with my generals and colonels. I was never in better form and after wining and dining well, we one and all dispersed to our respective quarters. ... I don't believe I ever slept sounder than on that night.*

Robert Parker wrote of the intervening hours of darkness 'We lay on our arms all night and next day, being 2 August [OS], we marched by break of day.'

34

The drum rolls that called the sleepy troops stiffly to their feet could be heard in the French and Bavarian camp, but seemed to cause no alarm. Remarkably, that very morning, Tallard on rising spent a few minutes dictating a letter to his private secretary to send to Louis XIV. In a memorable passage the Marshal predicted that the Allied campaign was, in effect, checkmated and that it was expected their army would withdraw towards Nordlingen and Franconia before very long:

It looks as if they will march this day. Rumour in the country expects them at Nordlingen. If that be true, they will leave us between the Danube and themselves and in consequence they will have difficulty in sustaining the posts and depots which they have taken in Bavaria.

How wrong the Marshal was, with his simple inability to grasp the intrepid character of both Marlborough and Eugene. So confident were the French and Bavarians that orders were even given for foragers to go out as usual that morning. Tallard was a good soldier, and so too were his fellow commanders, but their complacency and disdain for the vigour and daring of their opponents were soon evident.

Marlborough's plan for battle was simple, but very demanding. To get at the French and Bavarians he had to move through a narrow defile out onto a wide plain, in open view and within cannon range, and to deploy his army on a 4-mile wide front, then force the passage of the Nebel stream. It was too much to hope that he could do all this without interference, but the way in which his opponents lay in their camp indicated to the Duke that they would take some time to draw up in proper battle array. In this he was proved correct, and the valuable pause was used to deploy onto the plain before Tallard, Marsin and the Elector could properly react to his approach. Sitting in his coach at the roadside, as the marching army filed past in the early morning light, Marlborough conferred closely with Dubislaw Natzmer; the Prussian officer had been defeated on this very same ground only the previous year and knew the area well as a result. The British and German brigades that had held Schwenningen through the night joined the march, making another column on the left of the army, while the artillery made good use of the main road leading from Donauwörth.

It was Tallard's Wing on the French and Bavarian right that was to be the target of the assault launched by Marlborough, although this can only have been confirmed in the Duke's mind as the events of the morning unfolded. He undoubtedly had the outline of the plan of attack in mind as the army moved onto the plain, for the terrain here was open and gently rolling once the Nebel was passed. Assessing this as his army marched onwards, and the French and Bavarian camp came fully into view, Marlborough's plan was to deploy his own cavalry on the Allied left to crush Tallard in the open while Eugene pinned down Marsin and the Elector on the right. Eugene was directed, with the smaller Wing of the Allied army (about 20,000 men and 20 guns), to move across the face of the French and Bavarian position, with his left flank exposed to harassing fire, and to attack the Bavarian troops in the area of Lutzingen. If this assault was pressed with enough vigour, and Eugene could be depended on for that, then the Elector and Marsin would have no time or troops to spare to assist Tallard on the right of their army. The ground which Eugene had to cross was marshy and cut up with small streams, and patches of scrub also impeded progress. Not only would the Prince have to throw out flank guards in case of attacks from Marsin's troops near Oberglau, but his artillery would find the going difficult and take time to get into position.

As Marlborough's marching columns poured out past Schwenningen onto the approaches to the plain of Höchstädt, at least one of Tallard's officers was thoroughly alarmed. The Comte de Merode-Westerloo was just then awakening from his night's gentle slumber in Blindheim village. He wrote that:

> *I slept deeply until six in the morning when I was abruptly awakened by one of my old retainers – the head groom in fact – who rushed into the barn all out of breath. He had just returned from taking my horses out to grass at four in the morning. This fellow, LeFranc, shook me awake and blurted out that the enemy was there. Thinking to mock him I asked 'Where? There?' and he at once replied 'Yes – There – There.' Flinging wide as he spoke the doors of the barn and drawing my bed-curtains. The door opened onto the fine, sunlit, plain beyond – and the whole area appeared to be covered by enemy squadrons.*

Hurriedly dressing, Merode-Westerloo called his squadrons to attention and started to draw them up in a kind of order amidst the paraphernalia of their camp while the rest of the army were still shaking themselves awake. Tallard hurried past at one point and commended the Comte for his vigour. Signal guns were fired to bring in the foraging parties and picquets; all was hustle and bustle in the camp as the French and Bavarian troops tried to draw up into battle order to face the unexpected threat. The guns were heard by the Margrave of Baden at his headquarters before Ingolstadt some 40 miles to the east. He added a postscript to a letter that he was just then writing to the Emperor Leopold in Vienna: 'The Prince and the Duke are engaged today to the westward. Heaven bless them.'

Tallard, Marsin and the Elector hurried to the church tower in Blindheim village, from where they could view the Allied deployment on the other side of the Nebel. Tactically they were on the back foot, and they held a hasty council of war as the Allied columns grew longer and longer before their very eyes. It was plain that there was little time available to deploy their forces fully in battle formation, as the manner in which they had gone into camp was not an ideal arrangement from which to fight an active and dangerous opponent who might soon have them by the throat.

The Nebel ran across the plain of Höchstädt and provided a convenient obstacle against any direct attack on the camp. In 1704, without the benefit of modern drainage, the brook was boggy and the banks were treacherous underfoot, capable of being waded by infantrymen, certainly, but only with some difficulty and delay. Marsin felt it best to close his infantry right up to the stream and force the attackers to pay a dear price for every inch gained. Tallard, however, was intent on using his cavalry to best effect, and they could not operate very well in the marshy grass at the water's edge. He decided to hold his troops back from the stream on the slightly higher ground of the plain. Once Marlborough's army had scrambled across the water and was in place, he would throw his squadrons into the

Blindheim village church tower. The French and Bavarian commanders viewed Marlborough's advance from here.

attack and drive the Allies to destruction in the stream at their back. The Elector, mindful of the catastrophe at the Schellenberg, cautioned Tallard, 'Beware of these men [the British], they are dangerous.'

This was a sound enough tactic to adopt, provided that Tallard's cavalry, artillery and infantry were used in close cooperation. However, it also allowed Marlborough the chance to get across the Nebel without serious interference, and this was a necessary preliminary to the very kind of battle he had in mind. The two Marshals could not agree on the best course, so each went their own tactical way. Given numerical superiority and the natural strength of their position, neither commander was necessarily wrong, but the lack of a common approach was risky and the cooperation that was so vital between the arms in Tallard's Wing was soon to go adrift. However, at Tallard's request, Marsin did agree to detach sixteen cavalry squadrons to his support on the open cornfields between Oberglau and Blindheim, despite the risk to the horses of contagion from glanders. Tallard responded by sending two of his infantry battalions to help Marsin to garrison Oberglau adequately.

Despite their surprise at having to fight a battle at all, Tallard, Marsin and the Elector made their preparations with competent skill. The villages on the position, Lutzingen in the north, Oberglau in the centre and Blindheim to the south, were occupied by infantry. The cottages and barns were loopholed for muskets, and carts, furniture, logs, barn doors and debris were piled up as barricades in the entrances to the narrow alleyways. Fields of fire were good, although Blindheim was partially bounded by orchards and allotment fences. The open cornfields all around permitted fairly good observation, but the standing crops hampered the most advantageous siting of the French batteries. With no system of forward observers for artillery at this time, the gunners would not have been allowed to waste expensive roundshot by firing blindly through the corn. At least one six-gun battery, near Blindheim, got around the problem by firing obliquely across the slope at Marlborough's infantry as they gathered near to Unterglau. This hamlet, alongside the Nebel, was set alight by the French, as Weilheim Farm had been, to hamper the Allied deployment. Merode-Westerloo wrote that two small watermills close to Blindheim, where the Nebel divides to form a small reedy islet, were also put to the torch, although Robert Parker remembered that these were set alight during the course of the battle.

In Lutzingen, Count Alessandro Maffei, veteran of the Schellenberg fight six weeks earlier, deployed five Bavarian infantry battalions, and on the edge of the village a great battery of sixteen guns was established on a slight rise. From here an excellent field of fire was had across the lush cornfields and the Nebel stream towards Weilheim Farm, where Eugene's Danish and Prussian infantry were gradually taking up position and could be clearly seen in the morning sunlight. To the north, in the wooded hills beyond Lutzingen, seven French infantry battalions under the Marquis de Rozel were moving into place to anchor the line firmly on the left. Between Lutzingen and Oberglau, Jean d'Arco was in command of fourteen squadrons of Bavarian cavalry, while Count Wolframsdorf had thirteen more in support. To their right, in the open overlooking the Nebel, stood Marsin's forty squadrons of French cavalry and dragoons and twelve battalions of infantry. Oberglau was turned into a strongpoint packed with fourteen battalions of French and émigré Irish infantry, under the command of the Marquis de Blainville. Six powerful batteries were ranged alongside the village to cover the approaches from Unterglau and Weilheim Farm.

On the right of the French and Bavarian position, Tallard deployed sixty-four squadrons of French and Walloon cavalry on the plain of Höchstädt, leading gently down towards the Nebel. The slope would give impetus to their charge, when it came. Nine battalions of young French infantry stood near the Höchstädt road in support of the cavalry, although these soldiers' lack of experience might mean that they were not as steady as was needed. On the cornfield next to Blindheim, where the garrison was in the charge of the Marquis de Clerambault, were three battalions of the Régiment du Roi; nine more infantry battalions occupied the village itself. A further four battalions stood to the rear and eleven more were on the higher ground of the plain, ready to move forward when their support was needed. This was a sound position, made more secure by twelve squadrons of dismounted dragoons who threw up a sketchy breastwork on the right of the line, in the marshy grass leading the few hundred paces from the village to the edge of the Danube itself.

Once properly shaken out, the French and Bavarian army occupied a generally good position. The wide Danube shielded their right, and on this flank the strongpoint village of Blindheim was held by a numerous garrison under a veteran commander. On the other side of the plain of Höchstädt, Lutzingen was similarly fortified and occupied by seasoned Bavarian troops with a powerful battery in support. The wooded hills to the north of the village thronged with French infantry, so that flank was well held. The Nebel stream protected the whole frontage of the army and Oberglau, almost, but not quite, in the centre of the line, was packed with infantry. The French and Bavarian batteries were drawn up to cover the Nebel, although getting good points of observation remained a problem in places. Blindheim and Oberglau, in particular, were too far apart to achieve effective overlapping fire, but the problem was less acute between Oberglau and Lutzingen. The numerous squadrons of cavalry were drawn up on the rising ground above the stream, and, all things considered, by about 11am that day, the Elector, Tallard and Marsin could feel that they had recovered their poise rather well and were ready to fight. The position, on the face of it, was sufficiently strong and the army so well posted that many prudent commanders might not have attempted an attack on them at all. Francis Hare, Marlborough's chaplain, said afterwards, 'Almost all the generals were against my Lord's attacking the enemy, they thought it so difficult.' George Hamilton, 1st Earl Orkney, wrote, 'Had I been asked to give my opinion, I had been against it, considering the ground where they had been camped and the strength of their army. But his Grace knew the necessity there was of a battle.'

On the Allied side of the Nebel matters progressed rather unevenly. With the shorter distance to travel, and firm ground underfoot, Marlborough's British, Dutch, Danish and German troops got into place fairly quickly, moving up on either side of the smouldering hamlet of Unterglau. The Duke set his pioneers to bridging the stream, those rudimentary farm bridges that had existed having been torn down by the French picquets as they pulled back after setting Unterglau alight. In all, five of these makeshift causeways were constructed that morning, using 700 fascines cut the previous evening, and the banks were levelled in places to allow the Allied troops easy passage. While this was going on the French artillery near to Blindheim fired on the growing ranks of Marlborough's army, and at one point a roundshot struck the ground underneath the belly of the Duke's horse, showering mount and rider with dust. The Captain-General calmly looked around, suggesting to his brother, Charles Churchill, who commanded the infantry that day, that the troops should lie down to gain shelter from both the French gunners and the warm sun. Orkney wrote, 'His Grace rode along the lines to observe the posture and countenances of his men, and found them and the officers of all nations very cheerful.' Marlborough then dismounted to take refreshment with his staff officers, before ordering that divine service should be held at the head of each regiment. The French guns thundered away: 'A heavy cannonade was opened from every part of the enemy's right Wing.'

Eugene's troops, by comparison, struggled to get into place in good time; the ground did not make for rapid marching, and flank guards had to be placed to watch for any interference from Marsin's troops around Oberglau: 'Great difficulty occurred in bringing up the artillery, for the ground was extremely broken.' As the morning wore on, Marlborough became anxious for news; too much time was being allowed his opponents, and the precious tactical advantage snatched with the daring advance to the plain of Höchstädt could be lost if they took the initiative and moved out to the attack. At midday, the Duke sent William Cadogan to enquire after Eugene's progress. Reassured

Lieutenant-General Charles Churchill. Marlborough's younger brother and General of infantry at Blenheim and Ramillies.

that the Prince was getting into place, albeit slowly, the Duke ordered the bands of his army to strike up, both to cheer the soldiers as they patiently waited under French fire and to intimidate their opponents. The French bands responded, and a musical duel began across the plain as the musicians of each army sought to outshine the other. Marlborough's gunners were in action now, having been placed by the Duke himself to ensure that they had good fields of fire. Merode-Westerloo (who lost thirteen mounts that day) wrote that one of his favourite horses was a casualty of the Allied fire during this part of the battle: 'I was riding past Forsac's Régiment when a shot carried away the head of my horse and killed two troopers.' Despite this, the Comte could not fail to be impressed by the martial glory of the scene that had unfolded across the wide plain:

> *It would be impossible to imagine a more magnificent spectacle, the two armies in full array were so close to one another that they exchanged fanfares of trumpets calls and rolls of kettledrums. The brightest imaginable sun shone down on the two armies drawn up in the plain. You could even distinguish the uniforms of each successive unit; a number of generals and aides de camp galloped here and there; all in all, it was an almost indescribably stirring sight.*

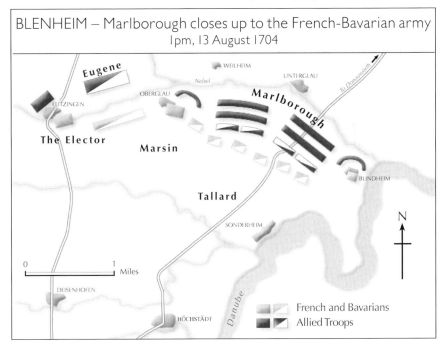

BLENHEIM – Marlborough closes up to the French-Bavarian army
1pm, 13 August 1704

At last, at about 12.30pm, a message came from Eugene that his cavalry and infantry were in place opposite Lutzingen and would go in on the Duke's command – 'The joyful news that Eugene was ready.' The Imperial artillery on the Allied right was still struggling across the broken ground and not yet in action, but the prince would attack anyway. The Allied soldiers were called to their feet, their dressing was checked under the barked commands of the sergeants, the cavalry took to their saddles, and to the blaring of trumpets and the tapping of side-drums, the battle began. At 1pm on 13 August 1704, Marlborough sent word to Lord John Cutts to press forward with his infantry and storm the village of Blindheim on the banks of the Danube. At the same time Prince Eugene was requested to assault Lutzingen on the Allied right flank. In this way, the Duke intended that the French and Bavarian infantry would be ruthlessly tied down left and right, and unable to take part in the crucial cavalry battle on the plain of Höchstädt.

So Truly Glorious

Lord Cutts (once described as being as brave and brainless as the sword at his side, and known popularly as 'the Salamander' for his liking of being in the hottest fire), gave the word and Archibald Rowe's British brigade rose from the edge of the Nebel stream, where they had been sheltering, and stepped forward across the boggy ground to the far bank. Clambering up the gentle slope towards the edge of Blindheim, they had some cover from the dip in the ground formed by the stream, and their approach was unhindered, apart from the French battery which fired on them from the slightly higher ground at the edge of the village. Simultaneously, James Ferguson's British brigade, led by the 1st English Foot Guards, shook out to the left of Rowe's men. They headed for a long line of logs, branches and overturned carts running from the cottages to the marshy edge of the Danube. This barricade was manned by dismounted dragoons from the Notat, La Reine and Maitre de Camp Régiments under command of the Comte d'Hautfeuille.

The dressing of the British regiments was carefully aligned, regimental colours snapped smartly in the breeze, and the two brigades went into the attack. John Deane remembered the day well:

About 3 a clock in the afternoon our English on the left was ordered by My Lord Duke to attacque a village on the left full of French called Blenheim which village they had fortified and made so vastly strong and barricaded so fast with trees, planks, coffers, chests, wagons, carts and palisades that it was almost an impossibility to think which way to get into it.

The discipline of the French during the British advance was superb; apart from the fire of the battery on the edge of the village, the approach was met with silence from the defenders. James Campbell, who took part in the attack with Rowe's Regiment, wrote two days later, 'We went throu the watter that was upon their front with little opposition and touck ane piece of cannon after that was mead a little halt and attacked the village that was upon their right called Blindheim.'

As the range closed, steady volleys of musketry poured out from the French barricades: many in the leading ranks of attackers tumbled down in the blast. Rowe had ordered his men not to return fire until he could touch the breastworks, but as he strode forward to strike an overturned cart with his sword, he was shot through the thigh and fell mortally wounded. Behind him his men closed up the gaps torn in their ranks and rushed onwards to exchange shots and bayonet thrusts with the defenders. Two officers, Lieutenant-Colonel Dalyell and Major Campbell, ran over to recover Rowe's body, but they were killed also. James Campbell went on: 'They received us with so hot a fire that they killed or wounded twenty officers our Brigadier is mortally wounded and his leg brock which is regretted by the whole armie.' Between the river and the village, the 1st English Foot Guards moved forward into a small orchard and were met with heavy volleys from the French dragoons. Colonel Philip Dormer was mortally wounded and the huge regimental colour of the Guards was 'all shott to pieces'. Ferguson's men recoiled from the terrible fire, and like Rowe's brigade, they fell back towards the Nebel stream to recover their shaken order.

At this dangerous moment, with Cutts's attack faltering, eight squadrons (sixteen companies) of the elite French Gens d'Armes, commanded by the veteran Swiss officer Beat-Jacques von Zurlauben, came sweeping in massed ranks across the slope from the plain of Höchstädt. They cut sharply in at the exposed right-hand battalion of Rowe's brigade, Rowe's own regiment (Royal Scots Fusiliers), whose ranks were ragged and officers flustered after their repulse from Blindheim. Now, von Zurlauben's troopers, resplendent in their laced red coats, rode among them, cutting and slashing with their long swords. The disordered infantrymen tried frantically to form square but they failed to do so in time and their ranks broke apart; the colour ensign, Will Primrose, was hacked down and the treasured regimental colour was lost to an exultant gendarme.

Wilkes's Hessian brigade was nearby, lying in the marshy grass at the edge of the stream. They rose to their feet and moved resolutely forward to steady the stricken British regiment. Their disciplined volleys, described by James Campbell as a 'peal of fire', and glistening bayonets drove off the Gens d'Armes, who were themselves now exposed and in some disarray after their

Blenheim. The British infantry advance on Blindheim village, 13 August 1704.

impetuous charge. The lost colour was dropped and returned safely to the regiment, while Cutts gathered his battered brigades into line again, ready for a fresh effort. Gallantly, the British and Hessian troops advanced once more to the barricades, but the French fire was unfaltering and the attackers' casualties were severe. They were thrown back towards the Nebel once more, without the satisfaction of having made any impression at all on the defence of the village.

The vigour with which the attack was pressed had its effect, however, as Clerambault grew increasingly nervous at the scale of the assault. He began to draw in all those French infantry battalions standing to the side and rear of the village, in the cornfields and gardens. These units had been placed where they could move to support either the garrison in Blindheim or, perhaps more importantly, the French cavalry in their battle on the plain of Höchstädt. So distracted did Clerambault become, under the remorseless pressure exerted by Cutts, that it seems he suffered some form of nervous breakdown that hot day. He went from one part of the village to another, questioning his officers, apparently unable to decide what to do for the best. As the afternoon wore on he gradually packed twenty-seven infantry battalions and de Hautefeuille's twelve squadrons of dismounted dragoons, perhaps 12,000 men in all, into the narrow streets and walled churchyard of Blindheim.

It soon became clear that the garrison in Blindheim was so strong that no attack by the Allied troops available on this flank, at that stage of the day, could hope to succeed. Marlborough had just ridden over from Unterglau to confer with Cutts and he countermanded an order to attack the village again. Instead, he gave instructions that Clerambault and his troops should just be kept occupied while the battle was won on another part of the field. Robert Parker of the Royal Irish Regiment wrote that the British infantry had:

> *Rallied, returned to the charge, and drove the enemy from the skirts of the village. They [the French] had not the room to draw up in any manner of order, or even make use of their arms. Thereupon we drew up in great order about 80 paces from them, from where we made several vain attempts to break in upon them, in which many brave men were lost to no purpose. It was not possible for them to rush upon us in a disorderly manner without running upon the very points of our bayonets.*

The success of the attack on Blindheim was such that no more than about 5,000 British and Hessian troops penned over twice that number of French infantry and dragoons to the defence of the place, helpless and unable to assist Tallard's cavalry in their battle nearby. Whenever the garrison attempted a sortie they faced the musketry of Cutts's infantry, sweeping the narrow exits between the cottages with a murderous fire. 'We mowed them down with our platoons,'

Parker wrote, and Holcroft Blood also had a couple of guns manhandled across the Nebel to support the Allied infantry outside the village.

At the same time that Cutts went into the attack on Blindheim, Prince Leopold of Anhalt-Dessau led forward four brigades of Danish and Prussian infantry against Lutzingen next to the wooded hills on the other flank. The place was well fortified, the Bavarian infantry had all morning to arrange their defences, and the great battery on the edge of the village had a good field of fire across the open ground stretching to Schwennenbach and Weilheim Farm. The attacking infantry came on in good order across open cornfields almost too open and level. The Nebel stream, broken into several small creeks, was no great obstacle at this point and it was crossed without serious effort. As soon as Anhalt-Dessau's brigades were across, however, they came under heavy volleys of musketry from Maffei's infantry and salvoes of canister from the Bavarian guns, both in front of the village and placed in enfilade against the wood-line to the north. Great gaps were torn in the attackers' ranks, but the Prussians rallied, pressed forward and attempted to storm the great battery. The Danish troops, commanded by Count Scholten, tormented by fire on their right flank, turned to drive the gunners and French infantry out of the copses beyond Lutzingen.

Eugene's first-line cavalry, under command of the Imperial General of Horse, Prince Maximilien of Hanover, picked their way across the stream. Hardly had the squadrons formed up on the drier ground than Marsin's French cavalry and their Bavarian comrades came sweeping forward to engage them. In a brief, hacking contest this counter-attack was held by the Imperial horsemen and then thrown back. The second line of Marsin's squadrons now came forward to the attack, and the Imperial squadrons were broken and scrambled back across the Nebel in confusion. This move uncovered the left flank of the Prussian infantry as they struggled to maintain a foothold on the great battery. Threatened with envelopment, two of the battalions were scattered and Anhalt-Dessau's troops had to fall back. As they did so, the Danes in their turn found that their flank was exposed, and they also had to withdraw. The Allied infantry tried to make a stand at the water's edge, but were pursued so vigorously by the Bavarian Life Guards that some panic took hold as Eugene's troops withdrew over the stream. Ten infantry colours were lost to the Bavarians and hundreds of prisoners taken. John Deane wrote of the repulse, 'The enemy did so bravely stand itt and so stoutly behave themselves, that Prince Eujeane was forced to give way.'

Eugene was only able to rally his shaken units on the wood-line at the foot of the Waldberg near Schwennenbach, well beyond their starting point. Despite the setback, his commanders re-ordered the ranks and they went into the attack once again, led by the second-line cavalry squadrons under the

Prince Eugene (Eugen) of Savoy (1663–1736)

François-Eugene de Savoie-Carignan, Prince of the House of Savoy, was born in October 1663 in Paris, the son of Eugene-Maurice, Comte de Soissons, and Olympe Mancini, the niece of Cardinal Mazarin. Refused a commission in the French army by Louis XIV (who thought he would make a good priest instead), Eugene absconded at the age of twenty to the Spanish Netherlands. Travelling on to Vienna he entered the service of the Holy Roman Empire. The Prince fought against the Turks at the relief of Vienna and in Hungary, where he was appointed Imperial commander. At the battle of Zenta (1697), Eugene destroyed a major Turkish army and his reputation as a general was made for all time.

Appointed to the Imperial War Council in 1703, Eugene met the Duke of Marlborough for the first time in 1704 and the two men became close friends. They campaigned successfully together, most notably at Blenheim (1704), Oudenarde (1708) and Malplaquet (1709). Eugene was also the victor at the battle of Turin (1706) where the French Marshal Marsin was killed, but he was less successful in the abortive campaign against the French naval base at Toulon in 1707. After the Treaty of Utrecht (1713), Eugene continued to lead the Imperial armies against the French along the Rhine. At the Peace of Rastadt (1714) he was appointed the Imperial Governor of the Austrian (previously Spanish) Netherlands. Campaigning once again against the Turks, Eugene won battles at Peterwardin (1716) and the capture of Belgrade (1717).

Although the Prince retired from active campaigning to become the principal adviser to the Emperor, he was appointed as the Imperial commander in the War of the Polish Succession in 1734–35, despite failing health. A lifelong bachelor (although fond of women), Eugene was a noted patron of the arts. He died in his sleep at his home in Vienna in April 1736.

Duke of Württemberg-Teck. They forced their way, at heavy cost, back across the Nebel, but were caught in a murderous cross-fire of artillery from the Bavarians around Lutzingen and Marsin's batteries at Oberglau and were again thrown back in disarray. The Elector of Bavaria attempted to follow this up with a sharp counter-attack, but his troopers responded rather lamely; the French and Bavarian cavalry on this part of the field were almost as disordered as their opponents, their horses were becoming tired and losses had not been light. For some time the commanders on both sides had to look just to restoring their soldiers' fighting zeal, and although the opposing lines drew close together from time to time, they did not seriously engage. Francis Hare saw both Eugene and the Elector vigorously exhorting their men for fresh efforts: 'The Elector of Bavaria was seen riding up and down, and inspiring the men also with fresh courage.' While Eugene's horsemen flagged, the Danish and Prussian infantry again stormed into Lutzingen and the wooded copses nearby. Fighting the French and Bavarians in a desperate stabbing, clubbing, hand-to-hand combat the Dessauer's men could not for long sustain this second effort without proper support and they fell back once again across the trampled mud of the stream to recover. This time Maffei's infantry, shaken by the ferocity of the attack, did not pursue.

With great effort, Marlborough's plan, sketched out in his mind at the Tapfheim church the previous afternoon and formed into full detail as his army moved through the Schwenningen defile, was taking effect. He had thrown heavy infantry attacks against both of his opponents' flanks, and although these had been bloodily repulsed, the French and Bavarian commanders were engrossed in these important but subsidiary actions. They had no freedom of manoeuvre, only Marlborough retained that, for Tallard's cavalry, the centre of gravity of the whole French and Bavarian army, was now devoid of proper support and exposed to attack by superior forces on the open plain. To this ripe target, the Duke now turned his attention.

While Clerambault was packing the French infantry into Blindheim, Marlborough in contrast began to move infantry away from the village, towards the centre of the battlefield: they had a role to play in the great battle to be fought there. Hulsen's Hessian and Hanoverian brigade, and Hamilton's British brigade, were moved across the Nebel to support the advance of Charles Churchill's infantry. Soon afterwards the dismounted British dragoon regiments of Ross and Hay were also detached from Cutts, and they marched to the centre of the field, while ten British cavalry squadrons under Henry Lumley soon followed. These were moved forward across the stream into position to cover Cutts's right flank from any further interference by the French Gens d'Armes.

Despite all the efforts of the Marquis de la Frequelière's French gunners, Charles Churchill got his Dutch, German and British infantry across the stream without very great difficulty, and they formed up on the edge of the cornfields facing the French squadrons massed on the plain of Höchstädt. The Allied cavalry followed and Marlborough's battle-line interlaced the cavalry with infantry in a novel manner, so that each arm could support the other. The Duke took care to see that sufficient gaps were left between the infantry battalions in order that his squadrons could pass and re-pass their lines without hindrance, whether moving forward to the attack or retiring to recover after a repulse.

The steady deployment of Marlborough's army did not go unchallenged. As the Allied troops lined up on the approaches to the plain, the French Gens d'Armes came charging forward once again, looking to rout Lumley's cavalry, who now linked Churchill's infantry with the column facing Blindheim. To split Cutts away from Churchill might seriously unbalance Marlborough's arrangements. As the elite French cavalry came on, they were faced with five British squadrons under command of Brigadier-General Francis Palmes. Although the French had the advantage of the slope, this was squandered as they halted their advance to fire their carbines at the British troopers before charging home. This ineffective tactic allowed Palmes time to throw a squadron outwards around each flank of the stationary Gens d'Armes, who suddenly found themselves threatened with being enveloped left and right, and were thrown back in terrible confusion. The gentlemen troopers then rather lost their nerve and galloped to the rear, careering through the ranks of those French infantry battalions that stood nearby to support them. Palmes attempted to follow up this success, but went too far and had to call off his squadrons hurriedly in the face of heavy musketry fire from infantry at the edge of Blindheim and fresh French squadrons who came cantering forward to challenge. The British horsemen were driven back in disarray, and one of the squadron commanders, Major Richard Creed, was killed. Creed's younger brother John tried without success to save him. He wrote to his mother three days later:

The enemy forst us to reteir & I mssing my Dearest Brother un ye retreat I advanced in haste toards the enemys squadrons with indeavour to rescew him but a dismall sight fund him strugling on the ground & one of ye enemy over him with his sord in his hand I shot ye enemy and dismounted and lifted up my Brother and brught him off but he neaver spoke more.

Despite this rather scrambled recovery by the French, the startling and ignominious repulse of such supposedly elite cavalry as the Gens d'Armes had a significant effect. Consternation was felt throughout the army and the Elector, on hearing the incredible news, said to an aide, 'What? Is it possible? The gentlemen of France fleeing. Go, tell them that I am here, in person. Rally them, and lead them to the charge again.' Such stirring sentiments went for nothing because the officer sent with the message, the Marquis de Montigny-Langost, was taken prisoner shortly afterwards while helping to rally the Gens d'Armes for a fresh effort:

I received two sabre cuts on the head, a sword thrust through the arm, a blow from a musket ball on the leg, and my horse was wounded. Thus, being surrounded on all sides with no hope of escape, I was taken by an officer, who taking one of my pistols said to me 'I give you quarter, follow me and I will see your wounds dressed.'

Having had to hand over his purse, the battered Frenchman escaped back to his own lines when his captor was wounded by a stray musket ball. The Marquis remembered watching in exasperation as the ranks of Allied cavalry grew longer on the near side of the Nebel stream: 'What a disappointment when I saw the English cavalry which had been repulsed returning to the charge, and again routing our Gendarmerie and the cavalry supporting them.' Tallard had watched the unexpected flight of the Gens d'Armes in alarm and rode across the field to confer with Marsin near to Oberglau. He warned his colleague that the main threat was clearly on the far side of the Höchstädt road and urged that Marsin detach more of his troops to reinforce the right Wing without delay. The younger Marshal, who had already sent part of his cavalry to help Tallard earlier in the day, now refused. Eugene's second attack was still in full flood and, even if repulsed, would no doubt be renewed before long. Columns of Dutch and German infantry could be seen moving towards Oberglau, held by Marsin's own troops, and Eugene's artillery was at last getting into action. The Prince's gun-line was established at Weilheim Farm, where fourteen artillery pieces were sited, and from here a slight rise in the ground gave the Imperial gunners a good field of fire over which to pound the French around Oberglau. So Marsin was under pressure too, his hold on the centre was not secure: Tallard would have to fight on alone.

While Tallard was engaged in anxious discussion with Marsin, his infantry were being taken into Blindheim by the Marquis de Clerambault who compounded his mistake by ordering the Régiment du Roi, still standing on the cornfields, into the village too. Tallard, fatally, then did nothing to rectify his subordinate's folly as the afternoon wore on. Soon, all that the Marshal had left to support his cavalry were the nine small battalions of young soldiers. These troops were substitutes for the veteran Swiss who had refused to cross the Rhine and were standing near to the Höchstädt road, presumably too far away for Clerambault to get his hands on them. Robert Parker commented on the growing confusion that afflicted the French command:

> *Tallard seeing his five [eight] squadrons so shamefully beaten by three [plus the squadrons thrown out around either flank], was confounded to that degree, that he did not recover himself the whole day, for after that all his orders were given in a hurry and confusion.*

All this time the long lines of Marlborough's cavalry and infantry steadily grew on Tallard's side of the Nebel. Von Zurlauben tried several more times to disrupt the deployment, his front-line squadrons darting forward down the slope towards the stream. The effort lacked coordination and real power, and the coolly delivered volleys of the Allied infantry disconcerted the French horsemen. Little was achieved, other than to tire the horses, although at one point several Hanoverian and British squadrons were temporarily thrown back on the left of their line. Von Bülow's Prussians stoutly rode forward to their aid, supported by the dragoons of Hay and Ross, so that the French cavalry withdrew a little, across the small Maulweyer stream, to recover their order and rest their mounts.

The Danish cavalry under command of the Duke of Württemberg (not to be confused with the Duke of Württemberg-Teck who fought with Eugene) had made slow work of getting across the stream near to Oberglau. Marsin's infantry struck several times at their harassed ranks as the troopers scrambled their horses through the mud, and the Danes were at first driven back. Count Horn's Dutch infantry brigades were nearby and they gradually forced the French away from the water's edge. It was evident that before Marlborough could launch his main attack against Tallard, he had to deal with the problem of Oberglau. The village, although smaller than Blindheim, sat squarely on the right flank of Churchill's infantry as they advanced from the line of the stream. It had been strongly fortified by Marsin, who had cleared the fences and hedges from around the cottages to improve their fields of fire.

At about 3pm, the Prince of Holstein-Beck was directed to move forward with two Dutch brigades and secure the village, but struggling through the stream they were confronted by a strong line of French infantry between the water and the cottages, and were unable to form a line of battle properly. The Dutch were then struck by a smartly conducted counter-attack mounted by the red-coated émigré Irish regiments of Clare, Dorrington and Lee. Such was the ferocity of this attack that the two leading Dutch battalions, those of Goor and Benheim, were routed and dispersed. Holstein-Beck called for assistance to some Imperial Swabian cavalry nearby, but their commander, Count Fugger, refused to move without orders. Valiantly trying to rally his soldiers, Holstein-Beck was mortally wounded and was taken away by the Irish soldiers on a hand-cart.

This was potentially a very serious development. For Marsin to complete the rout of the Dutch column would threaten to split the Allied army in two and give the French and Bavarians the one real opportunity that day to defeat their opponents in detail. Eugene's smaller Wing would be isolated from that of Marlborough and pinned against the wooded slopes of the Fuchsberg hill. A crisis was at hand, for the battle was at full tilt across the wide plain. Merode-Westerloo wrote of the moment, 'From one end of the armies to the other every one was at grips and all fighting at once.' Marsin had the chance to break Eugene and Marlborough apart: he ordered his cavalry to change front to their right and to strike at the open flank of Churchill's infantry, drawn up on the near side of the Nebel opposite to Unterglau. The French squadrons, tired after their efforts but still in good order, cantered past Oberglau and the Irish regiments, who opened ranks to allow them through. However, the haste of their advance, and the marshy ground, caused the cavalry commanders to pause and realign their troops for a proper charge. This was no doubt necessary, but it gave Marlborough just enough time to receive them.

The Duke had already crossed the Nebel on one of the makeshift bridges, and he had seen the repulse of Holstein-Beck's column. He ordered Hulsen's brigade to move forward to support the Dutch and these German battalions moved quickly into place. A Dutch cavalry brigade under Averock was also called forward and Blood had a battery dragged up to support them – 'Nine field pieces loaded with partridge [canister] shot,' as Robert Parker remembered. Averock's squadrons were soon under pressure and in danger of being overwhelmed by Marsin's more numerous cavalry, and so Marlborough sent word to Fugger to bring his cuirassier brigade down from Weilheim Farm to deflect Marsin's thrust at Churchill. The Count, who had previously refused to help Holstein-Beck, moved promptly forward at the Duke's request, and Marsin's troopers found that as they advanced they were threatened on their left side, the bridle arm (the weaker side away from the sword arm). The stream lay between the opposing squadrons, but the French could not ignore the threat and were forced to change front again to face the Imperial cuirassiers. The chance to strike with any real force at Churchill's infantry passed.

Marlborough now directed Count Berensdorf, who took command of the Dutch infantry in place of Holstein-Beck, to pen Marsin's French and Irish troops into Oberglau, so that they could not again threaten Churchill's flank as he advanced against Tallard. With the support of Blood's gunners, the Dutch, Hessian and Hanoverian infantry fought a tough battle to drive their opponents back into the village. The struggle was costly, with close-quarter bayonet fighting, but eventually this was achieved. The Marquis de Blainville, the French commander in Oberglau, was among those killed, while the Goor Regiment was entirely wrecked, with only fifty men left on their feet at the end of the day (the most severe unit loss in the Allied army). The next day Marlborough offered sympathy to the distraught regimental commander, saying that he wished he stood in Colonel Goor's place; the Dutch officer tartly replied that he too wished it, as, 'I would still have had a good regiment, and you would have been without one.'

Soon after 4pm, Marlborough sent Lord Tunbridge with a message to Eugene, who was in the saddle and fighting hand-to-hand with the Bavarian cavalry near Lutzingen, that all was well on the left of the field. If the Prince would just keep Marsin and the Elector occupied, he would now destroy Tallard's cavalry. Eugene was perfectly well prepared to do so, but he was increasingly exasperated at the failing energy of his own Imperial cavalry in the slashing fights along the Nebel. He had already threatened to shoot some of his own troopers who had hung back, and he now went off to fight with Anhalt-Dessau's infantry, muttering that he preferred to die among brave men: 'See, they don't retreat before the enemy, although they are attacked with a three-fold superior force.' Eugene's weary cavalry were left in position facing the Elector's equally blown squadrons on the other side of the stream. At Lutzingen, the Prince's wish was almost granted when a Bavarian trooper levelled his carbine at Eugene's head at close range, but a Danish soldier stepped forward to spit the Bavarian with his bayonet just before he could fire.

The Comte de Merode-Westerloo, who commanded the second line of the cavalry of the French right Wing that day, wrote of the imperfect ordering and slack handling of Tallard's French squadrons:

Our senior Generals had been pleased to leave too great an interval between our first and second lines. When the enemy attacked Blenheim in two-column strength, and the Gendarmerie charged ... I wanted to advance with the second line to support them, but the French high command would not allow. The broken, disordered cavalry poured through the intervals between my own squadrons; the Gendarmerie was undoubtedly soundly beaten, and the gallant Zurlauben received several grave wounds which caused his death two days later.

As the Allied cavalry deployment grew in strength, the Comte led his squadrons to the charge:

I came face to face with the enemy after he passed the stream, and my fresh, well-ordered squadrons charged and flung them back, right over the Nebel, following them up, we then attacked their second line, which also crumbled; but then we came up against a third, untired force, and my squadrons, disordered and blown by their exertions, were themselves defeated and pushed back.

According to Merode-Westerloo, the French squadrons on his left gave way too soon and allowed the Allied cavalry the chance to get onto the higher part of the plain:

They had given ground to the enemy, who were pouring over the stream and forming up on my flank in the very midst of our army, the centre of which was now under the command of the Duc d'Humieres, conspicuous in his fine gilt cuirass.

The time was about 5pm and the August sun shone on the striving soldiers across the plain with unrelenting warmth. With Clerambault's infantry crammed into Blindheim, unable to manoeuvre or use their muskets to any effect, while Eugene pressed remorselessly forward against the Bavarians defending Lutzingen, the time had come for Marlborough to launch his assault on Tallard. The French and Walloon cavalry on the plain of Höchstädt were hot and weary after the fruitless battles along the Nebel stream. They had few infantry supports, Clerambault had seen to that, but nine small battalions of young troops, the *régiments* of de Bellisle, de Beil and de Robecq, stood beside the Höchstädt road ready to offer what assistance they could. Tallard ordered three battalions forward to support his cavalry squadrons more closely, but nothing was done to help them, and the infantry fell back under artillery fire from Blood's batteries, leaving a trail of broken men behind them.

Marlborough glanced to left and right – all was ready, the two lines of cavalry had now moved to the front of the Allied line of battle, with the two lines of supporting infantry behind them. Francis Hare wrote:

> *The Duke of Marlborough had got the whole of the left wing of the allied army over the rivulet, and our Horse were drawn up in two lines fronting that of the enemy, but they did not offer to charge till General Churchill had ranged his Foot also in two lines behind the cavalry.*

The Duke now waved his cavalry commanders forward – Henry Lumley on the left with the first line of British horse and Graf Reynard Vincent van Hompesch on the right with the Dutch and German squadrons. Some 8,000 troopers rode forward in impressively good order, going quite slowly to conserve the horses' strength on the upward incline away from the Nebel. Höchstädt village was ahead of them, and the church tower, now picturesquely struck with the evening sun, could be dimly seen through the smoke and dust of the battlefield. Tallard's squadrons were ragged and tired, but the Allied cavalry were still fresh, due to the valuable support given by their infantry,

Blenheim. The Allied cavalry charge that broke the French squadrons at Blenheim.

whose volleys of musketry had broken up the French attacks with ruthless efficiency. Merode-Westerloo again:

They had brought their infantry well forward and they killed and wounded many of our horses. This was followed by an unauthorised but definite movement to the rear by my men – and I too would have been obliged to accompany them had not two musket balls killed my horse beneath me, so that he subsided gently to the ground. … One of my aides-de-camp and a groom came up with another horse after observing my fall and they soon had me hoisted onto horseback again. I then reformed some sort of a line, and placed four pieces of artillery in front of my position – I had noticed them trying to sneak off.

The Comte then rode over to Blindheim and ordered the St Second and Montfort Régiments out from the constricted alleyways and into the open to support his squadrons. For this presumption he was roundly abused by Clerambault, who ordered the infantrymen back into place, and Merode-Westerloo had to withdraw with as much dignity as he could muster. His fresh horse was killed shortly afterwards, but his groom soon got him mounted again.

The weary French cavalry pushed the first-line Allied squadrons back on their infantry supports once again. Nerves were stretched on both sides and the battle was not yet won – Marlborough had to rebuke gently one of his officers who was about to take his squadrons off the field in the face of the French resistance: 'Sir, you are under a mistake, the enemy lies that way, you have nothing to do but to face them.' Now, at the Duke's command, the Allied second-line cavalry under von Bülow and the Count of Ost-Friese went forward at a trot. The French, tired and dispirited, could not resist the approaching wave of fresh troopers. Robert Parker remembered, 'Our squadrons drove through the very centre of them, which put them to entire rout.' Their composure broke, panic gripped the French troopers, shouted commands were ignored and entire squadrons suddenly faced about and were seen galloping madly off the field, everyone attempting to escape the solid mass of Allied cavalry which followed close behind.

With their cavalry in full flight, the French infantry were abandoned on the open plain. These nine battalions had not been drawn into Blindheim, but had stoutly held their position to give support to Tallard's squadrons. Now those horsemen had fled, and the young soldiers had to face the full storm of Marlborough's army – horse, foot and guns – brought forward to destroy them. They fought with desperate valour. Earl Orkney wrote afterwards in admiration, 'They stood in battalion square in the best order I ever saw, until at last they were all cut down in rank and file.' Merode-Westerloo commented,

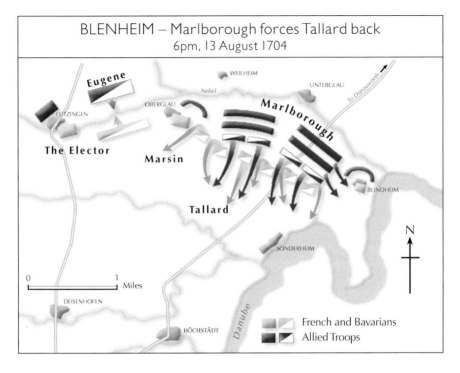

BLENHEIM – Marlborough forces Tallard back
6pm, 13 August 1704

Eugene

WEILHEIM

UNTERGLAU

Nebel

To Donauwörth

OBERGLAU

LÜTZINGEN

Marlborough

The Elector

Marsin

BLINDHEIM

Tallard

N

SONDERHEIM

0   1
Miles

DEISENHOFEN

Danube

HÖCHSTÄDT

French and Bavarians

Allied Troops

'These unfortunate battalions had found themselves completely isolated in the centre, and died to a man where they stood.' Meanwhile, the press of fugitive French cavalry was so great that his horse was borne up by others crowding in on either side – its hooves did not touch the ground for several hundred paces. The mass of horses and riders then tumbled down a bank near to the Danube. The unhappy Comte was trampled and bruised before escaping with his dignity very battered. Helped to his feet by his groom, Merode-Westerloo was soon back in the saddle. Numbers of the fleeing cavalry attempted to escape by swimming their horses across the river, but many who tried this desperate route drowned in the fast-flowing waters. Marlborough's comment on this tragic episode ran: 'We cut off great numbers of them, as well in the action as in the retreat, besides upwards of thirty squadrons of the French, which we pushed into the Danube, where we saw the greatest part of them perish.'

The Marquis de Gruignan attempted a counter-attack with some companies of the Gens d'Armes, but this was brushed aside by the triumphant Allied cavalry. Tallard was nearby with a small party of aides and he tried to rally

Camille d'Hostun, Duc de Tallard, Marshal of France (1652–1728)

Tallard was granted a commission in the French army at the age of fifteen; by the time he was forty-one he was a lieutenant-general, and was made a Marshal of France in 1702, after the victory at Speyerbach. Tallard was conscientious and did not lack bravery, but his friendship with Louis XIV sustained him in a position of high rank which his otherwise limited abilities perhaps did not merit. However, his calm influence as French Ambassador in London had been of great use to both William III and Louis XIV, and his expulsion in 1702 was an error. The bold operations to march his army  through the passes of the Black Forest twice during 1704 were well handled on the whole and a great credit to the Marshal.

A commander with a better tactical grip would surely not have permitted the Marquis de Clerambault to shut most of the infantry of the French right Wing into Blindheim village. Tallard was physically short-sighted, which may have hampered him in the smoke and dust of a battlefield. Taken as prisoner to England by Marlborough, he was kept in comfortable confinement in Nottingham, where his charm and good manners soon endeared him to the local gentry. The Marshal was disappointed with the local food provided and taught his gaolers to bake French bread. He also found celery growing wild and introduced it to the locals as a delicacy hitherto unknown in England.

On the signing of the Treaty of Utrecht in 1713, Tallard was released and returned to France. Nearly ten years had elapsed since the disaster to French arms over which he had presided. No one could predict the kind of reception he was to receive at Versailles. Louis XIV appeared to bear him no ill-will and, as Tallard stooped to kneel, the King took a step forward to receive him, a shocking and unprecedented gesture by that proud monarch. Lifting Tallard gently to his feet, the King murmured, 'Welcome back, old friend.'

Blenheim. Marshal Tallard surrenders on the banks of the Danube.

some of the broken squadrons, but his shouted entreaties were not heeded by the fleeing troopers. The Marshal sent the Marquis de Maisonelle towards Blindheim to try and draw out some of the infantry there to make a stand in the open. This was all far too late to be effective, even if it could have been done. In fact, the Marquis was never seen again, presumably killed on the way. A little later, as Tallard tried to escape from the field he was confronted on a track near Sonderheim by a trooper from Bothmar's dragoons and taken prisoner. The Marshal was conducted to the Prince of Hesse-Cassell and sent on under escort to Marlborough, who was near the Höchstädt road with his cavalry commanders, overseeing the pursuit of the broken French army.

With elaborate courtesy the Duke welcomed Tallard: 'I am very sorry that such a cruel misfortune should have fallen upon a soldier for whom I have the highest regard.' The Marshal murmured in reply, 'And I congratulate you on defeating the best soldiers in the world.' With crushing civility Marlborough said, 'Your Lordship, I presume, excepts those who had the honour to defeat them?' Tallard was then put into Marlborough's own coach and provided with refreshments. He was soon joined by some of his senior officers as the scooping up of prisoners went on through the evening. The day was doubly tragic for Tallard, whose own young son had been killed at his side that afternoon.

While Tallard's army was on the rack, the Danish and Prussian infantry under Anhalt-Dessau pressed forward again in a third attack on the Bavarian-held strongpoint at Lutzingen; just two squadrons of Imperial cavalry had come forward to shield their left flank. Prince Eugene went in with the infantry, while the Dessauer fought on foot, waving a shot-torn regimental colour above his head to encourage the troops onwards. As before, the Bavarian artillery was brutally efficient, but the Prussians disregarded their losses and stormed into the great battery; the gun crews fought them for possession of the pieces and were cut down without mercy. Beyond Lutzingen, Scholten's Danes drove the French infantry there for over a mile in a savage bayonet struggle, which left the groves thickly strewn with broken bodies clad in their blue, grey and white uniforms.

Despite the heavy cost, Eugene's infantry had now unhinged the left flank of the whole French and Bavarian line, and with Tallard in full flight on the far side of the plain, it was clear that Marsin and the Elector had to get their troops out or face annihilation. Merode-Westerloo, never slow to stress his own contribution to events, wrote that:

> *They ordered a retreat, which was carried out in good order; but I believe they would not have escaped so easily but for my men keeping the enemy's attention fully occupied. Otherwise the foe could have attacked the head and flank of our left Wing as it retreated towards Lavingen.*

The position occupied by Marsin was strong and his flanks were secure, at least until Tallard's army gave way. His troops were numerically superior than those of Eugene, and he was able to deploy at least as many guns as the Prince could drag into action. Marsin had nonetheless allowed himself to be fixed in position by the persistent attacks that came in across the Nebel stream from Schwennenbach and Weilheim Farm, even though the energy of the Imperial troops flagged as the afternoon and evening wore on. The Marshal, always a sharp critic of the shortcomings of others, had failed to deal effectively with Eugene, to support either Tallard on his right or the Elector of Bavaria on his left. Even Oberglau, strongly held by French and Irish infantry, he had allowed to be blockaded, so that Churchill's infantry could pass it by without interference as they advanced.

Tallard's army had broken and run away, and the French and Bavarians of the left Wing were now moving in full, if quite well ordered, retreat towards Diesenhofen and Morselingen. Any delay might mean a running fight to pass the gap between the hills and the Danube, and Marlborough had ordered van Hompesch to press them with his cavalry. These Dutch and German squadrons had fought hard and were tired, and in the failing light it was easy to mistake some of Eugene's Imperial cavalry, just then moving forward past Oberglau, for the French. The Prince made the same error. Robert Parker wrote of the incident:

Prince Eugene by this time had a good part of his troops over the morass [Nebel stream], and was just ready to fall on their rear, but perceiving the squadrons under Hompesch coming down that way, he took them to be some of Tallard's squadrons drawing down to join the Elector; whereby he halted, lest they should fall on his flank. The Duke also seeing Prince Eugene's troops so near the rear of the Elector's army, took them to be a body of Bavarians, making good the Elector's retreat, and there-upon ordered Hompesch to halt.

By the time the confusion was sorted out, Marsin and the Elector had opened a gap with their pursuers, achieving something of a clean break as they withdrew. Nearby, Merode-Westerloo, although bruised after his adventures at the river's edge, was sufficiently recovered to try and rally the surviving French troops of the right Wing:

I went into the square [of Höchstädt] where I found several French generals who had the nerve to tell me that I was pretty late. I retorted that they, for their part, had arrived too soon. . . . I then passed through the little town and came out on the ridge beyond the marsh [where Tallard had decided not to make his camp], and there I found all the debris of our cavalry in indescribable confusion. It was almost eight o'clock when I reached them; I at once settled down to work, as nobody else

63

was doing anything about the disorder. First, I posted a troop of twenty or thirty Gendarmerie on the road which I had followed to Hochstadt; it was only a narrow lane, but it offered the enemy the only approach to the town. One hundred paces back I drew up a second troop, and then another.

Despite these praiseworthy efforts, there was no disguising that fact that Tallard's cavalry was shattered both physically and morally as a fighting unit. The best that could be hoped for the rest of the army was that those who could still ride would get away to safety.

Meanwhile, the French infantry clung to their hold on Blindheim. With such narrow streets, many of the soldiers had no field of fire, and the Allied troops were pressing forward through the gardens and orchards around the village, sweeping the narrow exits with musketry fire. As the evening went on, Blood's guns were also brought up to batter the village and its defenders. The Régiment du Roi in particular, deployed on the edge of the Maulweyer stream which runs into Blindheim from the plain, had losses from artillery fire directed at breaking up the ranks of the Gens d'Armes, who had been posted nearby until they took to their heels. The growing numbers of the wounded and maimed in the village were thrust into the cottages for shelter. Even so, the British and German brigades had not enough strength to force their way past the French barricades, and Marlborough had to turn away from his pursuit of his broken opponents to direct Churchill to detach more infantry to move towards Blindheim and storm the place. This diversion may well have hindered the pursuit of the French squadrons, but panic lent speed to their flight, and there was little the Allied foot soldiers could do now to catch them. Orkney's infantry – Hamilton's brigade and St Paul's Hanoverians – moved across the trampled crops towards the cottages, and under this pressure the French fell back towards the centre of the village, where a bitter struggle with bayonet and musket butt erupted around the walled churchyard.

Soon Churchill had to send in the dismounted dragoons of Hay and Ross to add weight to the attack. Progress, where it was made at all, was hard won. Two battalions of Hanoverian Zell (Celle) infantry, under command of Colonel Belville, were also fed into the brawling battle in Blindheim, and their arrival steadied the resolve of the dismounted dragoons, who were being driven back by a smart counter-attack delivered by the regiments of Artois and Provence, under Colonel de Silvière. Tramping across the muddy Maulweyer stream once again, the rallied troops drove the defenders back at bayonet point through the smoking alleys towards the churchyard. With so much debris lying on the pathways, only a few men could advance at a time, and the French musketry took a terrible toll of the attackers. Many of the cottages were now burning – the repeated discharges of the muskets and the fire of the Allied gunners saw to that. Also, Orkney remembered, some cottages were deliberately set alight so that the defenders' field of fire should be obscured by smoke. The wounded men, who had hoped to find shelter, were now burning to death and their screams added to the mayhem of that ghastly evening. John Deane wrote later, 'Many on both sides were burnt to death. Great and grevious were the cryes of the wounded, and those suffering in the flames.'

Tallard, hearing the persistent roar of musketry from Blindheim, sent a message to Marlborough, offering to dispatch orders to the garrison to withdraw from the field. The Duke, in the saddle near Morselingen overseeing the attempts to disrupt Marsin's withdrawal, was visibly irritated at what he saw as the captive Marshal's presumption. His cool reply was: 'Inform M. Tallard that, in the position in which he now is, he has no command.' Nonetheless, as darkness came on, he was anxious for the outcome in the village. The garrison, infantry and dragoons had been abandoned in the chaos that enveloped Tallard – the Marquis de Clerambault was nowhere to be found and his aide afterwards told how he had drowned in a vain effort to swim his horse across the Danube: a crisis of command in the village was evident. The Marquis de Denonville had been wounded, and he and the Régiment du Roi were virtually cut off in the part of Blindheim that they held, having thrown Orkney's infantry back no fewer than three times. 'It came into my head to beat a parley,' the Earl wrote afterwards, and Denonville agreed to a temporary ceasefire where his troops stood to allow the wounded to be dragged out of the burning cottages. During this pause, Colonel Belville was sent forward by beat of drum to parley with the Marquis de Blanzac, who, in Clerambault's absence, took on the burden of this doomed command. The Marquis was conducted to where Orkney stood, with his grimy soldiers at the barricades. The Earl, although aware of his lack of numbers in the face of the powerful garrison, behaved with great coolness and pressed de Blanzac on the futility of continued resistance. Surely, he argued, to fight on would be to sacrifice needlessly the lives of his faithful infantry. The Marquis was not aware of Orkney's numerical weakness, and was reluctantly persuaded of the necessity to capitulate. As darkness fell, nearly 10,000 of France's best infantry laid down their arms and surrendered their colours.

One of Orkney's young aides, James Abercrombie, impetuously spurred his horse forward and attempted to seize the regimental colour of the Régiment du Roi: 'I rode up to the Royal regiment and pulled the colours out of the Ensign's hands.' Affronted at the insult, the French ensign struck Abercrombie a glancing blow with his sword across the outstretched forearm; the aide had to withdraw and wait for the formal surrender of the treasured symbol. As it was, the Navarre Régiment, in the bitterness of their disgrace, burned their colours rather than hand them over – a completely pointless gesture as they surrendered themselves anyway. The French capitulation came not a moment too soon for, at this late point in the evening, the battle for the village seemed far from won. Abercrombie wrote that:

My Lord Duke's Aide de Camp came and acquainted My Lord [Orkney] that his Grace had sent him to inform Him that he should lie upon his Arms that Night and that he would join Him next morning with all the Foot and Cannon He could get and Attack the Village.

Pausing in the direction of the Allied pursuit of the French and Bavarians, Marlborough borrowed an old tavern bill from an aide and, dismounting, scribbled a brief note on the back in pencil. He handed the makeshift dispatch to Colonel Daniel Parke, a volunteer from Virginia, to take to Duchess Sarah in London:

I have not time to say more but to beg you will give my duty to the Queen and let her know that her Army has had this day a glorious victory. M. Tallard and two other generals are in my coach and I am following the rest. The bearer, my aide

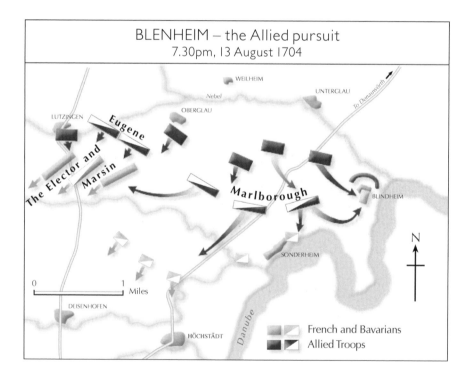

BLENHEIM – the Allied pursuit
7.30pm, 13 August 1704

French and Bavarians
Allied Troops

*de camp, Colonel Parke, will give her an account of what has passed. I shall doe it
in a day or two by another more at large.*

Eight days later that same scrappy note was handed to Queen Anne in the
long gallery at Windsor Castle. She learned in this way that, at her wish,
the Captain-General had destroyed one of France's main field armies in open
battle and that Louis XIV's war plans lay in ruins.

For much of the long day the two armies had been in close and deadly
combat. John Deane wrote, 'As for those killed upon the spot I believe few or
none can pretend to give that account being a thing seeming almost impossible;
butt this I can and will affirm that the earth was covered in a manner for
English miles together with dead bodys.' The night of the battle Marlborough
slept for three hours in a mill on the outskirts of Höchstädt that had been used
by the French to store gunpowder, but no accident or misfortune occurred to
disturb his rest. To the west, the Elector of Bavaria was writing to his wife with
news of the disaster to their fortunes. They had, he wrote, lost everything that
day: 'Wir haben heute alles vehrloren.' Louis XIV's scheming ally was now a

Blenheim. Marlborough writing the Blenheim dispatch. *Courtesy of the late Dr David Chandler.*

Blenheim. The Blenheim dispatch. Handwritten pencil note sent by Marlborough to the Duchess.

fugitive. The Comte de Merode-Westerloo, after a hectic day of battle, was able to relax a little:

> *Being in the saddle for thirty hours with neither sleep nor food and only one drink of water. My knee was swollen to the size of a man's head, although a bullet had been fired at me at point blank range, it had failed to penetrate thanks to my strong thigh boots with thick flaps down to the knees.*

The cost of the battle was extraordinary and added to the wonder with which the world greeted the news of Marlborough's triumph. The scale of the victor's casualties illustrates the vigour with which the French and Bavarians fought that day. Over 9,000 men from Marlborough's Wing were killed or wounded and nearly 5,000 from Eugene's smaller Wing. Of these, the valiant Danish infantry suffered a stunning 2,401 casualties (1,350 of them killed) in their bitter fight with De Rozel's French for possession of the woods beyond Lutzingen, while the British losses on the left flank were 2,234 killed and wounded. On the other side of the field, the loss to the French and Bavarian armies was simply staggering. Some 20,000 of their soldiers were killed or wounded and an amazing 14,000 unharmed prisoners fell into Allied hands (of whom 12,149 were French). No less than 40 general officers were taken prisoner, tamely surrendering themselves, so dazed were they at the day's awful events. The Allied booty included over 100 guns and mortars, 129 infantry colours and 110 cavalry standards, 5,400 wagons and coaches (some contained rather exotically dressed officers' 'ladies'), 7,000 horses and mules, and 3,600 tents. So great was the haul that much of the huge pile of camp stores, forage, food, ammunition, harness and campaign gear seized by the Allies could never be counted and was abandoned on the plain of Höchstädt to be pillaged or to rot.

Meanwhile, in Versailles a grand masque to celebrate the triumph of the river Seine over all the rivers of Europe was enjoyed by the court. Rumours abounded, though, that a reverse had been suffered in the Danube valley. French officers, now captive in Allied hands were writing home setting their affairs in order. When the dreadful news arrived, no one could credit the scale of the defeat and Louis XIV was so stunned by the news that it was thought at first that he had suffered a stroke. The Duc de St Simon wrote, 'One was not accustomed to misfortune ... what was the anguish of the King.'

Despite the magnificence of their victory, the Allied army had experienced a very severe test that day. Eugene wrote, 'I have not a squadron or a battalion which did not charge four times at least.' In truth, one army broke and ran, but only after putting up a hard fight. Once the victors had gathered themselves, and a distribution of prisoners and booty had been arranged between Marlborough and Eugene, the pursuit could begin in earnest. Some Allied regiments, however, were so shattered that they were beyond campaigning without full reconstitution and filling of the ranks with recruits. Many of the battalions of Marlborough's Wing, in particular, had suffered heavily at the Schellenberg fight and received no replacements since. Their ranks were even thinner after the heavy fighting on the plain of Höchstädt. The Comte de Merode-Westerloo was critical of the lack of a rapid pursuit by the Allies: 'If the foe had been quick enough, not one of us would have escaped.' Undoubtedly, the exertions of the Allied troops that day were such that the pursuit of their beaten opponents was less vigorous than might otherwise have been expected. The sorry remnants of Tallard's army, and the still more or less intact forces of Marsin and the Elector, were able to draw off without too close a harrying. Their spirit was badly shaken, of course, and desertions from the Bavarian ranks were numerous – the French were less inclined to desert as the local peasants would quickly lynch any they laid hands on.

All Bavaria was now under the control of the Allies and the Elector had to take what was left of his army to the Spanish Netherlands, where he was still the Governor-General, courtesy of Louis XIV. Marlborough pursued Marsin back to the borders of France, so far as the exhaustion of his army permitted. Plans for an autumn campaign against the fortress of Landau on the Rhine and in the Moselle valley were put into effect, but these went forward rather slowly. The French commanders recovered much of their poise and the Duke's subordinates fumbled some of the operations, although a firm base was established on the Moselle for a new campaign in the spring. The onset of cold weather saw the troops going to winter quarters, while Marlborough, after visiting Berlin, Hanover and The Hague, returned to London to receive his triumph in December 1704, along with Marshal Tallard and thirty-five of the more senior officers captured in the great battle. The regimental colours and cavalry standards from Tallard's shattered army were taken in grand procession to Westminster Hall and later removed to St Paul's Cathedral where they rotted away, quite neglected, so that within 135 years there was nothing left to be seen.

The Duke of Marlborough received a solemn address from the House of Lords, which gives a flavour of the sensation felt throughout the whole of Europe at the victory at Blenheim:

> *The happy success that has attended Her Majesty's arms under Your Grace's conduct in Germany in the last campaign, so truly great, so truly glorious in all its circumstances, that few instances in former ages equal, much less excel the lustre of it. Your Grace has not overthrown young and unskilful generals, raw and undisciplined troops, but Your Grace has conquered the French and Bavarian armies, that were fully instructed in the arts of war; select veteran troops, flushed with former successes and victories, commanded by generals of great experience and bravery.*

Among the rewards that came to the Duke of Marlborough after the victory, Queen Anne gifted her triumphant Captain-General the royal hunting estate at Woodstock in Oxfordshire, together with the funds to build a great palace there. The erection of this building, known as Blenheim Palace, took many years and became the subject of some controversy as the Duke's influence at court waned. This palace is the home of the Dukes of Marlborough to the present day and the quit rent paid every year to the sovereign is the standard of the French Régiment du Roi, which surrendered to Marlborough's troops in Blindheim village that summer evening in 1704.

Part 2

Ramillies, 23 May 1706

Introduction

On Whit Sunday, 23 May 1706, the battle of Ramillies seemed to contemporary observers to bear all the marks of nothing less than a miracle happening before their very eyes. The French and Bavarian army that took the field that day, commanded by François de Neufville, Marshal Villeroi, comprised 60,000 men, well trained and finely equipped. Their cavalry in particular was in good fettle, included the bulk of the elite Maison de Roi and would form a powerful striking force if used properly. On the day, by chance and courtesy of good march discipline and drying roads, Villeroi got his troops onto the field of battle ahead of his opponent, and settled nicely into a naturally strong defensive position. When the time came, the Marshal's soldiers fought well on the whole, in many cases with conspicuous valour.

Despite all this, Villeroi's army was utterly defeated in less than four hectic hours, shattered beyond hope of recovery by the 62,000 troops led by John Churchill, 1st Duke of Marlborough. Dazzled by the Duke's sudden and subtle moves and changes in emphasis, the French and Bavarian commanders simply lost control of the escalating battle, although, intriguingly, they did not realise that this was so until it was too late to attempt a remedy. Overwhelmed, caught in a tactical vice of enormous and unexpected force, their troops broke and ran for safety. 'Save yourselves!' was the cry. Villeroi lost all his guns, and it seems that fully one-third of his army ceased to exist, being casualties or prisoners by the end of the day. The demoralised rest still with their units were hardly recognisable as effective soldiers. Those that rallied at all were in such a state of shock at the sudden defeat that, as one of their senior officers wrote to King

Louis XIV the next day, 'The most awful thing of all is the terror that is in our troops.'

That warm Sunday, the Duke of Marlborough broke the operational ability and effectiveness of the only French army in the Spanish Netherlands. This was an army that had been substantially reinforced with cavalry just before the battle. There was nothing now to prevent Marlborough and his allies from pushing forward, as one later commentator so aptly wrote, 'as if the army had thrown itself upon an unlatched door and simply fallen through', and to conquer this rich and immensely important region over which a long and expensive campaign of many months, possibly even years, might legitimately have been fought. As it was, in the wake of Ramillies Marlborough took possession of the Spanish Netherlands in a lightning campaign lasting just a few short weeks, capturing such towns as Louvain, Brussels, Antwerp, Ostend, Bruges, Ghent, Oudenarde, Ath, Dendermonde, Courtrai, and even Menin on the French border. There was no army in the field to oppose him, and the only thing that held him back in this triumphal progress was the lack of speed with which his supplies and siege guns could come forward along the appallingly bad roads.

The political and military shape of Europe changed for ever that summer, and Louis XIV, who had lost the ability to win the war outright at Blenheim in 1704, but recovered his position quite well the following year, now lost the war itself at Ramillies in 1706. Of course, it remained to be seen whether he recognised this, and whether the partners of the Grand Alliance, with all their narrow self-interest, contrasting ambitions and jealous bickering, would realise what a glittering prize lay before them. With careful negotiation, would they have the sense to offer the French King a peace settlement that he could accept? Peace with honour and glory was almost certainly available after Ramillies, while peace through exhaustion might be the result of any prolonged delay.

The victory at Ramillies is of enormous importance to Marlborough's reputation as a great commander. The success was not only accomplished with verve and brilliance, but was achieved by the Duke without the assistance of his great friend and comrade Prince Eugene of Savoy, with whom he worked to such good effect on other battlefields. The Prince at this time was campaigning in northern Italy, and during that same summer would save Turin, and the Duchy of Savoy, for the Grand Alliance. Meanwhile, far away to the north, Ramillies proved in the starkest possible terms that Marlborough could rely on his own daring, calculation and skill, and did not depend on Eugene for victory.

Frank Taylor, in his most useful study of Marlborough's campaigns, wrote approvingly in 1915 of his pre-wartime visit to Ramillies and of how unspoilt the battlefield was. He hoped that it would long remain so. He would not be disappointed today, for the area, despite its quite close proximity to Brussels and Waterloo, is largely untouched by modern development. The small villages are, of course, rather more substantial than in 1706, but the vast plain to the south of Ramillies on which the great cavalry battle was fought is still laid to crops and looks very much as it must have done on that day. The marshy valley of the Petite Gheete stream to the north is drained now, but it still presents quite an obstacle to easy movement, just as it did to Marlborough's infantrymen on that long-ago Sunday in May, and it is easy to lose your footing when walking the slopes today.

The Fight at Elixheim

Any thoughts Louis XIV cherished that he could decisively win the War of the Spanish Succession were put at an end by the Duke of Marlborough's victory at Blenheim in 1704. No longer could France hope to exert its strength to knock out of the war any one of the main partners of the Grand Alliance – England, Holland or Austria – unless this could be managed in secret by negotiation. Blenheim marked a strategic shift in the war, assuming that there was not now some inexplicable and catastrophic error by the Allies. Quite apart from the massive losses in men, horses and matériel suffered by the French at Blenheim, and the blow to France's prestige, the King's main ally, the Elector of Bavaria was ruined and made a virtual fugitive. Louis XIV's other allies would not be at all encouraged by the course of events. It did not follow, however, that his opponents could achieve a conclusive victory over France; the immense resilience of the French King in the face of catastrophe, the strenuous efforts and, on the whole, skilful performances of his generals, had enabled France to recover its poise to a significant degree by the early summer months of 1705. In short, the Duke of Marlborough had been unable to make the most of his victory beside the Danube.

Emperor Leopold died in May 1705. This unavoidably complicated things for the Grand Alliance, even though his successor, his eldest son Joseph, was an admirer of Marlborough. The Allied campaigns in northern Italy and Spain failed to prosper, and the Dutch settled down to defend their borders and do no more for the time being. Meanwhile, the Duke's ambitious plans for a great campaign in the Moselle valley, with an advance into the heart of France, were foiled by both the careful defensive moves of Marshal Villars, who took up a strong position at Sierck, and the reluctance of his allies, in particular the Margrave of Baden, to join him in the campaign in good time and with the agreed number of soldiers. The effect was that in June, Marlborough could deploy only about 30,000 troops in the valley, rather than the 90,000 he had planned for, and supplies were short to feed those who were available (the Allied commissary officer in Coblenz had embezzled the funds and defected to the French to avoid retribution). The terrain was also poor – 'The terriblest country that can be imagined for the march of an army with cannon' – and the weather was bad. To add to these difficulties, Marshal Villeroi exerted pressure on the Dutch in the southern Netherlands by attacking and seizing the Allied-held town of Huy on the Meuse, before occupying Liège and threatening the citadel there. Veteran British soldier John Millner wrote:

> *The Duke of Marlborough received an Account from the States [General] of their Affairs in the Low Countries, the loss of Huy, and the siege of Liege began, and the Threats that those two [French] generals made, that they would recover all the former Conquests of the Allies.*

Marlborough had little choice but to abandon the Moselle operations, get his hungry army out from in front of Villars's defences and march northwards at best speed to join Veldt-Marshal Overkirk, who, lacking numbers, had gone into an entrenched camp at Maastricht. The Duke was able to disentangle himself from the Moselle without his rearguard having to fight its way out, but he bitterly regretted that this potentially promising campaign, offering the chance to bypass the massive fortress belt along France's northern border, had to be abandoned. However, given the shortage of supplies, the delayed appearance of Imperial reinforcements, bad weather and Villars's astute use of the formidable terrain, the campaign was already a dead letter by the time Marlborough was summoned north, even before Villeroi seized Huy and Liège to the alarm of the Dutch.

On 2 July 1705, Marlborough combined his forces with those of Overkirk, and the Allied army moved rapidly against Huy. Villeroi had already fallen back from the attempt to seize the citadel of Liège on learning of the Duke's approach, and he now went into camp at Tongres. Huy fell to Allied assault on 11 July: 'Neither side had above twenty men killed and wounded', and the French army then withdrew behind stout lines of defence that had been constructed over the previous eighteen months, known as the Lines of Brabant. These works stretched in a great arc from Antwerp in the north, past Louvain to Namur on the Meuse. From behind the defences, Villeroi confidently expected to defy Marlborough and Overkirk with impunity, although in their haste to pull back, the French troops under the Duke of Berwick also abandoned the small town of Leau.

Now that he had resumed campaigning in the Low Countries, a region in which major success had eluded him in the past, Marlborough was keen to regain the initiative. In consultation with Overkirk, the Duke drew up an

The Lines of Brabant

In the early eighteenth century, defensive lines of this sort were not continuous in the modern sense of a trench system or a row of fortifications, but were more a series of obstacles both natural (such as rivers or flooded meadows) and man-made (such as earth embankments and fortified farmhouses). The lines would be lightly garrisoned or patrolled by dragoons, and only manned in any force when a particular point was threatened by the approach of an opposing army. The presence of a major part of the defending field army in a given vicinity would, naturally, deter any serious attempt to breach the lines or risk heavy losses in the effort to do so.

Given their length, great ingenuity had to be employed in making these defences formidable but simple to defend, and engineers carefully plotted the course of the lines to take advantage of the natural strength of local topography, for example following the course of a particular river or canal. The weak point in the Lines of Brabant, one that Marlborough was astute enough to recognise, was a relatively narrow but perfectly usable watershed formed by high ground between the Petite Gheete and Mehaigne streams in the vicinity of Taviers and Ramillies. This was vital ground. Almost eerily, the French engineers recognised that an army occupying the position would naturally have to throw forward their wings to occupy the villages on either flank. Accordingly, any attacker approaching from the east would be able to switch troops from one side of the field to the other, cutting across the chord of the arc, thereby gaining an instant advantage over the defender, whose troops would have further to march when countering any such movement. As a result, the lines had been pushed forward by the French engineers nearer to Elixheim and Wanghe (close to the 1693 Williamite battlefield of Landen) in order to take advantage of the streams in that area and avoid the inbuilt weakness in the Taviers–Ramillies–Offuz position. The lines of defence were, as a result, rather more exposed than elsewhere, and so became the target for Marlborough's inspired attack in 1705.

imaginative plan to trap the French. As Marlborough expected, the Veldt-Marshal was at first cautious, aware that the States-General preferred to avoid open battles when they could, but was persuaded to cooperate; as Marlborough's chaplain Francis Hare shrewdly put it, the Dutch were prepared to 'follow him if he succeeded, to help him make his retreat if he miscarried, but not to share the danger'. Meanwhile, Villeroi had his field army well closed up, and was quite ready to shift this way and that as the threat from his opponents appeared to be most acute, first in one direction and then the other. On the afternoon of 17 July, Overkirk began to march his Dutch corps southwards, using pontoon bridges laid over the Mehaigne river, as if to threaten the French-held fortress of Namur. This movement was soon detected by French scouts, as was intended, and Villeroi took the bait; by nightfall he was marching his own army southwards to keep pace with the Allied advance and to cover Namur.

That same evening, Marlborough's troops were roused from their bivouacs and set to marching northwards on a diverging course to Overkirk's, heading for the section of defensive lines near the villages of Elixheim and Wanghe on the Petite Gheete stream. The Duke had quite deliberately divided his forces when in close proximity to the enemy, and this entailed some risk. However, Marlborough had assessed the character of his opponent well. The speed of the Allied operation allowed little time for Villeroi to reflect on these developments or to form any plan to interpose his own army between the two separate and temporarily vulnerable Wings of the Allies. He instinctively swallowed the notion that Namur was to be the target for Marlborough's attack, and took prompt action accordingly: 'This drew the Enemies main Force that way.' However, Villeroi was not so rash or neglectful as to leave his left flank and rear entirely denuded of troops, and a powerful mixed corps of French and Bavarian cavalry and infantry remained in place not far from Tirlemont under the experienced command of the Marquis d'Alegre. Villeroi also left strict instructions that these troops were to keep on the alert.

Marlborough's marching columns, British, German and Danish troops, found the night heavy with mist and light rain, and the roads were bad. Their guides got lost more than once, but despite this they made good time, so that by dawn on 18 July the grenadiers and pioneers of the army were wading the Petite Gheete and breaking down the palisades of the Lines of Brabant at Elixheim and Wanghe. A nearby French fortified post was rushed, and after a few scattered shots the squadrons of French dragoons in the vicinity took themselves off to raise the alarm. Marlborough's infantry commander, 1st Earl Orkney, wrote that 'Though the passages were bad, people scrambled over them.' With the loss of hardly a man, Marlborough had breached the French lines of defence by about 7am, but he had just thirty-eight cavalry squadrons and twenty battalions of infantry, under the immediate command of Count Noyelles. The troops were all intermingled together in broken country laced through with hedges and sunken muddy lanes leading up onto higher ground. The Allied troops were hardly able to form up in some sort of proper order, and then the inevitable counter-attack came in. One Scottish soldier laconically remembered, 'When we were over on their side, they attacked us.'

Yves, Marquis d'Alegre, an astute and skilful commander, had fifty squadrons of French and Bavarian cavalry under command, supported by Count Caraman with twenty battalions of Bavarian, Walloon and German infantry in the French service and some batteries of guns. This was just an advanced guard; the two commanders might have done well to wait for their supports to come up, and then to attempt to deliver the stroke with full power behind it. However, they rightly saw that Marlborough would benefit by any delay in getting his own army properly across the Lines and would position the troops to meet an attack. They might also have suspected that the Duke's intention was to combine with the Dutch, who, having marched south, were even now countermarching northwards to the crossings at Elixheim. Riders had been sent by d'Alegre to alert Villeroi to the Allied breaking of the Lines, but it would take most of the morning for them to reach the Marshal with the news and for the French field army to turn about in its tracks before hurrying northwards, along with everyone else that day, to the beckoning sound of guns, gradually increasing in urgent volume as time went on.

As it was, d'Alegre's corps was rather outnumbered at Elixheim, and many of the Bavarian squadrons in particular were understrength. As a result, it seems that the Marquis and Caraman moved into the attack with only about 10,000 troops and ten guns to challenge Marlborough, who was able to deploy (albeit in a rather hurried and unsatisfactory formation) some 16,000 men supported by a six-gun battery. The blackened armour worn by the Bavarian cuirassiers as their leading squadrons shook out for action could be plainly seen in the early morning light, and Marlborough, who could not have known for certain what a numerical advantage he had, was looking anxiously to the south for signs of Overkirk's leading Dutch regiments. He had thrown his troops over the formidable obstacle in the most audacious style with trifling loss; now the Duke had to hold onto the ground gained long enough for the Dutch to join him.

The French and their allies came on in good order, and a hard struggle broke out along the lanes and hedgerows in the area. Caraman's infantry drove Noyelle's leading troops back a short way, but Marlborough hurried forward his reserves and quickly recovered his force's composure; a sabre-swinging cavalry battle erupted in what little open ground there was available. Over the course of a two-hour engagement, the superior numbers Marlborough could deploy gradually told, and for all the dash and gallantry with which their opponents attacked, they were pushed back off the high ground. D'Alegre was wounded, and would have been bayoneted as he lay on the ground had not Lord John Hay recognised him, called his assailants off and taken him away captive. Without the guiding hand of the Marquis, the ordering of his cavalry in the broken terrain faltered, and many of the squadron commanders began to pull back into more open country where they might recover their composure. They were closely pursued by the Allied troopers, also keen to get out of the restricting lanes, and what began as a limited tactical withdrawal by the French became a bit of a scramble. At this point, as Marlborough pressed the advantage onwards with his squadrons, he was confronted by a Bavarian horse grenadier who aimed a mighty stroke at the Duke's head. The blow went wide and, the swing meeting no resistance, the soldier lost his balance and fell to the ground, whereupon the Duke's trumpeter leaped from his horse and killed him with his sword. 'Was it so?' Orkney asked Marlborough afterwards, 'and he said it was absolutely so.'

Pierre Caraman's infantry now found that their cavalry supports were melting away, but in a notably skilful manoeuvre they formed into a great square with the grenadier companies taking up position at each corner, and began a steady and superbly well-ordered withdrawal to the west, heading for the river crossings over the Dyle near to Tirlemont. Their musketry volleys deterred any close pursuit by Marlborough's infantry, and the perfect discipline of the square foiled all attempts by the Allied cavalry to interfere with Caraman's movement to the river. A British officer who watched the manoeuvre wrote admiringly, 'This shows what resolution and keeping good order can do.'

Marlborough had won a significant victory – 'Half a battle', one observer rather disparagingly noted, 'as only a half of each army were all that were involved.' Not only had the Duke burst through the vaunted Lines of Brabant with light losses, but he had repulsed a very well-handled counter-attack, inflicting hundreds of casualties and taken many prisoners, including the wounded French commander. Caraman's ten guns also fell into Marlborough's hands, and all this for the loss of little more than 200 killed and wounded. The regiments and squadrons with the Duke that day had all accompanied him in the Danube campaign, and the soldiers now crowded round his horse, shouting their cheers of triumph. 'See what a happy man he is,' Orkney wrote. 'I believe this pleases him more than Höchstädt [Blenheim].'

Marlborough did not pursue Caraman's infantry with as much vigour as he displayed on other occasions, and this had to do with the weariness of his own soldiers – they had marched all night and fought a hectic, if brief, battle in the morning. Also, Overkirk's Dutch troops were now arriving at the break in the lines, but these men had also had a hard march. The Veldt-Marshal, usually so cooperative, was short-tempered, and asked that his men be allowed to rest and eat something. The Dutch general Slangenberg (so often awkward and fractious) was all fire and energy this day, urging that a pursuit be mounted without delay: 'If we lie still, this is all for nothing.' Marlborough agreed with him, but would not overrule Overkirk, and so, by 10am, the Dutch had

Henry of Nassau, Count Overkirk, Dutch Veldt-Marshal and close colleague of Marlborough.

settled down to rest from their exertions. Although the Duke attracted criticism for this apparent inaction, he had little option when faced with Overkirk's reluctance to press on. He also had no way of knowing quite where the main French army was at this point in the mid-morning; Villeroi, having observed Caraman's masterly withdrawal from contact, was moving his troops back behind the comparative safety of the Dyle river, in such haste that he abandoned some of his artillery on the way, but Marlborough would not learn this for certain until later in the day. A British officer wrote, 'The Duke really neither knew nor indeed could know how near the Elector and M. Villeroi was with their whole army.' The moment to move in hard against the exposed flank of the marching French army, if it existed at all, had passed.

Suitably rested and refreshed, the Allied troops pressed forward to the river Dyle the next day, 19 July. Tirlemont had already been occupied by Marlborough's cavalry, who took some hundreds more French prisoners (some reports say the entire Régiment de Montluc) and scores of baggage wagons. However, Villeroi moved his army to shield Louvain, and bad weather now intervened to hamper Marlborough's operations. It was only on 30 July that the Duke was able to undertake a major crossing of the river in the vicinity of Neerysche. Villeroi moved promptly to block the operation, and the Dutch were reluctant to force a major action to sustain the advanced guard, which had already crossed to the far bank and was engaging the French with artillery. Frustrated, Marlborough pulled his troops back over the river with little loss to either side, and moved his army into camp at Meldert from where some useful time was spent in levelling the abandoned lines of defence. The Duke also took the chance to refresh his memory of the topography along the nearby Ramillies watershed. As it happened, Villeroi had done the same thing, and one of the plans that he periodically submitted to Versailles for consideration by the King included a scheme for his army to fight a defensive battle on that very ridge.

A couple of weeks later, Marlborough tried to engage Villeroi again. This time, by cutting loose from his supply bases and magazines and loading his carts with as much bread and ammunition as they could carry, he converted his army into an enormous flying column, able to move quickly and nimbly around the right flank of Villeroi's army as it lay covering Louvain. The Duke would be able to shrug off any countermove by the French against his lines of supply and communication, at least for a few days. As it was, Villeroi was puzzled by the sudden Allied dash to the south-west across the headwaters of the Dyle, from where Marlborough could, if he chose, threaten Mons, Charleroi, Valenciennes, Cambrai, or even turn northwards and attack Brussels.

Marlborough had neatly turned Villeroi's right flank, and the Allied army, although living on tight rations, now stood between the Marshal and the French border. Villeroi felt unable to uncover Louvain to a sudden thrust, but he moved a strong detachment under the Marquis de Grimaldi to cover the southern approaches to Brussels. This force was badly outnumbered by the advanced guard of the Allied army soon seen advancing past Genappes through the Forest of Soignes. However, Grimaldi was in a good defensive position: 'A deep muddy river [Yssche] in the front and the wood of Soignes in their rear ... close ground with hedges and ditches.' Nevertheless, as yet the Marquis was unsupported by Villeroi's main army, and he was unable to move closer to the Marshal as this would have uncovered Brussels to Marlborough's advancing troops.

There was some sharp skirmishing on 17 August, and the following day Marlborough had a good chance to overwhelm Grimaldi before going on to confront Villeroi, whose army was even now rapidly side-stepping to close the dangerous gap. To the Duke's intense annoyance, the Dutch generals were once again reluctant to engage and insisted on holding a council of war to discuss the intended attack. The following morning, when all had spoken, it was seen that Villeroi had managed to close his main army up to the Yssche position, which had been fortified during the night; no attack with a fair prospect of success was now possible. Marlborough carried out a careful reconnaissance and was fired on by French gunners, but there was little to be done; he commented that he felt 'ten years older than I was a few days ago.' The army's bread wagons were beginning to empty now, and a withdrawal across the Dyle was necessary. The Duke had to be content with completing the spoiling of the lines and laying siege to some minor French-held towns nearby.

In his disappointment, Marlborough wrote to the States-General, complaining of the obstructive attitude of their generals and of the field deputies who accompanied the army: 'I flattered myself, that I might soon have congratulated Your High Mightinesses on a glorious victory ... the opportunity was too fair to let slip.' The Duke hinted that he intended to retire, as his position was so much weaker than in the previous year. The Dutch general officers and their deputy colleagues attempted to excuse their behaviour, telling the States-General that Marlborough did not sufficiently consult them about his plans, that he 'without holding a council of war, made two or three marches for the execution of some design formed by His Grace, and we cannot conceal from Your High Mightinesses that all the Generals of the Army think it very strange.' As Marlborough knew well, they were unable to keep confidential anything told to them in confidence. The Dutch did have some grounds for complaint, however, given their own cautious inclination, for the Duke hoped, by keeping them in the dark, to overcome their reluctance by springing a promising opportunity on them, one which would be too good to resist – 'to cheat them into a victory', as one of his correspondents perceptively put it. To their credit, the States-General saw that the situation could not continue.

Public opinion in Holland, robust and courageous, was outraged at reports of the timidity of the Dutch generals and field deputies, and the more awkward among them were quietly removed from the army at the end of the year's campaign.

To Marshal Villeroi, despite his own doubts and an undeniable element of hesitation and fumbling in the recent campaign, it seemed possible to believe that he had, in fact, foiled Marlborough. This encouraging tale grew in the telling as he wrote his dispatches to his friend the King in Versailles. Villeroi extolled his apparent success at blocking the Allied army at the crossings over the Dyle and 'forcing' the withdrawal from the forest of Soignes, while heaping scorn on the Duke and his apparently flagging efforts. The vital, crucially hampering, part played by the cautious Dutch in ruining Marlborough's promising plans appears either to not have been recognised or was conveniently ignored. Louis XIV, hungry for good tidings and eager to be convinced, readily accepted the Marshal's rather spurious claims and was pleased for him in his success. The French Minister of War, Michel de Chamillart, visited Villeroi at this time and added his own dismissive comments on the Duke's abilities and performance, coming to the dangerous conclusion that Marlborough's successes in Bavaria and at the Lines of Brabant (either of which should have been warning enough) were due more to good fortune than to skill. 'I have a mediocre opinion of the capacity of the Duke of Marlborough,' a French diplomat wrote at this time. 'We find that Monsieur de Marlborough is less successful at war than he was last year.'

After the awful events of 1704, France had recovered her strategic poise quite well during 1705. Marlborough's inability to achieve another major victory, despite the undoubted success at Elixheim, seemed significant. Marshal Villeroi's modestly successful campaign, added to Villars's skill in holding the Moselle valley secure, French advances in Spain and northern Italy, and the growing pressure exerted on Savoy (the recently joined and most exposed partner in the Grand Alliance) all seemed good indications that the Alliance was growing stale. The glittering opportunity gained at Blenheim seemed to have been allowed to pass. 'The last campaign,' Colonel Jean-Martin de la Colonie wrote during the winter of 1705, 'had been so favourable to France, that she became convinced that the wheel of fortune was turning in her favour.' Louis XIV was now putting out peace feelers, particularly to the Dutch, whose expenses in the war had so far been ruinous. The French treasury was in a sorry state, Blenheim had been an undoubted shock to Louis XIV and he would now welcome a good peace, one that would offer concessions but enable his grandson to retain his domains in the Low Countries and the throne in Madrid. It seemed for a while that the French King would succeed in driving a wedge between the main parties to the Alliance, but the terms he suggested were so disproportionately unfavourable that nothing came of the approach, for the time being. Accordingly, in order to impress his opponents with the vitality of the French war effort and the huge resources that France could still call on, Louis sent instructions from Versailles to commanders in all theatres of the war, that they were to take the offensive everywhere in the next campaign season. The King wrote, 'I can think of nothing which can better induce them [the Allies] to come to an agreement which has become necessary now, than to let them see that I have sufficient forces to attack them everywhere.' All depended on the French commanders producing victory for their King; this was a dangerous course, and would inevitably diffuse the French war effort with consequent dire results not only in Flanders but in Italy and, to a lesser degree, in Spain also.

Marlborough was not yet to know all this, having kept busy through the winter months with a series of diplomatic visits to supporters of the Alliance, among them the Elector of the Palatinate who was persuaded to send a large contingent of troops to bolster the Allied campaign in northern Italy. Operating in the Low Countries, the Duke despaired of ever achieving very much at all, and on 26 March 1706, feeling that little was to be expected in the coming year, he wrote:

> The placing of the King of France's Household [cavalry] so that they may be sent either to Germany or Flanders is a plain instance that they intend to take their motions from what we shall do, which confirms me in my opinion of their being resolved to act in both places defensively.

The Duke prepared plans for a fresh attempt to advance into France through the Moselle valley, where Marshal Marsin had recently taken up the command, and he also considered going to the upper Rhine frontier to join forces with the Margrave of Baden and so threaten Alsace. That Marlborough ever thought, however briefly, of working with the awkward and obstructive Margrave again, he who had given such trouble in the Danube campaign and then not turned up for the Moselle operations the following year, shows how frustrated and doubtful he was of finding success while working with the Dutch. He even considered a plan, which the States-General did not know about for some time, to combine his British troops with those of Prince Eugene in northern Italy in an echo of the 1704 march to the Danube.

Marlborough crossed to Holland on the galley HMS *Peregrine*, landing on 14 April 1706, to prepare for the new campaign season. The war soon took a turn for the worse as news came in that the Duc de Vendôme had defeated an Imperial army at Calcinato in northern Italy on 19 April. French forces then moved to threaten Turin and the Duchy of Savoy. In early May, Baden was beaten near Landau on the upper Rhine by Marshal Villars, who had been reinforced with troops sent by Marsin from the Moselle valley. Baden lost his lines of defence, and important depots and magazines, and had to try to reform his battered army to the east of the river. With so many reverses, and French military power apparently reinvigorated in response to Louis XIV's urging, the Dutch refused to consider the Duke leaving their borders, whether the Moselle (where Marsin was now vulnerable after sending troops to Villars), the upper Rhine or even far-off Italy was his destination. Marlborough reluctantly shelved the schemes and looked forward again, without enthusiasm, to a fresh campaign in the Low Countries.

Marlborough was aware that the concentration of his army had been delayed, and many Dutch officers had not yet rejoined their units. Arrears of pay for the Danish troops were outstanding, and their King, not unreasonably, would not approve their use until these debts were settled. At the same time, the King of Prussia was pursuing private quarrels with both the Imperial court in Vienna and the States-General in The Hague; he kept his troops in their quarters behind the Rhine while the disputes rumbled on. The Duke wrote in exasperation to Queen Anne's Ambassador in Berlin, Lord Raby: 'If it should please God to give us victory over the enemy, the Allies will be little obliged to the King; and if, on the other hand, we should have any disadvantage, I know not how he will be able to excuse himself.' Meanwhile George, the Elector of Hanover, was also being uncooperative. His troops were not ready to take the field, and negotiations for fresh contingents of Hessian troops were not progressing well. As if all this was not enough, there was concern about maintaining an adequate supply of horses, and Marlborough's remount officers were scouring Schleswig-Holstein, Pomerania and the Protestant cantons of Switzerland for suitable replacements.

Amidst all these gloomy considerations, there was one ray of hope for the Duke. It was rumoured in the Allied camp that Marshal Marsin was sending cavalry reinforcements northwards to join the French army in the Low Countries and that he had moved his own headquarters to Metz, ready to march and combine with Villeroi. If that were so (and the reports were soon confirmed), then Villeroi might feel confident enough to move out and challenge Marlborough. In fact, as part of Louis XIV's desire to show a brave front to his opponents, the Marshal had recently received several letters from Versailles urging him to do just that. Villeroi soon became concerned that the King suspected him of hanging back at a time when Vendôme and Villars were operating in Italy and on the upper Rhine to such good effect. 'He had the feeling that the King doubted his courage, since he judged it necessary to spur him so hard,' wrote the Duc de St Simon. Even so, Marlborough had no great confidence that Villeroi really would advance to seek battle. He had always found the Marshal to be cautious, and he feared that, once again, Villeroi would cling to the protection of the river lines and avoid confrontation as he had done with reasonable success in previous campaigns.

The Duke left The Hague on 9 May 1706 to join his steadily gathering army, and wrote to a friend in London six days later:

I was assured I would find the army in a condition to march, but as yet neither the artillery nor the bread-wagons are come so that we shall be obliged to stay [and wait] for the English which will join us on Wednesday [19 May] and then we shall advance ... I have no prospect of doing anything considerable unless the French would do what I am very confident they will not.

The British troops made good time and joined the army a day earlier than the Duke expected, on the Tuesday. This promptness, the result of the improvement in the recent poor weather, was just as well. The Duke moved Overkirk's Dutch corps to Tongres, not far from Maastricht, although the Danish, Prussian and Hanoverian contingents had still not appeared.

In the meantime, the French had apparently uncovered a plot by a prominent citizen of Namur, a Monsieur Pasqieur, to betray the city to the Allies. Whatever unpleasant fate befell that gentleman is not known for certain, but nothing came of the plan itself, if it existed at all. However, Villeroi was sensitive to such indications that Marlborough intended to open his new campaign along

Ramillies. The plateau of Jandrenouille seen from Ramillies village. Marlborough's field HQ was at the farmhouse.

the line of the Meuse. When the French commander marched, he would naturally incline to the south, to be in a good position to counter any Allied attempt on Namur and to take practical advantage of the watershed at the Taviers–Ramillies–Offuz position. Possession of this valuable topographical feature would enable the French commander either to move eastwards onto the adjacent plateau of Jandrenouille, and so interpose his army between the Allies and the Meuse, or to stand and hold the villages on the watershed himself, denying its use to Marlborough. From that stout, seemingly unassailable defensive position, Villeroi would be able to threaten the Duke's flank if he tried to press on towards Namur. This would effectively check Marlborough's advance and leave Villeroi with a number of promising options to pursue. It must all have seemed very pleasing and plausible.

In the circumstances, Villeroi was responding in a perfectly satisfactory way to the persistent urging from Versailles to take action. However, to the Marshal's natural wish to demonstrate his energy to the King and so to take the field, and his own reasonable concern for the security of Namur, if that really was Marlborough's intended victim, should be added the Duke's own ardent desire for a decisive outright battle, wherever Villeroi could be found and made to stand and fight. The coming clash, if not at the Ramillies watershed then at some other convenient spot nearby, can be seen as almost an inevitability.

We May Have a Complete Victory

On 18 May 1706, Marshal Villeroi's army, comprising 60,000 troops with 62 guns and an engineer bridging train of 34 pontoons began to move forward from the vicinity of Louvain, crossing the Dyle river to challenge the Duke of Marlborough. Confidence was high, the army was well trained and superbly equipped, and reinforcements had recently been received from Marsin's forces in the Moselle valley. The French generals were heartened, both by the belief that Marlborough's success in 1704 had been due to luck rather than skill, evidenced by his comparative lack of progress the following year, and the certain knowledge that many contingents of Allied troops had yet to join the Duke's army. Villeroi at first moved towards Tirlemont, as if the intention was to threaten Leau, but he then turned southwards, heading for Judoigne. This line of march took the French and Bavarian troops towards the dry ground between the Mehaigne and Petite Gheete streams – 'a narrow aperture of but 1,200 paces' close to the small villages of Taviers and Ramillies which offered easy passage for marching troops between the small but marshy watercourses in the area.

From his scouts Marlborough learned of the French movement the day after it began, and set to completing the concentration of the two separate Wings of his army. As Villeroi was now moving to the south and east, it was almost certain that both commanders would be looking to gain the watershed between the Petite Gheete and the Mehaigne. Clearly the Allies and the French would be marching on a collision course, something that the Duke welcomed after the frustrations of the previous year. The Dutch generals, much more cooperative in the wake of Marlborough's anger the previous autumn, would place no hindrance in his way. Through the simple demands of geography and the physical need for firm passage for large bodies of marching soldiers, the choice of ground for the coming clash was almost obvious. Both commanders, for quite different reasons, were seeking battle, and their armies each needed the dry ground to advance in good order, so the collision at Ramillies was no real surprise. Serjeant John Millner, one of Marlborough's veterans, wrote, 'They striving and the Allies also, who should first possess themselves of Ramalies and the strong ground thereabout.' Despite this, neither Marlborough nor Villeroi quite appreciated how far his opponent had got on the march, each expecting to reach the Ramillies watershed first; the two armies, it might fairly be said, would soon stumble into one another.

Meanwhile, Marlborough had combined the troops in British pay with Overkirk's Dutch. The Duke also wrote with an appeal to the Duke of Württemberg, the commander of the Danish contingent: 'I send you this express to request Your Highness to bring forward by a double march your cavalry, so as to join us at the earliest moment, letting your infantry follow with all speed possible.' The Duke included in the message an assurance that the still outstanding arrears of pay would be made good, and astutely phrased the wording so that, if Württemberg should not be at hand to read the note immediately, any competent staff officer would not hesitate to get the Danish troops marching while the commander was found and asked to give the actual orders for such a movement:

In case Your Highness is not with the leading corps, the officer commanding that corps is hereby instructed to march without waiting further orders, and to forward this letter to Your Highness and all commanders in rear so that they can also conform.

In the event, Württemberg responded magnificently to the urgent summons, and his twenty-one squadrons of Danish cavalry, together with a second reinforcement of three more squadrons and six battalions of infantry, joined the Allied army in time for the coming battle.

Marlborough's order of battle was still not complete, and with several score Dutch officers still on leave at home, the battle would have to be fought without them. Despite this shortfall, the 62,000-strong Allied army – 123 squadrons of cavalry and 74 infantry battalions accompanied by 90 pieces of artillery and 20 mortars, and an engineer bridging train of 42 pontoons – was moving southwards on 21 May. Marlborough had to slow their progress near Corswaren to allow the Danish troops to catch up. By delaying in this way, he briefly surrendered the initiative to Villeroi, who got to the crucial ground first as a result. This was a very brief and shallow advantage for the Marshal, but it was an advantage all the same. What mattered more were the reactions of the opposing commanders when the actual clash came. With their armies more or less in balance numerically, and equal in the capabilities of their weapons and tactics, which of the two men would make good decisions the faster, whose touch in command of his army was the more sure, and whose procedures were best? The commander who took control, got a telling punch in first and then held the initiative and dictated the action would win.

That Marlborough foresaw, and welcomed, the coming battle is revealed in a letter he wrote on 21 May, less than forty-eight hours before the action:

> *The French, having drained all their garrisons, had passed the Dyle and were come to the camp at Tirlemont, which you may believe has quite broken the measures we were projecting at Maastricht; so that upon this news the army marched yesterday from Tongres hither, where the English joined us, and tomorrow we expect the Danes; then we design to advance to gain the head of the Gheete to come to the enemy if they keep their ground. For my part, I can think of nothing more happy for the Allies than a battle, since I have good reason to hope, with the blessing of God, we may have a complete victory.*

The Duke plainly expected to get across the Ramillies watershed and meet Villeroi in the area of Judoigne; he was not aware quite how far forward the French commander had advanced.

The weather had been bad in recent weeks with rain making the roads muddy, but they were drying steadily, and the armies made good time. So, in the early morning of Whit Sunday, 23 May 1706, the French army approached from the west the low ridge-line running from Ramillies northwards to the villages of Offuz and Autre-Eglise. Just beyond Ramillies, to the south of the village, was the mile-and-a-half-wide open plain stretching to Taviers, offering the coveted dry passage for moving from west to east. Marshal Villeroi was first on the ground, and plainly expected that a clash with Marlborough would take place, for the Irish soldier of fortune Peter Drake, serving with the Régiment de Courrière, remembered that sixteen rounds of ball ammunition were issued that very morning (an interesting clue to the degree of fire-power expected to be generated in a general action at the time). Despite this expectation of action, Villeroi's cavalry commander, Emmanuel Wittelsbach, the Elector of Bavaria and Governor-General of the Spanish Netherlands, was absent in Brussels, attending Pentecostal celebrations. He would not catch up with the army until later in the day, but would be in time to fight for his life before nightfall.

Across the marshy valley of the Petite Gheete stream from the marching French and Bavarian army lay the plateau of Jandrenouille, and cantering across those wide fields came William Cadogan, Marlborough's burly Quartermaster-General. He rode through the early morning mist and drizzle with an escort of 700 dragoons, looking for a suitable camping ground near Ramillies for the Allied army. The troops were still at their breakfast several miles to the east, having spent the dark hours in damp bivouacs between Corswaren and Merdorp. The Duke's intention was to move the army forward, past Ramillies and Taviers, and to occupy the plateau of Mont St André to the west of the watershed. From there, he would be well placed to close with Villeroi's army,

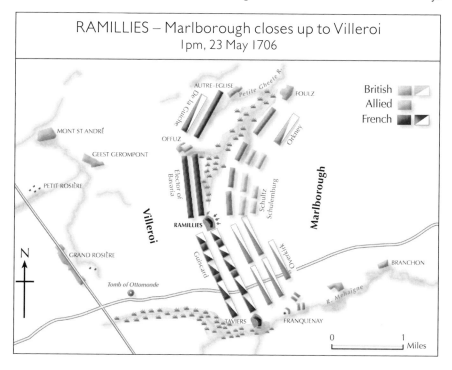

RAMILLIES – Marlborough closes up to Villeroi
1pm, 23 May 1706

thought still to be near Judoigne, a little to the north, and with good fortune he would bring them to battle before they could retire behind the Dyle once again.

Clearly, Marlborough was not aware that Villeroi had come so far forward, and the Marshal, in this respect, seems to have been one step ahead. At about 7am, Cadogan's escort clashed with some French cavalry troopers who were gathering forage on the edge of the plateau of Jandrenouille. After a brief exchange of shots, the foragers drew off to the west. Cadogan pressed forward, and was soon able to make out the smartly ordered lines of Villeroi's army as it moved majestically along the Ramillies–Offuz ridge-line, preparing to deploy across the watershed. As Colonel de la Colonie wrote, 'We were able to march our army on a broad front as we desired, and the result was a magnificent spectacle ... France had surpassed herself in the quality of these troops.' Alerted by reports of the brief opening clash on the plateau of Jandrenouille, the French commander quickly moved to deploy his army along the 4 miles of frontage from Taviers in the south, across the broad crop-covered plain to Ramillies village, and on to the enclosed gardens and orchards around Offuz and Autre-Eglise in the north where 'runs the river Geet which makes the ground in most places very swampy'. Villeroi could derive some satisfaction from the sure knowledge that he was first on the ground. 'Coming in sight of the enemy,' Peter Drake wrote, 'the cannon was ordered to the front to be placed on the proper ground to annoy them.' Getting the cumbersome pieces into place, even on firm ground, was a time-consuming procedure, so that,

Ramillies. Looking towards Autre-Eglise from the plateau of Jandrenouille. Petite Gheete stream in middle distance, shown by line of trees.

apart from some ranging shots by both sides, there was no real artillery work done until the afternoon.

Cadogan, meanwhile, had sent messengers hurrying back to Merdorp to bring Marlborough forward to a position where he could see the French army for himself. The Duke, accompanied by Count Overkirk, General Daniel Dopff and some staff officers, joined Cadogan at about 10am, by which time the mist had conveniently risen, allowing them a full and uninterrupted view of Villeroi's unfolding dispositions. One of the party was Sicco van Goslinga, a self-opinionated Dutch field deputy, and he apparently pointed out that 'the enemy's left could not be attacked with any prospect of success; for the hedges, ditches and marshes were a complete barrier to both sides; that therefore the whole of our cavalry should be massed on our left.' Marlborough accepted the civilian deputy's lecture with a polite smile, and promptly ignored his advice. To show his hand so soon, and so plainly, to his opponent would be folly, even if the exact details of his own plan were not, as they could not yet be, fully formed; a lot would depend on Villeroi's reaction to the first shock of the Duke's attack. The open plain to the south of Ramillies was, in any case, the obvious place to mass the bulk of the Allied cavalry, and the Marshal would do the same for precisely the same tactical reason; the more broken ground to the north of Ramillies offered limited scope for cavalry action, although as the day wore on it would prove to be not entirely impassable to horsemen.

Concerned not to let this promising opportunity slip, Marlborough called forward his leading echelons of cavalry to close up to the French as near as could be without actually bringing on a premature general engagement while the bulk of his army was not yet ready to support them. This cavalry advance, confident and forthright but not rash, would fix Villeroi in position and force him to commit to a battle that day. If he tried to draw off, the Marshal would risk an escalating and damaging running battle with the Duke's cavalry, something that could very easily tumble out of control amidst all the confusion of the baggage train before he could get his army back to the shelter of the Dyle river. If, on the other hand, the French and Bavarian troops on the other side of the Petite Gheete were just an advanced guard who had pushed on too far and too fast without real support, then the Allied cavalry might be able to give them a good mauling without too much trouble. Villeroi might then, in turn, have to come forward with his main army to save the detachment from destruction, and become obliged to stand and fight. On each count, Marlborough's rapid, almost instinctive, deployment of his cavalry was correct. As it was, it soon became apparent that the French and Bavarian army, in all its might, was just a short distance away, massing its strength to meet the advancing Allies.

The Duke was accompanied on his reconnaissance by a number of Walloon officers familiar with the area. They also warned that the ground to the north was too marshy to be crossed in the face of any determined opposition and that it was therefore not practical to try to attack in that part of the field. Marlborough, who was well aware of this problem having scouted the ground with care the previous year, paid no more attention to them than he had to deputy Goslinga's hints. As his army came forward to the edge of the plateau of Jandrenouille, it deployed from ponderous columns of march into eight nimble columns of attack, moving in the well-practised manoeuvre to form a line of battle. The soldiers found themselves marching over the debris of the Lines of Brabant, which they had demolished the previous autumn. The Duke directed the twenty-three battalions of British and Danish infantry towards Autre-Eglise and Offuz in the north; they were supported by fifty-four squadrons of British, German and Dutch cavalry. The forty-eight Dutch squadrons under Overkirk, together with nineteen battalions of their infantry and the Danish cavalry, went to the south to face the French squadrons massing on the plain between Ramillies and Taviers. In the centre, brigades of Dutch, German, Scots and Protestant Swiss infantry in the Dutch service closed up to Ramillies itself. As usual Marlborough took particular care with the correct siting of the batteries, and had thirty 24-pounder guns (some reports say twenty guns) dragged up into position on the highest point of the plateau of Jandrenouille, ready to open fire on the French artillery being deployed around the village.

On the other side of the tactical hill, Villeroi arranged his army with competent skill; the topography lent itself quite well to defensive action, with the natural bias of cavalry on the right and infantry on the left. The bulk of the powerful French cavalry, eighty-two squadrons in all, commanded by General de Guiscard was deployed on the plain to the south. The elite Maison de Roi cavalry and the red-coated Gendarmerie formed up as the front ranks, where their skill and mobility could be put to best effect on the wide cornfields, while brigades of French, Swiss and Bavarian infantry were ranged in their support. Additional batteries were placed on the edge of Ramillies, ready to sweep the open fields towards Taviers, where, presumably, the intention must also have been to site guns. The boggy ground of the Mehaigne stream, on the far right, would provide additional protection against any Allied flanking movement. Ramillies village, at this time a small cluster of thatched cottages, a few substantial farms and a church, would be an anchor for the left flank of de Guiscard's squadrons. Overall, in the south of the field the situation was as it ought to be, with a balanced mix of cavalry and infantry backed by powerful and well-sited artillery; all should have been well with careful management, and de Guiscard was certainly regarded as a safe pair of hands with the experience and skill to direct the battle there. However, Villeroi inexplicably neglected to clear away properly the baggage wagons, camp equipment and the attendant followers of the army, and these were allowed to clutter the area immediately behind the line of battle, 'heaped up between the two lines' as the Marquis de Feuquières remembered. At this point in time, this may have seemed of little importance, a minor administrative untidiness which could be attended to later, although it would plainly have been good practice to clear the whole area of non-essential wagons.

A little to the north of Ramillies, where the marshes of the Petite Gheete made the going difficult, Walloon and Bavarian infantry occupied the orchards and fields of the low ridge-line running towards Offuz and Autre-Eglise on the left of the position where woods and broken country covered that flank. In their support, on the plateau of Mont St André to the rear, stood the fifty cavalry squadrons commanded by the Elector of Bavaria, although four squadrons of cuirassiers were detached to support de Guiscard south of Ramillies. The villages were each packed with infantry and put into a state of defence, with the alleys barricaded and the cottages and walled farms loop-holed for muskets. Villeroi deployed his artillery with care, although the field of fire in the north, where the valley of the Petite Gheete dipped away immediately to the front, was rather limited. The powerful batteries established around Ramillies suffered no such disadvantage, and they enjoyed good fields of fire, able to cover fully the approaches from the edge of the plateau of Jandrenouille, which the Allied infantry would have to cross to come to grips. Robert Parker of the Royal Irish Regiment wrote rather dismissively, 'Along this river to the villages of Offuse and Autreglise which covered their left flank, was posted a thin line of the worst of their infantry, with squadrons after a scattering manner in their rear.' The captain was rather mistaken in his scornful assessment, and the stout defence mounted by the Walloon, French, Bavarian and émigré Irish infantry would put the British troops to the test before the afternoon was over.

The lie of the land, in a silent and subtly destructive way, actually worked against Villeroi, no matter how much care he took to arrange his army – yet, he had little notion that this was so. Tactically, it was imperative that he throw his flanks forward to occupy the villages of Taviers on his right and Autre-Eglise on his left; this all

Maximilien-Emmanuel Wittelsbach, Elector of Bavaria.

93

made sense, and he could do no less if his army was not to be exposed to a turning movement. By adopting this extended defensive posture, his commanders were, however, obliged to overstretch themselves, and in the face of so accomplished an opponent as Marlborough, this was risky. 'The position he had taken up,' wrote the Duc de St Simon, 'was well known to be bad.' For Marlborough, the broken ground to the north offered an obstacle to easy movement and narrowed the usable frontage, obliging him to take what seemed to be the most obvious course and deploy his cavalry on the left where it was awaited by the bulk of the French squadrons of the Maison du Roi, who were already settled comfortably into position. The staff officers riding with the Duke had already drawn his attention to this difficulty. So, the curious fact was that both commanders were deploying for battle on ground which, it was generally believed, was not suited to the type of operation they chose to undertake – defence for the Frenchman, attack for the Englishman.

All this while, Marlborough's army was closing up to the position. The Duke, with a slight numerical advantage, took care to ensure that his battle-line occupied a smaller frontage than his opponents'. This tight, potent formation (which was almost certainly no accident) had a double advantage, for the Allied blow, when it came, would be more concentrated and carry more weight. Also, due to the awkward topography of the battlefield, Villeroi had, in rightly occupying Taviers in the south and Autre-Eglise to the north, unavoidably thrown his flanks forward, and as a result his army stood in battle array in a shallow arc formation. Had he chosen to do so, the Marshal could have tried to envelop the flanks of the Allied army as it deployed; such an ambitious course, which would threaten Marlborough with encirclement, called for an early decision, and was at odds with Villeroi's rather sedate character. He chose instead to dig in his heels and wait for Marlborough's attack – not in itself a bad tactical choice. This meant that the French and Bavarians would have to stand the shock of the first Allied attack, letting their opponents exhaust themselves on the defences before moving forward in counter-attack. Given the natural strength of the position, and the fact that the Duke had only a slight advantage in numbers, the Marshal's decisions were perfectly satisfactory and justifiable. As with the situation to the south of Ramillies, where the French cavalry required adequate infantry support both to hold their ground and protect the flank in the marshes of the Mehaigne, active management was required to maintain the advantages of the position and Villeroi's initial modest success in getting in place before Marlborough.

One advantage offered by Marlborough's narrower frontage (given that Villeroi made no attempt to envelop his flanks) went unnoticed: the Allied soldiers could be moved from one side of the field to the other by cutting across the middle, whereas their opponents would have to take the long route, marching around the outside of the arc, if they tried to do the same thing. This tactical handicap, initially so slight as to merit almost no attention, would grow in importance as the events of the afternoon unfolded, and was commented on by the Duc de St Simon: 'There was a marsh which covered our left but prevented our two wings from joining.' The possible threat of Villeroi's throwing forward his army in a converging attack at the flanks of the Allies as they deployed remained just that, a possibility, and caused Marlborough no real concern. He judged his man well, for Villeroi was preparing to fight a defensive battle on the ridge-line. If he was not going to move forward and attack Marlborough on the plateau of Jandrenouille, the Marshal must fight and win there on the watershed. An orderly withdrawal under pressure was not open to him, with all the baggage of the army just to the rear of the French line of battle. Marlborough, much more agile in his approach, retained the options of advancing to the attack, or standing and inviting a French assault, or retiring eastwards and seeking battle on another occasion.

While the two armies made their dispositions and dragged their big guns into place, the morning sped by and a bright sunny afternoon came on. The hours before noon were by no means devoid of action: skirmishes and clashes broke out along the length of the line where the troops jostling to get into position had, occasionally, to push back the unwelcome attention of their opponents. Lord Ailesbury, an exiled Jacobite who lived nearby, remembered the morning well and wrote, 'Rising sooner than usual, we went to a hollow way just near the convent where we heard the musket shot most plain.'

Villeroi had now been joined by the Elector of Bavaria, fresh from church attendance in Brussels, who went to command the cavalry in the north of the field. Across the valley, Marlborough had completed his own close reconnaissance and deployed his army. Shortly before 2pm, he gave the order. The massed Allied batteries opened fire and Villeroi's gunners responded immediately, pounding the Dutch and German infantry brigades squaring up to Ramillies village as a terrific artillery duel broke out along the whole length of the line. Richard Kane, a veteran English campaigner, wrote, 'Our cannon being placed as most proper, they began cannonading and playing against the enemy, and theirs against us, very vigorous and smart on both sides.' Drifting smoke soon began to obscure the battlefield, particularly to the north along the broken country of the Petite Gheete valley; the fog of war, physical and psychological, inevitable and all but impenetrable to other than the keenest minds, settled over the field. The general who proved to be the more alert and have the surer touch would be at a distinct advantage.

The small village of Taviers on the far right of the French line of battle, amidst the boggy ground of the Mehaigne river and its tributary, the Visoule stream, had been occupied by two strong battalions of the Greder Suisse Régiment. This place had a particular importance for Villeroi – although he seems to have paid little attention to it – both to protect the otherwise unsupported flank of de Guiscard's cavalry on the open plain and at the same time to exert a threat to the flank of the Dutch and Danish cavalry as they came forward. This threat could be particularly effective if the French took the trouble to site artillery in the area around the village, in order to take Overkirk's squadrons in enfilade fire as they attempted to form up. Guns sited at Taviers could not achieve overlapping fire with the French batteries near Ramillies. They could still have done a lot of useful damage to the Allied cavalry, leaving little of the plain unswept by fire, impeding the Dutch and Danish advance, and going some way to redress the imbalance brought about by the relative, and growing, lack of infantry support for de Guiscard's cavalry as the battle developed.

Despite this weakness in his arrangements, Villeroi's attention was now almost entirely elsewhere, to the north of the battlefield where the British cavalry, dragoons and infantry, conspicuous in their red coats, were deploying. Louis XIV had written to Villeroi on 6 May 1706, 'Avoir une attention particuliere à ce qui essuiera le premier choc des troupe anglaises.' (Have a particular care to that part of the line which will receive the first shock of the English troops.) The Elector of Bavaria had warned, 'Beware of these men, they are dangerous.' Heeding this advice, the Marshal was at this early stage beginning to move his infantry away from the support of de Guiscard's cavalry to bolster the position held by the Bavarian and Walloon troops between Ramillies, Offuz and Autre-Eglise. This was already a naturally strong position, shielded to the front by the Petite Gheete stream and by the rising ground which, while not particularly steep to the ridge-line, was broken up with orchards and gardens – a good place to fight a defensive infantry battle. The advance of the British troops had a mesmerising effect on Villeroi, however, and on Marlborough's part this was almost certainly intentional. Richard Kane remembered that:

> *The Elector and Villeroy saw our right Wing marching down on their left, they were startled; whereupon they in a great hurry sent off from the plain a great many of their troops to sustain their left, which put the rest on the plain in some disorder.*

A breakthrough there, on the French and Bavarian left, would not only be serious in itself as a tactical problem on the field of battle, but, if developed successfully, would threaten Villeroi's line of communication with the Dyle river and Louvain. The Marshal was certainly not going into action while looking over his shoulder to a potential line of retreat; he intended and expected to win that day. All the same, a move by his opponents to turn his left flank appeared to be a matter more urgent than any corresponding threat to his right, where the power and mobility of de Guiscard's fine cavalry could be deployed to good effect on the wonderful open country to the south, which was ideal for mounted action. So, little attention was paid by Villeroi to the unfolding situation on the plain beyond Ramillies.

Significantly, the Marshal had not taken the chance that morning to occupy and fortify the hamlet of Franquenay, which was on the same muddy stream and just a few hundred paces forward of Taviers. It was a position now exposed to seizure by the approaching waves of Dutch infantry in their blue uniforms with orange facings. Rather belatedly, soon after midday several companies of Swiss troops were sent forward from Taviers to occupy the cottages and barns of Franquenay. The soldiers lined the adjacent hedges and gardens, but they were without real support – no guns or cavalry squadrons stood nearby, and the Swiss were too far ahead of Taviers to be supported by their comrades there. Hardly had they got into place when, at about 2pm, a brigade of Dutch Guards under command of Colonel Wertmüller (often incorrectly referred to as being a general at this time) came smartly forward from their forming up area near to the village of Boneffe in a resolute attempt to seize Franquenay for themselves. The four Dutch battalions were supported by two light field guns, boldly manhandled forward by their crews, and these were soon firing canister-shot into the ranks of the heavily outnumbered defenders. Shaken by the suddenness of the Dutch attack, the normally reliable Swiss did not hold their ground; they were quickly driven out of Franquenay and fled back across the boggy pastures, hampering both the field of view and the field of fire of the troops in Taviers. Hardly had the fugitives rejoined their comrades when the renewed assault by Wertmüller's Guards went in. A vicious battle at bayonet point erupted through the alleys and in and about the cottages and barns of Taviers.

Aware that reinforcements were being hurried to their aid, the Swiss fought back with determination, refusing to be driven, and losses on both sides mounted quickly, infuriating the soldiers in the close-quarter stabbing and clubbing contest. Colonel de la Colonie, standing with his regiment of grenadiers on the plain nearby, remembered that, 'This village was the scene of the opening of the engagement, and the fighting there was almost as murderous as the rest of the battle put together.' Such a fierce contest could not last long, and the superiority in Dutch numbers and fire-power soon told; by about 3pm they had pushed the surviving Swiss soldiers right out of Taviers and into the marshes of the Visoule stream, where, in their confusion, they were exposed to the musketry of the triumphant Guards. All was chaos on the right flank of Villeroi's army, now open and vulnerable, far away and out of sight of the French commander, who was absorbed with developments on his left. Rapid action was required to restore the situation.

The French cavalry commander on the southern part of the battlefield, General de Guiscard, was alert to the unfolding peril, and he took prompt, if rather ill-judged, action to recover Taviers. He ordered a swift counter-attack on the Dutch Guards by some of his own third-line troops, the fourteen dismounted squadrons of French dragoons from the Le Roi, La Reine, Notat and d'Aubigni regiments, who at that point were near the peculiar hillock or tumulus known as the Tomb of Ottomonde. Two more battalions of the Greder Suisse, under command of Brigadier-General de Nonan, were sent in their support by Comte de la Motte, the infantry commander on the plain. However, having to laboriously thread their way through the massed ranks of the Maison de Roi cavalry in their well-ordered formations, the Swiss infantry soon lagged behind the dragoons as they moved towards Taviers on foot. The counter-attack, instead of having real punch, was given no proper attention and quickly became a piecemeal and poorly coordinated affair. It failed miserably. 'The units were at some distance from each other,' de la Colonie recalled. 'Being uninformed as to whom they were to work with, each took their own line to reach the village, ignorant even as to whether there was a likelihood of its being defended.' Defended it undoubtedly was, as Opdham's and Holstein's regiments of dismounted Dutch dragoons moved forward to support Wertmüller's Guards, and together they poured in a heavy musketry upon the French dragoons as they struggled forward in their long boots. The Dutch guns added their canister fire, tumbling the French down in large numbers. Colonel d'Aubigni, who led his regiment into the attack, was mortally wounded, and the ranks wavered. At the same time, the leading squadrons of Württemberg's Danish cavalry, unhampered now by any fire either from Franquenay or Taviers, moved forward and cut in sharply at the exposed flank of the French dragoons. John Millner wrote, 'Wirtemberg at the same time being arrived with some Danish squadrons slipt in between the Enemies left and Taviers, and flankt them, but a marsh [the Visoule stream] in the way, he was obliged to stop a little.'

De la Colonie had also received orders to move his Grenadiers Rouges, together with the Cologne Guards with whom they were brigaded, from their post to the south of Ramillies so that they could support the faltering counter-attack on Taviers. Like the Swiss, these troops had to make their way through the lines of cavalry, although the Colonel noticed that their ranks were some-what thinner than was usual (de Guiscard had difficulty covering his wide frontage properly and with real depth). The veterans among the troopers cheered the grenadiers as they marched southwards, 'waving their caps with

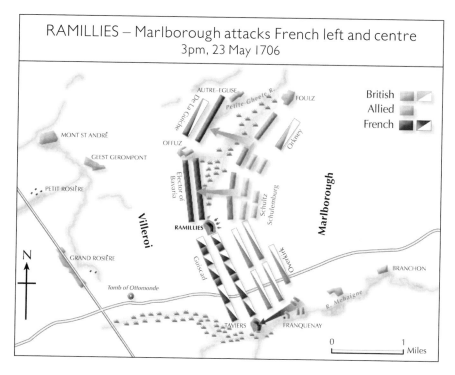

RAMILLIES – Marlborough attacks French left and centre
3pm, 23 May 1706

grateful applause', recalling their sterling performance at the Schellenberg fight in 1704 when, alone of the French and Bavarian troops that day, they had tried to stand firm as the defence on that hill collapsed in bloody disarray. However, as de la Colonie approached the marshy ground along the Visoule and Mehaigne streams, he could see that all was chaos ahead: the advance of the dismounted French dragoons and their Swiss infantry supports had broken down in the face of heavy Dutch fire and the movement of the Danish squadrons against their flank. Now his own brigade commander impetuously rode on ahead to test the depth of the marsh, but he went too far, got his horse stuck in the mud and was taken away as a prisoner by the Dutch. De la Colonie suddenly found himself in command of the brigade, and remembered that:

> We crossed fairly easily on foot, though in some parts were over knee-deep in water. Scarcely had my troops got over when the dragoons and Swiss who had preceded us, came tumbling down upon my battalion in full flight, just as the time when I was re-forming my men after their crossing ... My own fellows turned about and fled along with them.

Indignant at such craven behaviour in his men, the Colonel called on them to rally, seizing the regimental colour from a dazed subaltern: 'I was never more surprised in my life to find myself standing alone with a few officers and the colours.' Gathering together a small party of his nervous soldiers, de la Colonie drew them up at the edge of the Visoule just to the west of Taviers. From there they managed to extricate some of the French dragoons from the marshy ground where they had been providing target practice for the Dutch Guards. With a scratch force of his own grenadiers, who sheepishly came back into line around their Colonel and the colour party, and the remnants of the dragoons and the Greder Suisse battalions, de la Colonie was able to provide some limited support for the disrupted right flank of Villeroi's army at a time when the Marshal had no idea that things were going so badly wrong in the south. This was an entirely peripheral operation: the Dutch found that they could just shoulder aside the small detachment, leaving them to languish impotently beside the Visoule stream as the vast, surging cavalry battle roared away across the plain leading northwards to Ramillies village.

The failure of the inept French counter-attack on the Dutch Guards at Franquenay and Taviers left the cavalry of their right Wing, already struggling to cover adequately the frontage allotted to them, now much weakened by the wasteful destruction of the fourteen squadrons of dragoons; it also saw the ruin of four Swiss infantry battalions and the Bavarian brigade. The two villages had been lost, the flank exposed, and nothing achieved in return. Almost without effort, the French had got off to a very poor start in the battle and their cavalry was put at yet a further disadvantage. Richard Kane wrote afterwards of the tactical difficulty that now faced de Guiscard's squadrons: 'The intent of their interlining Foot with their Horse in the Plain, was to sustain the Horse in case of a Repulse, under the Shelter of whose fire they might easily rally again; for the Horse never care to come within the Fire of the Foot.' The failure on the French right flank would, presumably, have been attended to in time – it was certainly no minor matter. However, time was something that Villeroi and his generals did not have, and de Guiscard very soon had more pressing demands on his attention.

More Like a Dream Than the Truth

While Franquenay and Taviers were being lost by the French, at the other end of the battlefield the British and Danish infantry commanded by George Hamilton, 1st Earl Orkney, were formed up in two lines on the ridge opposite the course of the Petite Gheete stream. Across the marshy valley were the barricaded villages of Offuz and Autre-Eglise. Around these cottages stood the Bavarian and Walloon infantry, well posted in the gardens and orchards, and backed by strong reserves of the Elector of Bavaria's cavalry on the plateau of Mont St André. At about 2.30pm, the British infantry, who had been lying down to shelter from Villeroi's gunners and the hot sun, rose to their feet. Quickly picking up their dressing, with colours flying bravely and to the tapping of side-drums, they began the steady descent into the valley to their front, Orkney going forward on foot with his men. The second-line battalions, British and Danes, remained at the edge of the plateau of Jandrenouille for the time being. The bramble thickets that littered the gentle slope of the valley were found to be infested with Walloon picquets and these were cleared out, at some cost, with the bayonet. In the valley bottom, the pace of the soldiers slowed as they struggled through the boggy stream and were met with hedged bayonets and well-directed volleys of musketry from a tough brigade of Walloon infantry, sent forward from around Offuz by Major-General de la Guiche to dispute their passage.

Tom Kitcher, a Hampshire farm labourer who enlisted to serve with Meredith's Regiment, which formed part of the second line in the advance, remembered pioneers laying fascines to ease their passage over the wet ground. He was unable to avoid trampling on the bodies of his fallen comrades as he struggled through the mud: 'Many were shot and maimed, or killed, by the French outposts.' The opposing brigade were, in fact, Walloons, and they did not stand their ground for long; their aim had been to extract a suitably heavy price from the British for getting over the marsh, not to engage in an expensive and almost certainly doomed battle against superior numbers in the valley bottom. De la Guiche's troops fell back up the slope in good order, a difficult manoeuvre which they accomplished with great skill. However, Kitcher recalled, 'I spiked one of the Frenchies through the gullet, and another through the arse.' Hurriedly forming their ranks again on the drier ground, the British infantry pressed up the slope under a heavy fire, and began to break through the barricades around the cottages. 'I think I never had more shot around my ears,' Orkney wrote later. The Cameronians, on the right of the British advance, forced their way into Autre-Eglise. They were promptly driven out again by the Régiment du Roi, but this action seems to have been a rather brief affair, as Major Blackader of that regiment remembered he had very little to do all afternoon.

The defenders on the ridge comfortably outnumbered Orkney's attacking infantry, but such was the vigour of the British assault that it seemed they would break right through the line of villages and get out onto the plateau of Mont St André. Once there, unless adequate Allied cavalry came forward across the difficult ground of the Petite Gheete valley to support them, the soldiers would be at the mercy of the Elector's massed squadrons, ideally placed and patiently waiting for the moment to move forward and ride them down, disordered, hot and weary after their hard fight to claim their place on the Ramillies–Offuz–Autre-Eglise ridge-line.

Orkney wrote, 'The village of Autre-Eglise was in our grip, but as I was going to take possession I had ten aides de camp to [tell] me to come off.' Marlborough knew that the infantry's attack on the right, for all their local success, could not be properly sustained, while at the same time full support was being given to Overkirk and his cavalry in the south. If the British infantry were pressed too far out onto the plateau of Mont St André, a disaster beckoned at the hands of the Elector's numerous Bavarian and Walloon cavalry. Orkney could not know this, and to make sure that the order to withdraw was fully understood, an order that the belligerent soldier-earl might well disregard, Marlborough sent William Cadogan to deliver it. Heated words were exchanged between the two men, Orkney urging that his success, bought at the price of many of his soldiers' lives, be reinforced and pushed onwards with the assistance of Henry Lumley's cavalry, who were now picking their way across the marshy ground. Cadogan insisted that the Duke's order stood. Orkney reluctantly gave the word and his troops fell back down the slope, which was littered with the bloody wreckage of their attack, into the Petite Gheete valley and back up the rise to their starting point on the edge of the plateau of Jandrenouille. 'It vexed me to retire,' Orkney wrote. 'However we did it very well and in good order, and whenever the French pressed upon us, with the battalion of [1st English Foot] Guards and my own [regiment], I was able to stand and make them retire.'

Once securely back on the ridge facing Offuz, Orkney and his officers could see the wider plan, for in response to Marlborough's summons the second-line battalions, shielded from their opponents by a slight fold in the ground formed by the La Quivelette stream, began to move southwards towards the centre of the field to support the attacks on Ramillies. These British and Danish troops of the second line were commanded on the day by the Dutch Brigadier-General van Pallandt, a valiant, hard-fighting officer in whom Marlborough had the highest confidence. He reportedly ordered that the regimental colours be left in place at the edge of the plateau to reinforce the impression that the troops were still there in full strength and ready to renew the attack across the stream at the right moment.

Marlborough was now throwing his full weight onto his left. Marshal Villeroi, by contrast, remained concerned at the security of his own left around Offuz and Autre-Eglise. He was still moving reserves of infantry away from the plain to the south of Ramillies and up onto the plateau of Mont St André, where, unknown to him, the Allied effort was coming to a halt. Richard Kane, a noted tactician, wrote, 'Without firing a shot he [Marlborough] obliged them to break the Dispositions in their Centre, where they had placed the greatest Dependence of the success of the Battle.' The infantry support available for de Guiscard's cavalry was really getting thin, even before allowing for the destruction of the Swiss battalions, the French dragoons and the Bavarian brigade in their failed attempt to retake Taviers. A French officer wrote that now, 'The whole weight of the battle fell upon the right Wing of the army, where the troops of His Majesty's Household [cavalry] were placed.'

While Orkney's attacks on Offuz and Autre-Eglise gathered pace, the assault on Ramillies went in under the direction of Marlborough's younger brother and General of Infantry, Charles Churchill. 'He ordered four brigades of foot to attack the village,' remembered Captain Robert Parker of the Royal Irish Regiment. Under heavy French artillery fire, twelve battalions of Dutch infantry, commanded by Major-Generals Schultz and Spaar, moved resolutely forward, supported by two brigades of Saxon troops under Count Schulemberg. A Scottish brigade in Dutch service led by 'Red' John Campbell, 2nd Duke of Argyll, and a small brigade of Protestant Swiss (who had first been posted to the south of Ramillies to support the Dutch cavalry) also moved into the attack. The disciplined French gunners lowered the muzzles of their pieces and switched from roundshot to canister as the range closed, and the attackers, soon losing the meagre protection afforded by the slight rise in the ground on the edge of the plateau of Jandrenouille, began to go down in scores with each salvo.

Ramillies was strongly held: twenty French and Bavarian infantry battalions were supported by Clare's émigré regiment of Irish dragoons and a small brigade of elements of the Cologne Guards and the Bavarian Guards, commanded by the Marquis de Maffei. The garrison put up a tough and spirited defence, driving back the attackers with heavy losses. Gallantly, the Dutch infantry and their allies renewed the assault and came on again, bayonets levelled, but they struggled forward in an absolute storm of musketry and canister-fire, and were unable to make any impression on the defenders.

As the attackers recoiled from the French barricades at the edge of Ramillies, one of Argyll's Scottish battalions, Borthwick's, was driven back in such disorder by the Régiment de Picardie that the ensign carrying the regimental colour, James Gardiner, was shot in the mouth and left for dead alongside the churchyard wall (he survived the dreadful wound, and was killed at the head of his own regiment at Prestonpans, thirty-nine years later). The colour, treasured symbol of regimental pride, was lost to a French soldier and only recovered after a bitter hand-to-hand struggle in a sloping field of rye next to the church – the grenadier company of Collyer's Regiment also became engaged there before the French could be driven back. The soldiers suffered heavy casualties in the fierce contest where bayonets and clubbed muskets

Ramillies. Ramillies village seen from the south. The great cavalry battle was fought on these fields.

were used freely, and their dead and wounded lay in thick droves in their greyish white and red coats along the lanes and hedges around the churchyard. The French grip on the village, for the time being, was unshaken.

Seeing that Schultz and Spaar were faltering with their assault on Ramillies, and that there was every likelihood the attack would fail completely, Marlborough sent for a brigade of Orkney's reserve infantry, who were standing on the ridge overlooking the Petite Gheete stream, to add their weight to the effort. These troops had not gone into the attack on Offuz and Autre-Eglise, although Orkney would, in other circumstances, have called them forward before long to provide the essential second echelon to move through and exploit the hard-won success. The three battalions (Churchill's, McArtney's and Mordaunt's) were now brought to the centre of the field to support the attack there, and others would soon follow. Robert Parker watched the move and remembered, 'As soon as our rear line had retired out of sight of the enemy, they immediately formed to the left, and both horse and foot, with a good many squadrons that slunk out of the first line, marched down to the plain, as fast as they could.'

A subtle and powerful shift in emphasis by Marlborough had begun: he drew more and more troops to his left, and the weight of his attacks grew in the south and correspondingly lessened in the north. The escalating cavalry battle on the plain, and the opportunity presented by the glaringly exposed right flank of Villeroi's army, required Orkney to call off his attack against Offuz and Autre-Eglise. Crucially, it would be some time before the French commander appreciated the vital change in emphasis in the Duke's effort. Whether he could respond in good time to the unfolding threat to his right, as he simultaneously reinforced his own left, remained to be seen.

At about 3.30pm, while the Allied infantry attacks in the centre and the right ground steadily forward, Veldt-Marshal Overkirk led his forty-eight squadrons of Dutch cavalry onto the open plain to the south of Ramillies. They were supported on their left by the twenty-one Danish squadrons who had already taken up a position beside Taviers. The massed squadrons advanced at a steady pace – care was taken not to tire the horses prematurely that hot afternoon. Colonel de la Colonie remembered that the Dutch seemed 'like solid walls, while we had but three lines, the third of which was composed of several squadrons of dragoons.' This technique, used to such good effect by the Allied cavalry that day, was known at the time as riding 'en muraille', and involved the troopers keeping well closed up, knee to knee in formation, with arms outstretched and swords thrust forward, coming on at a gentle trot and then gradually increasing speed until the moment of impact. The squadrons meeting a charge performed in this highly disciplined way would, unless they were led forward in a similarly resolute fashion to meet it with full vigour, literally be overthrown and driven back. 'I now saw the enemy's cavalry squadrons advance,' de la Colonie wrote. 'The Maison du Roi decided to meet them for at such a moment those who await the shock find themselves at a disadvantage.' The Dutch, able to deploy greater numbers in the first line, had an obvious advantage, regardless of whether de Guiscard's squadron commanders could properly employ the same masterful technique.

Overkirk's ability to mass his full strength in this initial attack, in contrast to the French arrangements, was also commented on by the Marquis de Feuquières. He described the 'en muraille' technique used at Ramillies rather well:

They advanced in four lines to our right Wing of cavalry ... As they approached they advanced their second and fourth lines into the intervals of their first and third lines; so that when they made their advance upon us, they formed only one front, without any intermediate spaces. This motion was performed so near us, that our right had no time either to close themselves, in order to fill the intervals by that contraction, or to supply [reinforce] them with the second line, which, beside their immoderate distance from the first line, were incapable of making that advance on account of the several equipages left, through mere negligence, between the two lines.

Despite all this, the valour of the French cavalry was not in doubt, and Overkirk's horsemen were to have a hard struggle in the dust and heat of the afternoon. It was their lack of numbers, made worse by Villeroi's stripping away the reserves of infantry in his absorbing concern for the left flank, that would become the telling handicap as the day wore on. Such a drastic structural disadvantage defies bravery and energy in the putting to rights.

Now the lack of support was felt most forcefully. The French first-line cavalry responded magnificently to the Dutch and Danish advance, coming forward to meet them with great dash, but de Guiscard's squadrons were soon thrown into disorder and driven back by superior numbers. They retired upon the support of their second line to recover their order and rest their horses, but the French second line was almost immediately under pressure also and had to retire on the inadequate third line and the few infantry battalions that remained on the plain. Still, the French troopers recovered their order, and, Richard Kane wrote, 'Here the cavalry charged each other for a considerable time, with various success, the Foot on both sides often stopping the squadrons in their career.' The troops on both sides fought well, and whatever advantage was gained from time to time was dearly bought.

These cavalry were the best the French had, superbly mounted and well-trained elite squadrons of the Maison du Roi – the Gardes du Corps, the Royal Carabiniers, the Mousquetaires, the Grenadiers à Cheval and the Gens d'Armes, supported by four squadrons of Bavarian Cuirassiers, 'riding closen liken to a brassen wall' as one observer remembered. All were under the superb leadership of de Guiscard, who exerted himself in positions of the greatest peril all afternoon, and they rallied more than once and returned to the charge with whirling and slashing swords, thrusting back the Dutch in forthright and quite unexpectedly successful local counter-attacks. This day there were none of the time-consuming pauses to fire off pistols and carbines that so often hampered the French cavalry, and on Overkirk's right flank, closest to Ramillies, ten of his squadrons suddenly gave way and were scattered, riding to the rear to recover. A crisis threatened in the centre, as the left flank of the Swiss brigade and German brigades trying to break into the village was exposed. A brief chance offered for de Guiscard to throw his cavalry forward with all its might and split the Allied army in two. The threat was real enough, and Marlborough could not yet know that the French squadrons had insufficient strength by this time to make their blow really count.

The Duke was nearby, watching the progress of the milling cavalry battle, well aware that the day was not yet won. He had just given orders for eighteen squadrons of Dutch cavalry, held back in reserve near Ramillies, to move to Overkirk's assistance, and he now called for all the cavalry of his right Wing, except the British squadrons under Henry Lumley who remained in support of

Earl Orkney, to come southwards also. While he waited for the fresh squadrons to travel the short distance to get into position, Marlborough was almost alone. Just a couple of aides and his trumpeter were in attendance when the French squadrons suddenly came surging towards his party. Marlborough turned and spurred towards Murray's Swiss brigade, which stood a few hundred paces away, but in the confused press of riders his horse stumbled and the Duke was thrown heavily to the ground. The French could not mistake him, a conspicuous figure in his faded red coat and Garter sash. 'They fired their long pistols' and dashed forward to hack him down. 'Milord Marlborough,' Orkney wrote later, 'was rid over.'

It was Marlborough's custom to wear comfortable linen gaiters, rather than the more common high boots, and on this occasion they served him well. Scrambling to his feet with an agility that did credit to a 56-year-old man just thrown from his horse, the Duke ran towards the nearby Swiss brigade, closely pursued by sword-swinging French horsemen. A British officer remembered that 'The Duke when he got to his feet again saw Major-General Murray coming up and ran directly to get in to his battalions.' It was a race for his life, a race that the Duke narrowly won, finding shelter in the ranks of the Swiss who then resolutely threw back the pursuing troopers, some of whom had been so close behind that their horses careered on and were impaled on the waiting bayonets. Murray offered Marlborough his own horse, but his aide de camp, Captain Robert Molesworth, hastily led up one of the Duke's own remounts, and he was soon back in the saddle, rather bruised and a little breathless from the escapade, but otherwise unharmed. After the slightest pause, Marlborough could look around and attend to the positioning of the cavalry reinforcements feeding down from the north of the field in increasing numbers. Their arrival to the south of Ramillies accomplished the dramatic shift in the tactical balance on the battlefield, a shift of which Marshal Villeroi was still blissfully unaware.

Soon afterwards, as Marlborough changed horses once again, a French roundshot fired from a battery on the edge of Ramillies neatly decapitated his aide, Colonel James Bringfield, who was helping the Duke into the saddle. The unfortunate colonel's headless body, fountaining blood, fell to the ground at Marlborough's feet, a grisly episode that was commemorated in a remarkably lurid set of playing cards that subsequently enjoyed great popularity in England. 'The ball took off Major Brinfeilde's head just by my Lord Duke's side,' wrote John Deane of the 1st English Foot Guards.

Serving as a staff officer to the Duke was plainly no quiet sinecure. Young Robert Molesworth, who, alone of Marlborough's aides, had been with him in the dash to the shelter of Murray's brigade, was almost hacked down in the mêlée around the hedged bayonets of the Swiss square – this in addition to the very real danger of being shot down by his own troops. Captain Parker of the Royal Irish wrote, 'The Captain, being immediately after[wards] surrounded by the enemy, from which danger (as well as from our own fire) he was, at last, providentially delivered.' The time was about 4.30pm, and the two armies were in close contact across the whole wide battlefield from the grubby skirmishing in the marshes of the Visoule stream, through the vast cavalry battle on the open plain, to the desperate infantry fights for Ramillies in the centre and at Offuz and Autre-Eglise to the north, where the soldiers of Orkney and de la Guiche faced each other across the Petite Gheete stream, ready for a fresh onset of the battle. Villeroi was off balance, and this uncomfortable fact should now have been dawning on him as the Allied cavalry deployment in the south grew in strength and reached out around his flank. The French and Bavarian army was fixed tactically; it was fighting well, but fighting for its life. Marlborough alone retained the initiative, and the next moves were entirely in his hands.

The French cavalry, for all their valiant efforts, were gradually being worn down in the battle to the south of Ramillies. Richard Kane remembered, 'The Household Troops who had hitherto behaved with great Bravery, rallied and came again to the Charge; but the French Fire [spirit] which on all first onsets seemed very furious, was now spent.' They had, from the very start, struggled to cover the frontage allotted to them, and the rapidly growing list of casualties inexorably added to their problem; the French squadrons shrank in size, and as they did so, the frontage they could cover shrank too. General de Guiscard's cavalry were becoming tired, and their numerical inferiority was telling at last: Veldt-Marshal Overkirk's troopers found that they could thread through the wide intervals between the squadrons, engage them from the flank, and even, on occasions, hack at them from the rear. Unlike their more fortunate opponents, the French cavalry could not fall back on the protection of their infantry supports to catch their breath, recover their order and rest their horses.

By late afternoon, as the losses among the French squadrons mounted, the fatal gap had opened wider on the right of the line where the earlier, uncorrected failure to hold or retake Franquenay and Taviers had already exposed the flank. Into this gap Colonel Wertmüller's Dutch Guards had been thrust, and they were supported by Dopff's, Holstein's and Opdham's regiments of dismounted dragoons. With this support, the twenty-one squadrons of the Duke of Württemberg's Danish cavalry slipped through, right past the flank of de Guiscard's horsemen, whose attention was almost entirely fixed on holding back the Dutch. Virtually without any hindrance, apart from some fugitive remnants of the French dragoons who had been dispersed earlier in the afternoon (many of whose untended horses managed to find their way, unaided, to the comfort of their own stables twenty or so miles away), the Danes formed up in the area of the Tomb of Ottomonde. The troopers turned to face northwards towards Ramillies and the plateau of Mont St André beyond, where the equipages (as the Marquis de Feuquières put it), the baggage and tentage of Villeroi's army was still carelessly left lying about.

As evening came on, there was a pause in the pace of the fighting across the wide battlefield. The Allied army, ideally placed to deliver their blow, caught their collective breath and readied themselves for the great effort. Their French, Walloon and Bavarian opponents were grateful for the brief chance to try to recover their order. Weariness was playing its part, certainly in the south where the French squadrons could hardly raise their blown horses to the pace of a gentle trot, and aides were hurrying northwards to find Marshal Villeroi and urge that assistance be sent from the ample reserves held back behind the villages. The Dutch, after a hectic afternoon, were not much better placed, although these squadrons still had the advantage of proper infantry support, and the Danish cavalry nearby were comparatively fresh.

The garrison in Ramillies, all but irrelevant now to the wider battle, were battered but still firmly in possession. Now the attackers gathered their strength for another attack. From the ridge-line to the north, Orkney's troops

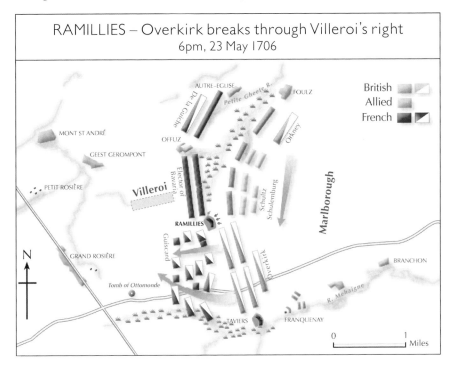

RAMILLIES – Overkirk breaks through Villeroi's right
6pm, 23 May 1706

looked across the valley of the Petite Gheete at de la Guiche's infantry and the Elector's massed cavalry. Standing behind Offuz and Autre-Eglise they had played no really active part in the battle. According to Richard Kane, 'Their left Wing and the Front Line of our Right, where our Regiment was, stood looking on all the while, without striking a stroke.' So, time that was vital to Villeroi in reordering his army and getting fresh troops into the right position to meet the unfolding threat to his right Wing was allowed to go to waste, while for Marlborough this inactivity simply added to his chances of success off to the south. The longer the Duke kept Villeroi's attention occupied in the north, the greater the likelihood that he would achieve the desired outcome. His final reinforcement of the cavalry in the south had now moved into position, and the only movement of real note across the whole 4 miles of battlefield was in the calm ordering of the ranks of the Danish cavalry near the Tomb of Ottomonde: they looked with grim determination towards the exposed flank of Villeroi's army. The Marshal was now dreadfully out of position, held in place by the combination of Marlborough's concurrent attacks and bewildering shifts in emphasis throughout the afternoon.

The movement of the Danish cavalry around the French right flank had not gone unnoticed by any means; such a substantial body of horsemen would be very visible in open country such as this, even at a distance of a mile or so. Until this point, Villeroi may have felt that he had fought a rather good battle: the Allied infantry attacks had been held or bloodily thrown back, while Overkirk's Dutch squadrons had been roughly handled by de Guiscard's troopers in their fight in the south of the battlefield. Furthermore, the Marshal had plenty of reserves, both cavalry and infantry, in good order and ready to hand behind Ramillies and Offuz. Now, though, he was suddenly brought to realise that the loss of Taviers and Franquenay, to which no proper attention had been given and no sustained effort made to recapture, had fatally exposed his army to a flank attack of crushing force, a blow that he could not hope to counter with some late rearrangement of his troops. His opponent had massed cavalry in overwhelming strength on a part of the field that was simply too far away for Villeroi to redeploy his reserves in good time to meet the threat. The Marshal was off-balance, merely reacting to Marlborough's skilled moves and with no real chance of recovery. It was all too late.

The French right Wing were very ragged after their efforts, and, increasingly, men began to glance behind them, disregarding the shouted orders and entreaties of their officers, seeking an avenue of escape from what was fast looking like a trap. At about 6pm, Villeroi and the Elector of Bavaria, having ridden over to Ramillies from their watch over de la Guiche's infantry around Offuz and Autre-Eglise, found that fugitives were streaming past them, heading for the roads that led to the north and west. Urgently, the two commanders

A kneeling British Grenadier gathers captured French colours.
(*From the Blenheim Tapestry. By kind permission of his Grace the Duke of Marlborough*)

The Schellenberg Tapestry.   (*By kind permission of his Grace the Duke of Marlborough*)

The 1st English Foot Guards wade the Nebel stream to attack Blindheim village.

Houses in Blindheim village, contemporary with the battle in 1704.

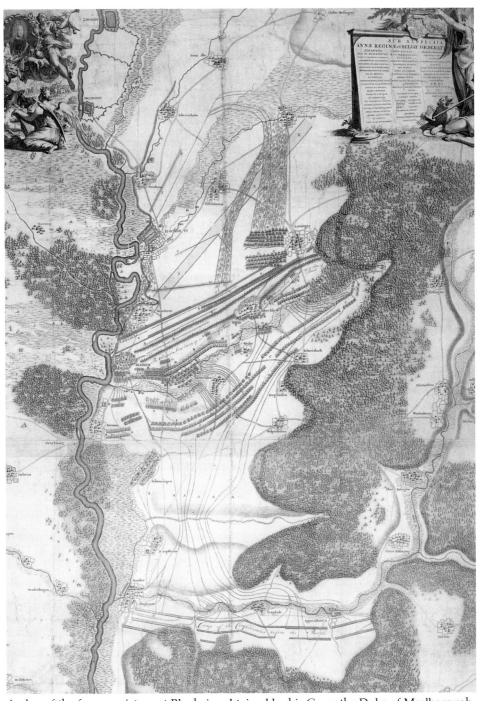

A plan of the famous victory at Blenheim obtained by his Grace the Duke of Marlborough over the Elector of Bavaria and Marshals Tallard and Marsin, the 13th August 1704.

The Duke of Marlborough on
the field of Blenheim.
*(From the Blenheim Tapestry.
By kind permission of his Grace
the Duke of Marlborough)*

Ramillies. Marlborough's
horse stumbles, and the Duke
is thrown to the ground.

Ramillies. Marlborough and his staff oversee the cavalry battle.

(Courtesy of the Marquess of Anglesey)

Walled farmhouse in Offuz, scene of Earl Orkney's infantry attack, 23 May 1706.

The great cavalry pursuit after Ramillies.
(Courtesy of the Marquess of Anglesey)

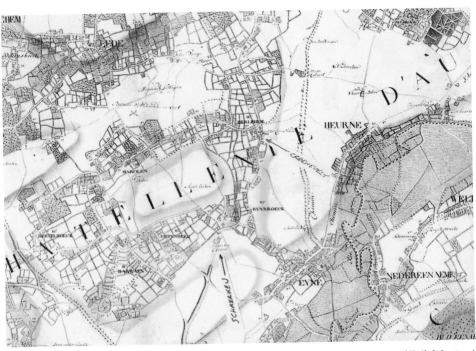

18th century map of the Oudenarde battlefield.
(Courtesy of Erik Wauters)

The Oudenarde Tapestry at Blenheim Palace.
(By kind permission of his Grace the Duke of Marlborough)

The Allied and French infantry struggle for possession of the Bois de Sars Triangle at Malplaquet.

Prince Eugene of Savoy, Marlborough's comrade and close friend. A contemporary cartoon portrait. *(Author's collection)*

began to draw out from the plateau of Mont St André the reserves of cavalry and infantry held in idleness there, and tried to form a new line facing to the south, bent back at right angles to the original dispositions that were now of so little relevance to their survival as a fighting force. The baggage and wagons, so neglectfully left lying around in the area behind the village, hampered the attempted re-ordering of the left Wing of the army, but it was probably hopeless anyway. The irresistible dynamics of Marlborough's fast-unfolding plan were taking hold.

Only Marlborough held the initiative now, for his cavalry, the Dutch and the Danes to the south of Ramillies were about to deliver a death blow to the French and Bavarian army. Marshal Villeroi, for all his competent arrangements and recent energy, could only watch it happen; nothing he attempted now would take any effect before Marlborough's awful cavalry stroke went in against the right Wing of the French army. Near the Tomb of Ottomonde, meanwhile, nothing was rushed, although a stunning victory of unimaginable scale beckoned the Allied commanders; nothing was to be thrown away by rashness or mismanagement. The dressing and alignment of Württemberg's Danes and Overkirk's Dutch, their horses standing in a great arc from just south of Ramillies to the hamlet of Ottomonde, was checked, the barked commands of officers and NCOs mingling with the groans and pleadings of the wounded lying scattered around on the trampled cornfield. The Duke had now joined the Veldt-Marshal, and at the word of command the vast imposing array of horsemen surged forward against the outnumbered and weary French squadrons. 'Up comes the Danish Duke of Wirtemberg with the Danish Horse,' Richard Kane wrote, 'also falling on their flank ... charg'd them with such a fury that it put them into great disorder.' Even with the squadrons that were being scrambled together by Villeroi to form a new line of battle to face the Allied onslaught, de Guiscard's cavalry could not resist the new attack. The Marquis de Feuquières recalled, 'They were now thrown into a general disorder by the squadrons of the enemy's second line, and by those who charged them in the rear.' Turning their horses' heads northwards, the exhausted cavalry of the French right Wing broke ranks and fled from the field in wild disorder, trampling down anyone – foot soldier, cannoneer, servant or camp follower – who got in the way.

Villeroi's army, which just half an hour before had been fighting well and in good order, now ran for their lives. 'The cry went up,' according to Peter Drake, 'Sauve qui Peut! Then might be seen whole brigades running in disorder.' In moments, what had been a huge disciplined body of soldiers dissolved into a frantic mob. 'The Elector and Villeroi did all that was possible to keep them from breaking,' Robert Parker wrote, 'but our troops stuck so close to them, that they were put to the rout.'

In Ramillies the Allied infantry at last broke through the defences in a renewed attack, the Duke of Argyll being among the first to clamber over the barricades, and the garrison were driven out at bayonet point. The Régiment de Picardie stood their ground, though, and were caught between Borthwick's (now reformed) Scots-Dutch regiment and part of a fresh British brigade brought down from the north. Colonel William Borthwick was among those killed in the fighting here. So, too, was the exiled Irish Jacobite Charles O'Brien, Viscount Clare, now in the French service with his regiment of dragoons when 'engaged with a Scotch regiment [Collyer's Scots-Dutch] between whom there was a great slaughter'. The Bavarian Grenadiers, who had been moved to the southern edge of the village as the threat developed on the plain, were routed and driven in confusion back through Ramillies by Spaar's Dutch infantry, but they rallied with the small German brigade composed of two battalions of the Cologne Guards and the Bavarian Guards under command of Alessandro Maffei. He vainly attempted to make a stand from the shelter of a sunken lane that runs from the village onto the plateau of Mont St André, and even got some companies of infantry back into nearby Haute Censée farm, which had recently been abandoned. Their musketry held the Allied infantry back for a while, and in this way Maffei hoped to provide an anchor of a sort for the

Ramillies. La Haute Censée farm, Ramillies village. Maffei's HQ.

disordered French cavalry, upon which they could recover and fight back. It was all in vain, as the Marquis rather drily remembered in his journal:

I then saw coming towards us a line of hostile cavalry, but as this cavalry was coming from the side from which I naturally had expected our own cavalry to arrive, I thought at first they must be our own people ... I did not notice the green cockade they wore in their hats [the Allied field recognition symbol] which was indeed so small that it could hardly have been discerned at any distance ... I went towards the nearest of these squadrons to instruct their officers, but instead of being listened to was immediately surrounded and called upon to ask for quarter.

Maffei was led away by the Dutch cavalry. His brigade soon afterwards joined in the flight from the battlefield, but got entangled in the marshy ground at the head of the Petite Gheete stream; most of the men became prisoners of the advancing British infantry. The roads leading to the north and west were, in any case, now choked with fugitives, and the sunken lanes, which are such a feature of the area, quickly became blocked with abandoned wagons and carts, adding to the confusion. The Allied cavalry followed close behind, cutting and slashing at the fleeing soldiers. The pursuit by the Danish horsemen was particularly savage, as news had recently come in that numbers of their countrymen had been massacred after surrendering to the Duc de Vendôme at the battle of Calcinato in northern Italy in April, and the cry for revenge was on everyone's lips.

Despite the smoke hanging about on the northern end of the field, Orkney could make all this out from the ridge-line to which his infantry had withdrawn a little earlier after being brought back from their attacks on the villages. The right and centre of the French and Bavarian army were plainly in chaos, as were the rear areas. The Earl did not wait for fresh orders but sent his troops back across the valley to storm their triumphant way into Offuz, where de la Guiche's infantry had begun to melt away in the confusion of the evening. Seven squadrons of the Bavarian Horse Grenadiers and the Electoral Guards moved forward to block their advance, but were driven off, with many empty saddles, by well-aimed volleys of musketry from Orkney's leading battalions. On the right, the dragoons of Hay and Ross picked their way across the difficult ground of the stream and, taking the rare chance to charge at full tilt, put to flight the Régiment du Roi as this elite infantry unit withdrew. 'Our dragoons,' John Deane wrote, 'pushing into the village of Autre-Eglise made a terrible slaughter of the enemy.' The French soldiers had paused to recover the knapsacks they had dumped on the ground when moving forward earlier in the day; now they were ridden down and dispersed by the charging dragoons.

The Bavarian Horse Grenadiers and Electoral Guards had withdrawn a little way after being driven off by the British infantry. They formed a shield around

Marshal Villeroi (1644–1730)

Born in April 1644, François de Neufville, Duc de Villeroi, was the son of a noble French family that first came to prominence in the reign of King Charles IX. His father, Nicholas de Neufville, had been the governor of Louis XIV when he was a minor, and François and the Sun King remained close friends, having known each other since those early, troubled times. Villeroi was a polished courtier, an elegant, witty and cultured man. His military career was long and quite distinguished, if not spectacular, and in 1695 he succeeded Marshal Luxembourg, on that soldier's death, as commander of the French army in the Low Countries. Villeroi had

François de Neufville, Marshal Villeroi, defeated at Ramillies, 1706.

a reputation for great personal bravery, and was made a Marshal of France at this time, but he found William III to be a formidable opponent, and his efforts against him were rather unsuccessful.

Prior to the outbreak of the War of the Spanish Succession, Villeroi was sent by Louis XIV to northern Italy as commander in place of Marshal Catinat, but his army was beaten at Chiari by Prince Eugene. Soon afterwards, the Marshal was surprised in camp at Cremona and taken prisoner, although he was soon exchanged. Villeroi campaigned in the Spanish Netherlands against Marlborough in 1703, and the following year shadowed the Duke's march up the Rhine, eventually joining Tallard in Alsace before that Marshal went to historic defeat in the Danube valley. Villeroi moved forward into the Black Forest to help extricate Marshal Marsin's battered army and the remnants of the Elector of Bavaria's forces in the wake of that disaster. This was a well-handled, if rather unglamorous, operation by Villeroi, but it is generally overlooked. During 1705, Villeroi once again commanded the French army in the Low Countries, on the whole foiling Marlborough's efforts either to seize large amounts of territory or pin his opponent down to battle in open field. Urged on by Louis XIV to confront Marlborough in May 1706, Villeroi was soundly defeated at Ramillies by the Duke, an incomparably finer commander. On his return to Versailles, the Marshal was kindly received by the French King, but was never again offered a military command.

In 1714, Villeroi was made a Minister of State, and during the minority of Louis XV he was governor and mentor to the young King. He fell from favour after scheming against the volatile Regent, the King's uncle, the Duc d'Orléans, who had Villeroi arrested by officers of the Mousquetaires Gris and unceremoniously bundled away from court in a sedan chair. The Marshal was subsequently made governor of Lyons, almost a post of internal exile for such a prominent person. He died there in July 1730.

the Elector and Villeroi, and tried to present a properly formed front as the British cavalry surged forward. They were charged by Henry Lumley's squadrons – 'a la hussarde, sword in hand, at a gallop' – near to Autre-Eglise and scattered. So too were the Spanish (Walloon) Guards, whose commander, the Marquis de Guertiere was taken captive. This left the British cavalry free to move on and drive a wedge into the flank of the seething mass of fugitives streaming away from the field. One of their commanders, Lieutenant-General Cornelius Wood, saw both Villeroi and the Elector nearby in the crowd but, not recognising them in the fading twilight, he turned aside to secure some other senior French officers as captives: 'Had I been so fortunate to have known, I had strained Corialanus [his horse] on whom I rode all the day of battle to have made them prisoners.' The Queen's Regiment of Horse did, however, seize the well-known black kettle-drummer of the Bavarian Electoral Guards; some reports say the drummer was mortally wounded in the process, others that he was immediately pressed into Queen Anne's service.

Among the cavalry and dragoons engaged on this flank was the Irish female soldier Christian Davies, who had followed her husband to war by masquerading as a man in the ranks of Hay's Dragoons. Now, her career as a soldier came to an abrupt end. She recalled, 'An unlucky shell from a [church] steeple struck the back part of my head and fractured my skull.' Too stunned to conceal her sex from the surgeon who tended her, Davies was dismissed from the regiment, but on account of her good conduct while serving as a soldier, she was allowed to stay with the army as a sutleress to the war's end.

The British cavalry rout the Elector of Bavaria's squadrons. Afternoon, 23 May 1706.

Although a number of French and Bavarian units gamely struggled to make a stand and staunch the flood of the Allied onslaught, the furious pace of Marlborough's pursuit could not be resisted for long. For the victors, no orders could possibly be given by their commanders as the evening sped on; individual officers just drove their troops forward, allowing their beaten opponents no chance to recover. The Allied infantry could not keep up, so fast was the chase: the cavalry were off the leash, with the Duke and his staff riding among the pursuers, heading through the gathering night for the crossing places over the Dyle river, beyond which Villeroi's fleeing army, even in its shattered state, might find shelter. Orkney wrote of the difficulty of gathering his troops quickly enough to overtake the fugitives: 'If I could only have got up in time we should have taken eight or nine battalions ... All night we knew nothing of one another, and Mr Lumley and I had resolved to march straight to the Dyle to their Lines.' At last, shortly after midnight, Marlborough called a halt several miles to the north, rather closer to Louvain than to Ramillies. Weary after nineteen hours in the saddle this eventful day, he lay down to sleep on the grass in the corner of a field, sharing his cloak with field deputy Sicco van Goslinga. No one in his party was quite sure where they were by then, so hectic had been the pursuit. 'In short,' veteran Scottish officer Jemmy Campbell wrote, 'it is a most glorious victory.'

Colonel de la Colonie was still on the edge of the Visoule stream to the west of Taviers, and under no real pressure as the Allied pursuit rushed away to the north and west. He withdrew during the night, with the survivors of his brigade and those dragoons and Swiss who had been gathered together to the French-held fortress of Namur. The Governor, although quite astounded to receive the appalling news of such a defeat, was sufficiently alert to send out working parties with teams of horses to drag off several of the abandoned artillery pieces that littered the quickly emptying battlefield.

The Allied army lost 1,066 killed and 2,597 wounded at Ramillies, an astonishingly light total considering the scale of their victory. The French and Bavarian army, by stark comparison, suffered more than 12,000 killed and wounded – the precise total could never be calculated, so complete was the collapse of the army that day, and it was reported that another 10,000 unwounded prisoners were taken by the victors. John Millner, seventeen years after the battle, reckoned that 12,087 of Villeroi's men were casualties with another 9,729 taken prisoner or defected to the Allied cause. In addition, hundreds of soldiers were fugitives no longer with their units. Fifty-two of the sixty artillery pieces in Villeroi's army were lost, as was their entire engineer pontoon train. Marlborough captured no fewer than eighty regimental colours, as well as almost all the campaign gear of the French army and a vast haul of ammunition, matériel, camp stores, baggage and other booty. A third of the

French and Bavarian army had ceased to exist, and the morale of the remainder was so shaken that their effectiveness as a fighting force was in shreds. 'The most dreadful thing of all,' the Elector of Bavaria wrote the day after the battle, 'is the terror that is in our troops.' Marlborough's army, on the other hand, was buoyed up by their success and would soon receive substantial contingents of fresh German troops as reinforcements left their cantonments along the Rhine and hurried to join the campaign.

That Sunday night, the Marshal and the Elector met by torchlight in the square of Louvain with those senior officers who had eluded Marlborough's cavalry. There was stunned despair at the scale of their unprecedented defeat, and no one believed that the line of the Dyle could be held; the Senne river, the next practical line of defence, might also be lost before long. Peter Drake remembered, 'We never halted until break of day, near Louvain where we crossed the river dispirited and weary, having been on our feet twenty-four hours without the least rest.' Instructions were immediately given to set fire to the huge stocks of ammunition and matériel in the town and to dump what

Ramillies. Marlborough receives the captured French standards after Ramillies.

could not be burned in the river. Orders were issued for what was left of the army to fall back to the Dender river; there, perhaps, a stand might be made. So scattered were the French and Bavarians that fewer than 15,000 troops rallied to the colours in the days immediately after the battle. Villeroi could hope to do little more than save what was left of his army, which, with better fortune, might live to fight another day.

The letter announcing the extraordinary victory, sent by Marlborough to his Duchess the day after the battle, read:

> *On Sunday last we fought and that God Almighty has been pleased to give us a victory. I must leave the particulars to Colonel Richards, for having been on horseback all Sunday, and after marching all night, my head aches to the degree that it is very uneasy for me to write.*

The Duke had ordered his victorious troops to close up to the Dyle; he was heading to cross the water obstacle without delay. Coming immediately after a tumultuous battle and demanding pursuit, this was a demanding logistical operation, but the officers of Marlborough's engineer train were equal to the task. By nightfall, 24 May, the Duke's troops were at the gates of Louvain, and the town yielded the following day. After a brief pause, Marlborough lunged forward again, his cavalry columns taking several individual routes, each commander seeking the line of least resistance. In the event, resistance was not really there at all; Villeroi's fugitive army were mostly concerned with drawing away from the peril in which they stood. The French commanders were walking through a waking nightmare, and those who had thoughts for anything other than flight to the fortress belt along the French border simply hoped to find a place where they could make a stand of some kind.

The Senne was reached and Marlborough crossed that river on 26 May, summoning the magistrates of Brussels to surrender. Villeroi and his officers had ridden off, and the Governor of the city replied to the Duke that day:

> *The States of Brabant and the Magistracy of Brussels, have taken the Resolution to send Deputies to you; they have desired me, Sir, to write to you, most humbly to desire you to send a Trumpeter, to conduct them in Safety, where you shall think fit to receive them. I have the Honour, Sir, to say more to you concerning my Particular Interests, and those of the other Persons of Quality, who seem resolved to stay there if you approve of it.*

The hint, dropped rather heavily to the Duke, that the Governor was inclined to change sides is quite plain. The keys to the city were ceremonially handed to Marlborough on 28 May, and the States of Brabant did the same, the Duke assuring them, on behalf of the Archduke Charles, that their ancient rights and privileges would be maintained. That this was not entirely to be the case in practice would be the cause of some trouble two years later in the prelude to the Oudenarde campaign.

Marlborough wrote to Robert Harley, the Secretary of State, on the day that Brussels submitted,

The consequences of the battle is likely to be of greater advantage than that of Blenheim; for we have now the whole summer before us, and with the blessing of God, I will make the best use of it ... We had no council of war before this battle, so that I hope to have none this whole campaign.

The Duke's intention was clear; with the French in disarray and such glittering prospects ahead, Dutch caution, understandable as it might have been on earlier occasions, was not to be allowed to interfere with the decisions he now made. In fact, the field deputies (van Cotton, van Rheede and van Goslinga) were almost besides themselves with glee at the triumph, writing to The Hague:

The Confusion the Enemy were in, after the Battle, cannot be expressed, as we are informed by the Seigneur de Gravenmoor, who was an Eye-Witness thereof ... in short, the Victory is complete and the happy Consequences thereof begin to appear.

In Versailles the dreadful news of defeat did not arrive until Wednesday 26 May. It was greeted with incredulity. Rumours of a battle had been heard sooner, as Villeroi had thoughtfully written to a friend at court that his son, although wounded, was in no danger of his life. Matters were made worse by the arrival of messengers to announce that an attempt to recapture Barcelona, recently stormed by the Allied army in Catalonia, had failed. Now, 'Days seemed like years in the ignorance of everyone as to the details,' according to St Simon, and, as the awful truth came in, the King was 'forced to ask one and another for news, here and there'. The Elector of Bavaria wrote to Louis XIV with an account of the events at Ramillies:

Your Majesty's household [cavalry] and my cuirassiers broke no less than three times the enemy's left ... The only consolation, sir, in my misfortune, is, that I have done nothing contrary to your orders, which Marshal Villeroy cannot but acknowledge, as well as all the officers of the army, who have seen me expose myself as much as the meanest soldier.

The King was reticent in his comments about the lamentable performance of Villeroi, his old friend, but many others stepped forward to denounce the Marshal's incompetence at Ramillies. Prominent among these critics was Michel de Chamillart, the Minister of War, who had so recently urged Villeroi to go out and seek battle. He was sent to Courtrai on 30 May to confer with the

Marshal on what was to be done for the best. On the way he drew up a list of Villeroi's mistakes: he had sought battle without ascertaining his opponent's real strength; he had fought without waiting for full reinforcement from the army on the Moselle; he had failed to reinforce his right Wing and had placed insufficient infantry on the right; he had inefficiently deployed the right Wing so that they had inadequate supports; and so on. De Chamillart was busily scheming to deflect any possible criticism of himself, for his erroneous judgement of Marlborough's performance in 1705 might well come back to haunt him. His views on Villeroi's tactical failures, while correct, were so obviously reached with the benefit of hindsight that they were worth little comment, and the first two considerations were plain nonsense – the Minister for War had been among those who urged Villeroi on to battle, and, cautioned to wait for cavalry reinforcements, the Marshal had done so, despite being impatiently urged by Versailles to get on with things.

Louis XIV was affronted by reports of how his household cavalry, the Maison du Roi, had galloped off the field of battle in such indecent haste, and he eagerly seized for consolation on anecdotes of individual bravery and gallant conduct. St Simon remembered, 'He sent word to the Guards that he was contented with them, but others were not so easily satisfied.' Marshal Villars, campaigning on the upper Rhine, commented that the French defeat in the battle was the most disgraceful thing he had ever heard. This judgement does less than justice to the French cavalry, to their commander, General de Guiscard, whose performance that afternoon was selflessly valiant, and to Marlborough, whose sparkling and dynamic tactics were so successful.

In the meantime, Villeroi found it impossible to hold the line of the Dender, and attempted to establish a new position on the Scheldt to cover Ghent, Bruges and the northern part of Flanders. Before he could do so, Marlborough's advanced guard (twelve squadrons of cavalry and dragoons together with a picked force of 2,000 grenadiers) cut across the Marshal's right flank, passing the river at Gavre, just downstream from Oudenarde on 31 May. That town capitulated soon afterwards, and with his lines of communication and supply into France under threat, Villeroi had no choice but to abandon Ghent and Bruges. De Chamillart and the Marshal met at Courtrai on the Lys river, where the remains of the army fell back to recover their composure. Given the catastrophe that had been suffered, and the fact that the French troops were in little condition to offer organised resistance to the Allied advance, de Chamillart approved Villeroi's plan to abandon the region and withdraw inside the dense fortress belt along France's northern border. It was therefore necessary to disperse many regiments to occupy the various fortresses that now lay in Marlborough's path, and before long the French army had almost entirely gone into static defence. Only Mortagne, Armentières and

Dendermonde were to be held as forward posts and, for the time being, the Duke was not faced with a French force capable of sustaining anything like a general action. Constrained only by logistics, he could go where he pleased.

Faced with the stark facts of the destruction at Ramillies of his army's operational ability, Villeroi remained convinced that he had done nothing with which to reproach himself. He had been instructed by his King to go out and fight Marlborough, and had done so; he had been warned to pay particular attention to the deployment of the British troops, and had done so. He had done his best. When driven from the field of battle, he had given ground regardless of his own reputation to save what was left of his army for future operations – in his own eyes, a creditable thing. The one alternative after such a defeat was to fight another action, which, in the now enfeebled state of the army was plainly not advisable. Given all this, the Marshal saw no reason why he should not continue to enjoy the trust of his King and remain in command in the Low Countries. He appeared blind to the fact that no one had faith in his abilities any more. Louis XIV would spare his feelings as much as he could, but Villeroi had to be replaced as soon as possible. When, at last, it was found that the Marshal would not give up his command, it was given out by Versailles that he had asked to be replaced. In effect, he was 'resigned'.

The fortnight-long hectic pace of Marlborough's pursuit, impressive though it undoubtedly was, was influenced to a large degree by the logistical demands of his army. There was little, if any, formed body of French troops immediately in front to oppose the advance, although some rearguards were posted by Villeroi, trees were felled and bridges broken down in a game, but rather futile, attempt to slow the Duke's armies. The pressing daily need to feed his troops, with supplies dragged along bad roads, exerted the only real brake on progress. Fortresses and towns submitted to his commanders – Alost, Oudenarde, Mechelin, Ghent, Bruges, Courtrai – in some cases with hardly a shot being fired. The Marquis de Vallée, Governor of Dendermonde at the junction of the river Dender with the Scheldt, decided to put up a fight, however, and these vital waterways, so useful in bringing forward guns, powder, food and matériel, were denied to the Allies for the time being. Marlborough, aware of the value of the place, wrote on 1 June, 'I am endeavouring to make the Governor propositions that may tempt him to declare for King Charles.' It was a vain hope, and the fortress stood firm for precious weeks. The Marquis's robust response was that 'The place being well garrisoned and provided with all necessaries for its defence, he hoped to merit his Grace's esteem, by discharging his duty and the trust reposed in him.'

News was coming in to Marlborough that the contingents of Prussian, Hanoverian and Hessian troops, so long delayed for reasons which may have been good or bad, but whose absence on the day of battle might have had such serious consequences for the outcome, were now pressing forward to take a hand in the campaign. 'This,' the Duke wrote drily, 'I take to be owing to our late success.' The reluctance of their rulers to commit the soldiers at the start of operations had evaporated with the triumph at Ramillies, and all were eager to participate and share in whatever glory was to be had. In the meantime, Marlborough received assurance from London on a matter that had been troubling him. His friend Sidney Godolphin wrote, 'You may depend that Her Majesty will not fail to take care of poor Bringfield's widow.'

The great port of Antwerp did not submit immediately, but the resistance of the garrison did not last long. The Governor, the Marquis de Tarazena, declared for King Charles III on 6 June, as did most of his Walloon troops and in this way seven of these excellent battalions joined Marlborough's army; the French in the garrison were permitted to march away without giving their parole. Overkirk then moved on to attack Ostend with the assistance of a Royal Navy squadron whose bombardment soon set the town alight. On 4 July, the defences were stormed by a Dutch infantry battalion, led by a forlorn hope of fifty British grenadiers. The seizure of the port provided Marlborough with a valuable direct route to the Channel for communication and supply. In the meantime, the Elector of Bavaria, having recovered his spirits a little, slipped some reinforcements into Dendermonde, elbowing aside a rather feeble attempt to oppose him, much to Marlborough's annoyance. He wrote with gentle sarcasm, 'The Elector of Bavaria has taken advantage of the siege of Ostend and the army's being there to cover it, to put a reinforcement of about four hundred foot and one hundred dragoons into Dendermonde. Brigadier Meredyth was upon his guard, but had not the strength to prevent it, he had five or six men killed, and as many, with a captain, taken prisoners.' The operations against the town were delayed, and an eight-day bombardment at the end of June failed to intimidate the Marquis de Vallée. The conditions were particularly difficult: sufficient troops to invest the town were lacking, as was ammunition, and the weather was very hot. Operations were reduced for the time being to a simple blockade. Dendermonde has strong water defences, and Louis XIV scoffed that the Allies had better use ducks if their siege was to succeed. Only when William Cadogan and Charles Churchill went to take charge a few weeks later did the defences begin to fail.

The powerful Vauban-designed fortress of Menin, close to the French border, had been invested by 23 July, and on 6 August the digging of the trenches began. Meanwhile, the Duc de Vendôme, one of Louis XIV's most bruising field commanders, had arrived from Italy and began to scrape together a field army once more. The task was daunting, and Vendôme commented bitterly on the low state of morale among the troops, even those who had not been at Ramillies. He wrote to Michel de Chamillart from Valenciennes:

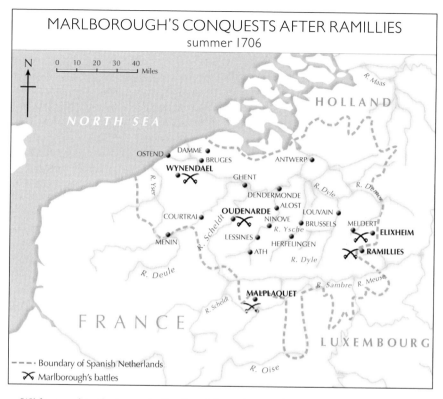

MARLBOROUGH'S CONQUESTS AFTER RAMILLIES
summer 1706

With regard to the troops in the Spanish service, no one can answer for them; but that grieves me far less than the sadness and dejection that appears in the French army. I will do my best to restore their spirit, but it will be no light matter for me to do so, for everyone here is ready to take off his hat at the mere mention of the name of Marlborough.

By the second week of the month the Allied bombardment of Menin was under way, but Vendôme moved forward on 15 August with a fairly substantial force gathered together from the garrisons in Lille and Tournai to threaten the Allied foraging parties and lines of communication. Vendôme had no intention of being made to stand and fight a battle, but in the skirmishing that followed Cadogan was taken prisoner by a French cavalry patrol. He was released soon afterwards, to Marlborough's great relief, in exchange for Lieutenant-General Pallavacini, a Savoyard officer in the service of France who had been captured earlier in the campaign. Vendôme (in many ways a somewhat uncouth man) speeded up the exchange, as he knew how much

Marlborough valued Cadogan's services. A week after the covered way at Menin was stormed, the garrison commander, Count Caraman (veteran of the fight at Elixheim), capitulated and was permitted to march away with his troops to Douai.

With Vendôme's arrival, Marshal Villeroi had been replaced as army commander in Flanders. His reputation was in ruins after Ramillies, but Louis XIV was forgiving, greeting his friend on return to Versailles with the kind words, 'At our age, Marshal, we must no longer expect good fortune.' Forgiven, but now quickly forgotten as a commander, Villeroi never led an army in the field again; he was a brave, honest soldier who had the misfortune to meet in open battle an opponent so immeasurably his superior. His rather sad comment to the King was that he could now look forward to only one happy day, that of his own death.

Dendermonde held out beyond the month of August, and this became a real concern for Marlborough because it exerted a stranglehold on the free use of the Scheldt and Dender. The resistance by the garrison was a creditable achievement as the Allies were helped by unusually dry weather which depleted the water-defences. A British officer remembered, 'Old men up to seventy years observe that they never saw such a drought, or the waters so low about the town.' The Allied trenches were opened on 1 September, and de Vallée submitted six days later. Within twenty-four hours heavy rain began to fall, flooding the trenches and making them uninhabitable. The waterways were at last open to use by Allied supply barges and the French grip on those vital arteries of war was prised loose at last.

By 9 September, Marlborough was shifting his attention from Dendermonde to laying siege to the town of Ath. The heavy artillery came up the Scheldt to Oudenarde, and on 16 September the place was invested by Overkirk with his Dutch corps. The trenches were opened on 20 September, and a lodgement made on the covered way a week or so later, after a well-executed counter-attack was beaten back. The governor submitted on 2 October, rather than face a storm, and the garrison went as prisoners of war to Holland to await exchange. Meanwhile, news came in to the Allied camp of Prince Eugene's stunning victory at Turin earlier in the month – he had saved Savoy for the Grand Alliance and killed Marshal Marsin in the process.

With the arrival of the first week of October, the Dutch were looking forward to their winter quarters; much had been attempted and much achieved, and they had played a major part in the successes of the year. Still, Marlborough wanted one more effort, despite heavy rain which turned the roads to quagmire and marooned the heavy guns of the siege train: he planned to seize the important fortresses of Charleroi and Mons, close to the French border. For all his urging, the Dutch deputies refused to do more, and Marlborough, after reviewing his victorious regiments, sent them off to their quarters. The autumn sped onwards, and the astonishing year drew to a close. The Duke could reflect with pride and perfect justice on his achievement. The French had not been expected to fight at all that year, and a dismal prospect had loomed ahead as the Allies took the campaign trail. To general surprise, Villeroi came out to fight and his army was shattered in one short afternoon. He had then chosen, quite rightly, to save what was left of his army, and had abandoned the Spanish Netherlands almost entirely. Those garrisons that he left behind put up, in the main, a poor resistance. Louis XIV would rebuild his strength along the northern border of France, but this would take time, as regiments and generals were summoned from distant theatres of war, surrendering hard-won gains elsewhere, to hold the line. In the meantime, the initiative in the war once more lay with the Grand Alliance.

Increasingly, Louis XIV looked for ways to get out of what was fast becoming a ruinous war for France, unaware that the Grand Alliance had neither the wit nor the will to conclude a peace on terms that would satisfy both claimants to the throne in Madrid. With French military power broken in the Spanish Netherlands (for the time being), and the King's prestige damaged in the aftermath of the disaster at Ramillies and the defeat at Turin, a peace tolerable if not actually advantageous to both sides was a real possibility. It was not to be. The year's heady successes raised expectations throughout the Grand Alliance, which became greedy; the utter defeat of France, unimaginable in other circumstances, now seemed to be achievable, and so the war went on.

Part 3

Oudenarde, 11 July 1708

Introduction

The year that followed Marlborough's great 1706 campaign of conquest proved to be one of surprising disappointment. So much had been achieved in the battle and its glorious aftermath that anything seemed possible. It appeared that the war for Spain was won: Louis XIV must submit – surely he could do little else. The parties to the Grand Alliance, so firm and steadfast in adversity, now began to look more to their own narrow interests. For his part, the French King proved resilient, as did his generals. In the Spanish Netherlands the Duke of Marlborough tried to bring the French army to battle once again, but his opponent, the cunning and adept Duc de Vendôme, evaded him month after month, drawing things out until the season for campaigning in 1707 had passed without any real result. Meanwhile, in Spain the Allied cause suffered a heavy blow with the defeat of the Earl of Galway's army at Almanza by a Franco-Spanish force under Marlborough's nephew, the Duke of Berwick. The campaign to secure the throne in Madrid for the Archduke Charles never really recovered.

In 1708 things certainly changed; in part this was because the Allied cause in Spain was foundering and significant resources had, of necessity, to be diverted to that arid and thankless theatre of war. Also, the French had spotted a glistening opportunity to seize important towns in northern Flanders, and the Duc de Vendôme did just that, very publicly wrong-footing the Duke of Marlborough in the process. How different it all was for the Allies from the happy days of Ramillies in the summer of 1706, but the Duke and Prince Eugene rose magnificently to the occasion, forcing the river lines at a fast marching pace to confront the unsuspecting French army near to Oudenarde on the Scheldt in July 1708, while they were still on the move. Vendôme's tactical handling of the battle that ensued was lamentable: the veteran campaigner lost his head and allowed his troops to drift into the very kind of tumbling, uncontrolled battle that should have been avoided. The lack of command and control among the French leaders that day stood in stark comparison with the sure, almost carefree handling of the fighting by Marlborough and Eugene, working together in complete understanding and harmony. At the end of the day those French that could run did so, either as a beaten army or fugitives fleeing through the darkness. They laid bare the frontier of northern France in the process.

Marlborough had in mind a grand plan to immediately advance deep into northern France and confront his opponents at the gates of Paris or Versailles. This was far too adventurous for his generals, and they were probably right – the French were down but they were not out, and they would be dangerous again, given time. The Duke turned his intentions instead to capturing the great city and fortress of Lille, cherished conquest of Louis XIV's younger days and Marshal Vauban's engineering masterpiece. In a huge and bewilderingly complex operation lasting over four harrowing months, Marlborough not only sustained his army deep inside France, with his lines of supply and communication often threatened and even cut by his opponents, but conducted the massive siege and held off French armies in superior numbers who were attempting to stop him. Lille, that 'Pearl among Fortresses' as it was described, fell early in December 1708, and the Duke went on to recapture quickly the towns in northern Flanders that had been lost earlier in the year. Field deputy Sicco van Goslinga, often a critic of Marlborough, wrote, 'Thus ended this dangerous and remarkable campaign, one of the most glorious that was ever made.'

This was the Duke of Marlborough at the height of his confident powers and influence. He commanded the operations of the Grand Alliance's main field army in the theatre of war that mattered most, the Spanish Netherlands, while conducting Britain's foreign policy almost single-handedly. Louis XIV had, in effect, lost the war, and was in despair at the end of the year as Marlborough's armies rampaged through northern France. Only a dreadful miscalculation by the Grand Alliance, made arrogant by repeated successes, in drafting absurd terms for a negotiated peace drove the French King to fight on at the risk of courting disaster for his country. Marlborough laid a victory at the Alliance's door but, tragically, it was allowed to slip away.

We Shall Advance, Tomorrow

The astonishing year of victories, 1706, when the Duke of Marlborough seized all but a few odd corners of the Spanish Netherlands and Prince Eugene saved Savoy for the Grand Alliance with his victory at Turin, seemed to hold out bright promise for the new campaigns in 1707. As so often with alliance warfare, matters proved not to be that simple. The Imperial Court in Vienna was concerned that the Dutch should not gain too great an influence, or tax-gathering powers, in the Spanish (Southern) Netherlands. The region was, nominally at least, a possession of the Austrian claimant to the Spanish throne, Archduke Charles. To the States-General in The Hague, on the other hand, the area provided a cherished strategic shield against French aggression – the 'Barrier' to which they, quite understandably, attached great importance. Furthermore, the victory at Ramillies, which had led to the conquest of the Spanish Netherlands, had been achieved in no small part because of Dutch efforts and Dutch casualties, whereas no Imperial troops had been engaged. Now, the States-General were affronted to learn that the Emperor in far-away Vienna had, without consulting them, offered the Governor-Generalship of the region to the Duke of Marlborough (Louis XIV's appointee, the Elector of Bavaria, being a virtual fugitive in the wake of defeat). Although Marlborough prudently declined, mistrust and suspicion resulted, while the council of regency that was appointed instead on behalf of Archduke Charles proved to be both inefficient and ineffective. Louis XIV, with an exhausted treasury, undoubtedly now wanted peace for France, and he offered tempting terms of a kind that would have been eagerly snapped up by his opponents before Marlborough's triumphs at Blenheim and Ramillies made them so greedy. Dazzled by success, the Grand Alliance spurned the French peace overtures, and the war went on.

Marlborough had been engaged on a series of diplomatic visits, perhaps the most significant of which was to persuade the volatile Swedish King, Charles XII, to stay out of the war. The Duke joined his army at Andschot in mid-May, hoping to force a battle on the French commander before long. Once the 1707 campaign in Flanders started, Marlborough once again faced the Duc de Vendôme, a formidable and astute soldier. The Captain-General, just as in 1705, cherished hopes of mounting a campaign in the Moselle valley, well away from the French fortress belt, but the Dutch would not agree. They, perhaps, had good reason for their renewed caution, as the French had taken the offensive along the middle and upper Rhine, where Marshal Villars had breached the Lines of Stollhofen and gone raiding into central Germany. The Imperial commander, the Margrave of Bayreuth, scattered his forces into garrisons instead of trying to confront Villars, and the many minor German princely states that provided such excellent mercenary troops for the Grand Alliance were in a considerable state of alarm. 'We had an account this morning,' Marlborough wrote on 30 May, 'of the misfortune of the German troops on the Rhine, who had let the French pass that river by surprise.' So deep did the French cavalry raiders go that some of the officers even went sightseeing on the Schellenberg hill above Donauwörth, scene of the bitter fighting there three years before. A week later, Marlborough complained to Robert Harley in London, 'If [only] they had a good general in Germany, I am persuaded they can bring together troops enough of their own to oblige the French to retire over the Rhine.'

The affairs of the Grand Alliance were also ailing elsewhere. In northern Italy the Austrians concluded a separate private truce with the French early in the year, permitting over 20,000 of Louis XIV's troops to leave the region, free to campaign in other theatres of war. This did, however, also release some Imperial troops to pursue the arid campaign in Spain, but Vienna turned its main attention instead to the strategically rather irrelevant task of seizing Naples, while neglecting the Rhine frontier. In Spain, Philip V's forces were gaining ground, and, most significantly, the young Frenchman was gaining the sympathy and support of the people. In April, the Anglo-Portuguese army had been heavily defeated at Almanza by the Duke of Berwick, and Valencia and Aragon were lost to the Allies, who were reduced to holding on to Catalonia and some scattered fortresses elsewhere. Such a sorry list of reverses had a distinctly dampening effect on the spirits of the Dutch. 'Our friends will not venture,' the Duke wrote, 'unless we have an advantage, which our enemies will be careful not to give.'

Vendôme however, had instructions from Versailles to avoid a general engagement, and he was not to be caught. As hard as Marlborough tried, the French commander proved able to slip away and avoid being fixed long enough to have to stand and fight. A summer of intense frustration ensued, the Dutch increasingly seemed content with what had been achieved after Ramillies, while the Allied war effort everywhere flagged. In southern France, a grand plan for Prince Eugene and the Duke of Savoy to attack Toulon, in conjunction with the cruising squadrons of the Royal Navy, proved an expensive failure in the face of solid resistance by Marshal Tessé's troops, although the French Mediterranean fleet was beached or burned at anchor to prevent its capture – a worthwhile achievement in itself. Also, substantial French forces had to be drawn away from campaigning in Spain to help defend the port, preventing recent successes there against the Allies from being fully exploited. So, the attempt on Toulon, while a disappointment for the Allies, was not entirely without benefit, although this is seldom recognised.

By early August, Marlborough learned that French units were also being sent from Flanders to assist in the defence of Toulon. This news encouraged the Dutch to agree to a fresh attempt to corner Vendôme, and on 10 August the Duke moved forward from near Louvain to Hal with about 90,000 troops. The French army, which lay at Perwez, fell back towards Seneffe as soon as the Allied advance was detected, but Count Tilly, the very able Dutch cavalry commander, was sent on ahead to engage and pin down the French rearguard near to Nivelle on 12 August. The weather was bad, Tilly received the message to move late in the day, and the instructions were ambiguous, so that Vendôme got his troops away without too much trouble. 'The enemy escaped out of our hands,' a British officer commented ruefully. The French settled into a new defensive position between Mons and Ath, while the Allied army halted at Soignies, waiting for the foul weather to clear. On 1 September, Marlborough advanced again, crossing the Dender river at Ath to turn the left flank of the French position. Vendôme then withdrew behind the Scheldt, but Marlborough got across that river on 5 September. As a result, the French commander fell back to the Marque river, inside France itself, not far from Lille. Despite Marlborough's advance, no serious engagement had resulted, the season for campaigning was being eaten up unproductively, and Vendôme was playing quite a skilful and cautious game. As the French army now stood, the Allies would be hard put to attack them with any real prospect of success.

For all the astonishing successes of 1706, which the Grand Alliance had perversely failed to make the most of, Louis XIV might yet succeed in securing the throne in Madrid for his grandson. Friends of the Duke of Marlborough noted that he appeared to be out of sorts and ill-tempered as he returned to London at the end of the year, and this is perhaps not surprising. His mood cannot have been lightened by the increasing friction between Duchess Sarah and Queen Anne. The Duke's position had at its base the unstinting support of the Queen, and this was undoubtedly weakened as the old friendship between the two women cooled and gradually became bitter.

Early in 1708, Louis XIV attempted to distract the attention of Great Britain (as it now was with the passing in 1707 of the Act of Union between England and Scotland) by launching an expedition to land the Jacobite Pretender, Queen Anne's half-brother (known in France by the courtesy title of the Chevalier de St George), on the coast of Scotland. A French force of 6,000 troops was embarked at Dunkirk in a flotilla of ships commanded by Comte Claude de Forbin. The departure was delayed while the Pretender recovered from measles, and contrary winds blew over, but on 17 March the ships were at sea. De Forbin was intercepted by a Royal Navy squadron off the Scottish coast, and after some inconclusive fighting turned back for Dunkirk after losing a ship. Still, this was a period of danger and possible Jacobite rebellion, a most unwelcome distraction because, while preparations for the new campaign were in progress, Marlborough was obliged to divert ten battalions of infantry from the army in Flanders to bolster the rather meagre military strength in Britain. However, the alarm was soon over and they returned to their camps. Although not very much came of the attempted Jacobite incursion, it backfired on the French King. Public opinion in Great Britain, which had been cooling towards the expensive and seemingly interminable war for Spain, was outraged at the brazen French attempt to interfere in British internal affairs. Elections in mid-May strengthened the Whigs in Parliament, the more ardent supporters of the war. The Duchess of Marlborough favoured the Whigs and their support of the Duke's campaigns, but the same politicians were distrusted by Queen Anne, and this added to the growing tension between the monarch and the Captain-General. Things were made worse by attempts to force the appointment of advisers whom she disliked but who were sympathetic to Marlborough's view of how the war was to be fought and won. 'Why may I not be trusted,' the Queen burst out, almost plaintively, 'since I mean nothing but what is equally for the good of all my subjects?'

The Devil Must Have Carried Them

Dutch caution in the year after the Ramillies triumph had thoroughly exasperated the Duke of Marlborough once again. Still, the States-General were at their most positive and eager when preparing for the 1708 campaign. Assured by Antonius Hiensius, the Grand Pensionary of Holland, that the Dutch generals and field deputies would be entirely cooperative, Marlborough was resolved to force the issue in Flanders 'to endeavour by all means a battle, thinking nothing else would make the Queen's business go well.'

The Allied plan of campaign in Flanders for 1708 was agreed in conference at The Hague in early April, and was, on the face of things, quite simple. Suggestions that Prince Eugene should go to command the Allied armies in Spain were put aside. Instead, he would gather some 40,000 Imperial troops in the Moselle valley. Eugene would then bring this force north to combine with Marlborough, so that the two friends could confront and defeat Vendôme before the French, in turn, were reinforced from elsewhere. George, the Elector of Hanover (one day to be George I of Great Britain), would hold the upper Rhine frontier secure in the meantime with another Imperial army. The plan was almost an open secret, and had little subtlety about it; however, it was still a good one, and Louis XIV had to be careful not to permit major troop movements to bolster Vendôme's forces in Flanders until he was sure that Eugene was indeed committed to taking his army north. Otherwise, the main Allied effort might suddenly switch back to the Moselle, where the, by then weakened, French forces would be caught at a disadvantage. As a result, both sides had to bide their time, watch each other and employ patience while the various plans took effect.

As the fine weather of spring dried the roads and allowed the armies to deploy, Vendôme could put about 110,000 troops into the field. He had, for the time being, a distinct numerical advantage over Marlborough who had at his disposal only some 90,000 men until Eugene arrived. Vendôme was hampered, however, by having to share the command of the army with the Duc de Bourgogne (Burgundy), the 26-year-old eldest grandson of Louis XIV and eventual heir to the French throne. Burgundy was accompanied by his younger brother, the Duc de Berri, and the Chevalier de St George. The King was anxious that his grandson should become better known to the officers and soldiers, and nominally at least the young man held the command of the army, just as he had done in 1702 and 1703. Still, Burgundy had little talent or appetite for being on campaign, and he and Vendôme heartily disliked each other, and neither had the wit to hide the fact. They engaged in as little day-to-day contact as could be managed. Burgundy had instructions from his grandfather to be guided by and to heed Vendôme with all his vast experience, but in practice this did not happen. There could be no mistake, of course, that Vendôme was the army commander, but the presence of the royal prince, who was not slow to express his, often inexpert, opinions, and the natural deference that he was shown as the King's grandson, inevitably made command and control on all occasions difficult and prone to hesitation and contradiction. This fractured leadership in the French army was highly dangerous, and hampered effective operations; the two men, and their respective staffs, exchanged as few words as possible.

Vendôme would have preferred to shift operations eastwards into Brabant, closer to the Meuse to threaten Huy or Liège where the more open terrain than was found in much of Flanders would suit the numerous French cavalry. This move would also close the distance between Vendôme's army and that of Marshal Berwick on the Moselle. Burgundy, on the other hand, favoured a direct march on Brussels, although this would almost certainly bring on a general action with Marlborough on ground of his own choosing. Given the French numerical superiority at this point, this was not an entirely unattractive choice. As neither man would agree to what the other suggested, the decision was referred to the King in Versailles. The matter was settled as a tempting plan emerged, one too good to resist, to surprise and retake the towns of northern Flanders, which had been lost by Philip V and France in the dreadful summer of Marlborough's successes in 1706.

By 21 May, Marlborough had gathered his troops at Anderlecht, ready for the new campaign. The French army had concentrated near to Mons, and on 26 May Vendôme advanced to Soignies on the Haine river. Marlborough directed his army towards Hal, seeking to cover the southern approaches to Brussels. Vendôme then moved through Nivelles to Braine l'Alleud, as if to threaten Louvain. Marlborough again shifted to block the way, his troops marching through pouring rain to Terbanck – 'Very tedious with wet and dirt and extraordinary great rains,' as John Deane remembered. By 3 June, Vendôme had halted near Braine l'Alleud, apparently foiled by his opponents' confident countermoves, and the opposing armies settled down to keep watch on each other. On 25 June, Marlborough was dismayed to learn that Prince Eugene would not begin his march northwards, bringing a force only 15,000 strong to combine with the Duke's army, before the end of June. There were good practical reasons for this, one of which was the offence taken by the Elector of Hanover at being left out of things. The lack of reinforcement hobbled the Duke's campaign for the time being; he had gone into a camp at Terbanck, where both Brussels and Louvain could be covered, and had to employ patience and bide his time. With his comparative lack of numbers, and particularly with regard to the French superiority in cavalry, he was unable to venture forward and engage Vendôme with any real chance of success. Marlborough wrote to London on 28 June, 'Since the disappointments Prince Eugene has met with have lost us above a month, and that the enemy knows too much of our designs, the best thing we can hope for is, that we may be able to oblige them to come to some action.' The Prince began his march from Coblenz the next day, but the Duke of Berwick was soon hard on his heels with 27,000 French troops. Marlborough wrote to James Brydges, the Paymaster-General, on 2 July:

> I believe our long continuance in the camp has been a great disappointment to our friends at home. I assure you it has been no less to me, after the measures I had concerted with the Elector of Hanover and Prince Eugene, in April last, but I hope we shall be able in a little time to send you some good news for I have an account [that] the Prince Eugene's Army has been on the march towards us these four days. The Prince designs to be at Maastricht the 4th, in order to come directly to the camp.

At this time, Marlborough was unwell with migraine headaches and a fever, and the delay in making progress with opening the campaign, the success of which depended upon quite a tight timetable, depressed his spirits. The Duke had taken measures to improve the security of Antwerp earlier in the summer, and the Comte de Merode-Westerloo, now in the service of the Austrian claimant to the Spanish throne, wrote of having given a warning to him that the French had new plans to take the offensive in northern Flanders: 'I received news from a reliable source advising me to take good care of Ghent and Bruges, which were soon to be betrayed to the enemy ... He [Marlborough] treated my news as something of no account, telling me that it was impossible.'

It was not impossible at all, for on 3 July a French force under the Marquis de Grimaldi crossed the Senne at Hal and Tubize, as if to forage in the lush

135

country to the west. The next day, strong detachments of French cavalry and dragoons under Comte de la Motte and the Marquis de Chemerault crossed the Dender at Ninove and were riding hard towards Ghent and Bruges, where the garrisons had recently been reduced to augment the Allied field army. The citizens of these two important towns, exasperated at oppressive Dutch tax-gathering, gladly threw open their gates to the French, although the small Allied garrison in the citadel of Ghent held out for some days. De la Motte went on to seize Plas Endael on the Bruges canal, taking control of the road to Ostend, but the Allied troops in nearby Damme refused his summons to submit. At a stroke, Marlborough had lost control of much of this region and the important waterways so valuable for the movement of men and supplies. 'The States [General],' the Duke wrote, 'have used this country so ill, that I no ways doubt but all the towns will play us the same trick as Ghent has done.' He had been unable to alert or reinforce the Allied garrisons in the two towns in time, but now quickly sent fresh troops to both Dendermonde and Oudenarde to prevent a similar fate there. 'I desire,' he wrote to Brigader-General Murray early on 5 July, 'that you immediately upon receipt of this cause Sir Thomas Prendergast to march with his regiment to Oudenarde.' This town was of particular value – situated on the Scheldt, it exerted a latent threat to the French lines of communication and supply to northern France. The Governor, Brigadier-General Chanclos, was a tough no-nonsense soldier who made it

Oudenarde. View towards Oudenarde across the Scheldt near to Eyne.

plain to the citizenry that he would burn the town around their ears before he saw it given up to any French *coup de main*. Not surprisingly, the place remained calm.

On 5 July, the main French army crossed the Senne, and the Dender at Grammont was reached early the following day. Marlborough, certain now that Vendôme was marching westwards, was in close pursuit, and tried to attack the French rearguard between the two rivers. Time was lost on the road, a wrong turning was taken, and a skilful withdrawal by the French enabled them to avoid serious contact, although part of their baggage train and some 300 prisoners were taken by Marlborough's cavalry. The Duke's response might have been sharper, and Vendôme pushed rather harder, had William Cadogan been present to command the Allied advanced guard, but he had been sent to meet Prince Eugene at Maastricht and conduct him straight to the Allied camp. This very neat French operation, taking Ghent and Bruges right out from under Marlborough's nose and then slipping out of his grasp, had undone much of what had been achieved immediately after Ramillies. A certain air of gloom settled over the Allied camp – this time, it seemed evident, they had come off worst, and the Captain-General's normally sure touch had been lacking. 'The blow which the enemy dealt us,' wrote the Prussian Brigadier-General Grumbkow, 'did not merely destroy all our plans, but was sufficient to do irreparable harm to the reputation and previous good fortune of My Lord Duke.' However, the undoubted French success also had the corresponding, rather inconvenient, effect that it drew the French army to the north-west, away from its own depots and magazines in the fortress belt along France's northern border. Successful at this stage in the campaign, Vendôme was now operating at full stretch, and this would have serious implications if his opponent suddenly sprang into life.

The French commander, quite naturally, wished to cover his recent conquests, but Marlborough's army, by marching in a straight line to a point on the Scheldt somewhere between Oudenarde and Tournai, could stand closer to the border than did their opponents. The Duke still had to cover Brussels, of course, and he moved his army to Assche to do so, but with the extended French lines of supply and communication now exposed to interference, it would plainly be prudent for Vendôme to move closer to his own depots while holding on firmly to the conquests in northern Flanders. Burgundy preferred to try to recapture Menin, close to the border with France, but Vendôme was reluctant to go quite so far south, leaving Ghent and Bruges relatively exposed. He wanted to attack Oudenarde on the Scheldt instead as this would remove any threat from the garrison there to the French lines of supply. Either choice of action was, arguably, as good as the other; each had its merits, but the important thing was for the French to press on with their campaign, to continue to dictate the pace of action, and not to lose time and impetus. Almost inevitably, the two men again could not agree on the best course, and the matter had to be referred to Louis XIV in Versailles for a decision. In the meantime, plans were made to lay siege to Oudenarde and heavy guns were ordered forward from Tournai, while the army held the line of the Dender river, to cover Ghent and Bruges from any countermove by Marlborough.

Vendôme, so energetic in recent days, was now too slow, although he had no obvious pressing need to seek a battle – after the recent successes in northern Flanders he could afford to hold his ground and wait for Berwick to turn up with the reinforcements from the Moselle. The resistance of the Allied garrison in the Ghent citadel (which did not submit until 8 July), of short duration though it was, delayed French operations, and time was not now on their side, for Eugene had ridden with Cadogan ahead of his marching troops, and joined Marlborough at his camp at Assche on 6 July. Although he brought only a small cavalry escort – some wild-looking Imperial hussars – his arrival lifted the Duke's spirits, and Eugene shrugged off the importance of the loss of Ghent and Bruges: what would really count, he insisted, was a victory in open battle. An Austrian biographer of Eugene commented, 'The Prince was astonished to see such despondency in a general like Marlborough, over a misfortune not relatively very important.' In fact, Marlborough was still not

at all well, but this encouragement from his friend was just what he needed to hear; he and Eugene quickly agreed to advance and confront Vendôme without waiting for the arrival of the troops from the Moselle. They would be giving up the hope of achieving a temporary numerical superiority in exchange for the chance to force the pace and catch the French commander off-guard.

After conferring with Marlborough, Eugene went to Brussels to pay a fleeting visit to his aged mother. He then hurried back to the campaign. The two Allied commanders could see that a direct advance to the Dender, in the vicinity of Ninove or Alost, could be countered by the French without difficulty. The crossings over the river to the south at Lessines, on the

Arnold Joost Van Keppel, 1st Earl Albemarle. Favourite of William III, and highly capable Dutch cavalry commander.

other hand, were a long step for either army, but the commander who got there first could dictate the pace of the unfolding campaign. An operation to hold the road to Brussels on the Allied right, while throwing a hard marching punch with the left to get across the Dender, could well take the French by surprise. Marlborough might force Vendôme back upon the Scheldt and at the same time relieve Oudenarde, even if he could not get him to stand and fight. However, if the French commander was alert enough, he could move forward quickly to hold the line of the Dender.

Although Marlborough kept to his tent on 8 July with a fever, eight days' supply of bread was baked – a double ration – and loaded onto the battalion carts of the army in readiness for a move. That evening, the advanced guard of the army, commanded by the ever-dependable William Cadogan, was set marching southwards at a fast pace on the road from Assche through Herfelingen and Ghislengien towards the Dender river crossings at Lessines. The main army followed a few hours later, while the baggage trains were covered by thirty squadrons of Albemarle's Dutch cavalry and the grenadiers of the army; Earl Orkney stayed in Brussels with a stout brigade of infantry, in case of a French raid on the city. 'We began our march again at 2.00 o'clock in the morning,' Marlborough wrote, 'and about noon came to this camp [Herfelingen], where we shall only halt till about 7.00 in the evening, and then pursue our march towards Lessines.' The Allied troops were marching on the curve outside that the French would have to take to reach the river crossings; they had further to go but they were on the road first and making better time.

Eugene rejoined Marlborough while the main body of the army was resting at Herfelingen. He was pleased to find that the Duke had recovered his customary good spirits, and Frances Hare wrote that, 'In all appearances, he was very well.' The Duke wrote to Lord Treasurer Sidney Godolphin before resuming the march:

I am continuing my march, as I intend to do all the night, in hopes of getting to the camp at Lessines before the enemy, who made yesterday a detachment of sixteen thousand men for the investing of Oudenarde. If I get to the camp at Lessines before them, I hope to be able to hinder the siege, being resolved to venture anything.

From this it seems clear that it was not yet regarded as a certainty that Marlborough's rapid march to the Dender river crossings would succeed, and that he was still, quite understandably, concerned for the security of Oudenarde. The strong detachments of cavalry under Albemarle and the infantry under Orkney, two of the Duke's most capable field commanders, also indicate his clear concern at this critical time that Vendôme might suddenly cut across the rear of his marching army in an attempt on Brussels. Such a move,

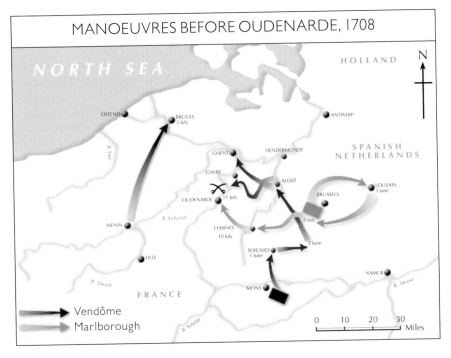

MANOEUVRES BEFORE OUDENARDE, 1708

apparently an obvious choice when viewed on the map, depended entirely upon his being determined to retain the initiative in the campaign. Instead, taken up with the happy success at Ghent and Bruges, Vendôme was intent on holding on to these gains while making sure of his lines of communication with France. It was now Marlborough who was driving the campaign forward. By perverse coincidence, the French commander felt quite secure, while the Duke was still anxious for the safety both of Brussels and Oudenarde.

Cadogan's fast pace had the desired effect, and by break of day on 10 July he stood in the streets of Lessines – his troops had secured the Dender crossings, having covered 30 miles in less than thirty-six hours. French cavalry were soon spotted approaching from the north-west, but these troopers drew off on seeing that the Allied soldiers were already across the river. Although Marlborough had further to march than the French, the admirable pace set by his advanced guard had told, and Vendôme had lost the line of the Dender. The French commander was understandably furious; his first thought was to close with Cadogan and attack him straight away, before Marlborough's main army could come up. Such a bold course of action had a good chance of success, but Burgundy thought it too risky and would not agree. Frustrated, and aware that he had been foiled by his opponent, Vendôme began to march his army to the crossings over the Scheldt at Gavre, a few miles downstream from Oudenarde. Once safely across that river, he could select a good defensive position, probably on the nearby high ground at Huyshe, and await Marlborough's next moves with confidence. Northern Flanders would be covered, while Vendôme could use the obstacle of the wide marshy Scheldt to cover a move to both attack Allied-held Menin and secure his lines of supply and communication – it was no longer practical to attempt anything serious against Oudenarde, with the Allied army so close. So, for all Marlborough's bold advance, Vendôme was still in a sound position, able to manoeuvre to cover the crossings of the Scheldt, as long as he remained alert.

Marlborough was with the main body of his army on the road to Lessines, and received confirmation that the French had started to invest Oudenarde. This now caused little concern – it was also confirmed that Chanclos had got reinforcements into the town (Prendergast's infantry and Waleff's dragoons) and he was tough and dependable. In any case, Vendôme had lost the protecting line of the Dender river, and no serious siege of Oudenarde could be carried out now. The Duke wrote from Lessines, 'I should think myself happy, since I am got into this camp, if they continue with their resolution of carrying on that siege.' The continued French operations against the town would have a beneficial effect for the Allies of keeping the army in that area. Marlborough was now less concerned for the security of Brussels, as Eugene's cavalry had begun to arrive in the city, and the rearguard of the Allied army could start to close up to Lessines.

In the early hours of 11 July 1708, Cadogan was sent forward by Marlborough with his advanced guard along the 15 miles of rough road from Lessines towards the Scheldt and Oudenarde. The Quartermaster-General had with him six British battalions of infantry under Joseph Sabine, four Dutch and two Scots-Dutch battalions commanded by van Plattenberg, and the four battalions of Evans's Prussian brigade. They were accompanied by eight squadrons of Hanoverian dragoons

William, 1st Earl Cadogan. (1665–1726). Marlborough's Quartermaster-General.

141

commanded by Jorgen Rantzau, thirty-two light 'battalion' guns, squads of pioneers and the whole engineer pontoon bridging train of the army loaded on long oxen-carts. In all, Cadogan had only about 10,000 troops in the advanced guard. Marlborough soon followed them, getting the main body of his army on the march at about 8am. The road was poor, but no French patrols or scouts were encountered, and the soldiers made good time. By 10am that fine morning, Cadogan stood on the high ground at Eename, overlooking the Scheldt near to Oudenarde. Glancing to his left, he could see the town was securely held by Chanclos and his small garrison, while beyond the river was the still peaceful, low-lying and intensely cultivated terrain – 'Ground encumbered with hedges and bushes,' according to Christian Davies – cut through by the marshy Norken, Marollebeek and Diepenbeek streams, all bounded by the high ground at Huyshe to the north and the rounded hill known as the Boser Couter to the west. By comparison, 6 miles downstream at Gavre, off to Cadogan's right, the massed columns of the French army could be made out, preparing to cross the river on pontoon bridges; blithely unaware that the Allies were bearing down on them, they were clearly in no real hurry, and had even sent out foragers into the water meadows alongside the Scheldt. Immediately, riders were sent by Cadogan back along the road towards Lessines to find Marlborough and his cavalry escort. If the army moved quickly enough, the Duke could catch the French as they crossed the river, and a general action might be forced on them there and then. Prussian Major-General Dubislaw Natzmer wrote, 'We received the cheerful news that Cadogan had thrown bridges over the Scheldt at Eename, near Oudenarde, without any resistance.' A great deal depended on how quickly Marlborough's army could get to the Scheldt crossings, but at the very least Vendôme's rearguard should be caught and engaged.

Without delay, Cadogan set his engineers to bridging the Scheldt with the pontoons, the invaluable 'tin-boats' that had been laboriously dragged along with his advanced guard. This work was completed in admirably short time, so that by midday five bridges were laid and the British and Dutch infantry could begin to cross. Working parties were also sent into Oudenarde to help Chanclos strengthen the two stone bridges in the town and to add two more pontoon bridges, so that they could be of use when the army arrived. During this whole vital period there was no noticeable French interest or interference in the work, and Vendôme and his generals appeared to be quite unaware of the growing threat as they moved in their stately, even leisurely, progress over the Scheldt and on towards the nearby heights of Huyshe. If the presence of Cadogan's engineers at the water's edge near Eename caught their attention at all, it seems that they were mistaken for working parties sent out from the Oudenarde garrison rather than the advanced guard of their opponent's main

Oudenarde. View towards Oudenarde from high ground at Huyshe.

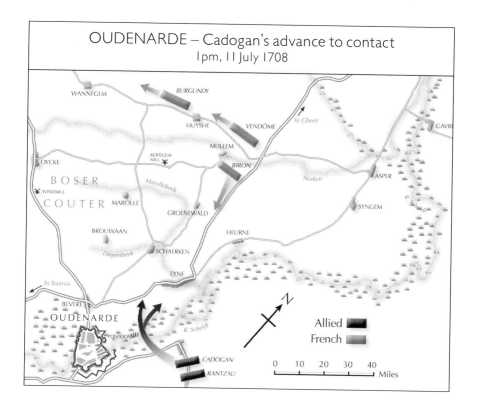

army. With this welcome indifference on the part of his opponents, Cadogan was able to push his infantry out of the constricting bridgehead by about 1pm, beginning to form a line of battle of sorts. The first, most acutely dangerous, phase of the Allied operation had passed safely.

Marlborough and Eugene joined Cadogan at about this time, accompanied by an escort of twenty squadrons of Prussian cavalry commanded by Natzmer. The Duke quickly approved the Quartermaster-General's dispositions, and instructed that the small hamlet of Eyne, just downstream from the pontoon bridges, be occupied and that his infantry should close up to the Diepenbeek stream, which runs to its confluence with the Scheldt nearby, to guard against French interference with the river crossings. They were to occupy 'a marshy piece of ground full of trees and brushwood', as Robert Parker recalled – the first natural line of defence for the bridgehead. Natzmer's Prussian squadrons were posted to watch the road from Lessines in case of any sudden French attempt to intercept the marching columns. The Duke was not overly concerned for the security of the pontoon bridges themselves as they were well guarded by the Prussian infantry of Evans's brigade. Confident that Cadogan had things well in hand at the bridgehead, Marlborough paused to order a battery of guns into place on the left of the incomplete Allied line near to the hamlet of Schaerken, and then rode off with a small escort to scout the high ground of the Boser Couter feature to the north-west of Oudenarde. 'The Duke, on this occasion, having no time to give exact dispositions for attacking the enemy, order'd what was up as they were, to begin the attack, and the rest as they came up to fall in accordingly,' wrote John Millner.

The flank guard for the French army on this march comprised two brigades of Swiss infantry commanded by the Marquis de Biron – seven good-strength battalions from the Gueder, Pfeiffer and Villars Régiments, about 4,000 men in all. He had been entrusted with the seemingly undemanding task of preventing any harassment of the line of march by the garrison in Oudenarde. In support stood twenty squadrons of cavalry, the closest at hand being the Royal La Bretache Régiment, who had been foraging along the Ghent road, but were now resting their horses near to Heurne. Natzmer's leading Hanoverian dragoons began to brush with the French foragers, and shortly before 2pm Biron sent his leading brigade, four battalions under Major-General Pfeiffer, through the marshy water-meadows to take up a position in Eyne. The leading Swiss companies soon encountered large numbers of British and Dutch infantry, who were making their own way forward from the pontoon bridges to the line of the Diepenbeek stream. A fierce close-range musketry battle blew up as Pfeiffer's troops, who had been marching at ease, unaware of the close proximity of superior numbers of their opponents, hurriedly attempted to form a line of battle. 'They cut down a number of trees, and laid them in a manner to prevent our coming at them,' according to Robert Parker. The Swiss were confronted by Plattenberg's Dutch and Scots troops, while Sabine's British battalions, nearer to the Ghent road and going into battle for the first time under the Union flag, threatened to turn their right flank. Casualties mounted, and the Swiss position was soon made completely untenable by the blue-coated Hanoverian dragoons, who had been fanning towards the Ghent road, but were now drawn towards Eyne by the persistent firing. Pfeiffer's outnumbered troops were roughly handled in the sudden fighting and they drew off to try to recover their order, but Rantzau's dragoons were now nipping at their right flank. The Swiss fell back in haste and confusion, looking to rally on the three battalions of Biron's other brigade, which had not yet moved forward and were still in place near to Heurne.

Chased and ridden down by the sword-swinging Hanoverian dragoons, Pfeiffer's men lost all order as they fled across the meadows. Biron, alerted by the musketry, had come

Master-General Joseph Sabine. Commanded British infantry at the crossing of the Scheldt before the Oudenarde battle.

forward from Heurne to find out what was going on, and from a nearby windmill he could see not only the wreckage of Pfeiffer's brigade in their flight, but the evident growing deployment of Allied infantry on the near side of the river. This was plainly not an insignificant affair of skirmishing between outposts, or even a sortie by the garrison of Oudenarde itself to harass the French army while on the march; troops in large numbers – horse, foot and guns – were streaming down from the high ground at Eename towards the river crossings.

Thoroughly alarmed, Biron sent messengers hurrying back to Vendôme, who was at this time enjoying a light lunch at the roadside near to Gavre while his army marched past on its way towards the higher ground. Burgundy and his elegant party of staff officers were nearby but carefully keeping themselves aloof. Vendôme's scornful response to the news of the Allied approach was, 'If they are there, the Devil must have carried them, for such marching is impossible.' However, looking towards the river it was apparent that the clouds of dust boiling above the hills beyond Eename indicated a great force on the march. The French commander's mood cannot have been improved by

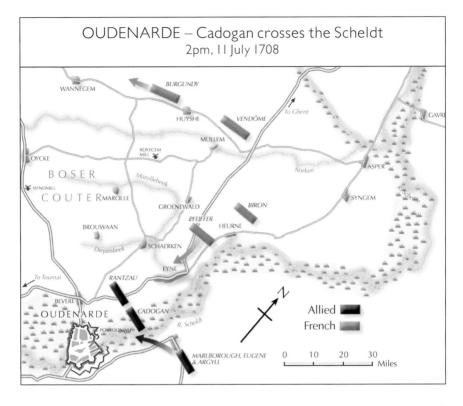

OUDENARDE – Cadogan crosses the Scheldt
2pm, 11 July 1708

the simple knowledge that his opponent had, quite literally, stolen a march on him, and this must have been evident to everyone standing around. The time was about 3pm when Vendôme sent an order to Biron to move forward immediately and hold the flank of the army firm while a proper effort to eliminate the Allied bridgehead was organised; the army commander would summon the nearest cavalry of the right Wing to come to his support once he moved off. Vendôme had been caught off-guard, but he was in no doubt what had to be done. A forthright French attack at this time, sent in overwhelming strength, would almost certainly succeed, wrecking Cadogan's small advanced guard and inflicting a damaging, if limited, defeat on the Allies. However, such a success, though gratifying, would have been relatively minor in the context of the whole campaign – unless, of course, the French commanders really gathered their wits and quickly formed a plan to allow a significant part of Marlborough's army to come across the Scheldt before striking with full might, forcing the Duke to fight a general action with the handicap of a major water obstacle at his back. Given the fractured nature of the command of the French army, such a ploy, however potentially attractive its possibilities, had little chance of being considered.

The Marquis de Biron did not lack initiative or energy by any means; he was a brave and experienced soldier, and had already moved his reserve brigade to support Pfeiffer and restore the situation in Eyne. As the soldiers went forward, the Marquis de Puységur, Vendôme's Chief of Staff, rode up and ordered the advance to halt. The ground ahead, he declared, was too marshy to be practical for cavalry, and Biron's troops would be unsupported as a result. Soon afterwards Marshal Matignon arrived, and he readily agreed with Puységur; Biron was to suspend his advance. The chance to strike swiftly and hard at Cadogan's bridgehead was being carelessly frittered away. An anonymous French dragoon officer who was on the field that day wrote later that:

We let them come over the River quietly, which they would not have ventured to do, had we, in any tolerable Manner, offered to dispute their Passage, but seeing us standing still, they were encouraged to prosecute their Design and began to pass over two Bridges, which they had laid.

As things stood, the French had two perfectly good options open to them, and they were rather better placed than Marlborough and Cadogan. If

Oudenarde. View across the Scheldt to Eyne. Cadogan laid his pontoon bridges in this area.

Vendôme gathered his army in its full strength, and launched a proper attack on the Allied bridgehead, then, given the disparity in numbers at this time, he could hardly have failed. At the very least, Cadogan's advanced guard would have been driven back over the pontoon bridges, with all the chaos and casualties that such a withdrawal under pressure entails. Marlborough's spirited attempt to surprise the French and regain the initiative after the humiliating loss of Ghent and Bruges would have been dealt a really damaging blow. Alternatively, Vendôme could just ignore the Allied bridgehead for the time being, and draw his army up on the heights of Huyshe, occupying a good defensive position from which to defy Marlborough to attack him. Despite the Captain-General's shining successes on other occasions, if he was faced with so adept an opponent as Vendôme, who had superior numbers to deploy, the result of such an attack would be no foregone conclusion. In the event, through mismanagement the French adopted neither of these promising courses of action, but allowed their opponents to continue to dictate the course of events.

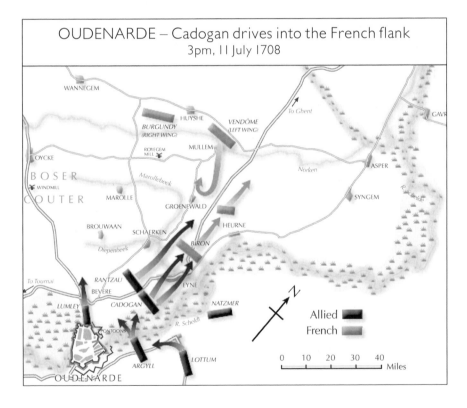

OUDENARDE – Cadogan drives into the French flank
3pm, 11 July 1708

148

More battalions of Allied infantry were now coming along the road from Eename down to the pontoon bridges; Evans's Prussians were released by Cadogan from their watch on the crossings, and were sent across the Ghent road towards the small hamlet of Groenewald (Craenevelt Farm) near to the Marollebeeck stream. Once they were in position there, the rather exposed left flank of the Allied bridgehead would be more secure. In the meantime, Rantzau could not restrain the high spirits of his dragoons after they dispersed Pfeiffer's Swiss infantry; the men charged headlong down the line of the Ghent road, and went at full gallop into the ranks of the Royal La Bretache Régiment, dispersing them, taking the standard and killing their colonel. The Hanoverians now went on too far and became embroiled in an unequal contest with the cavalry of the French right Wing, which formed the rearguard of the marching army and were now being deployed across the Norken stream to meet the growing threat to this flank. The Electoral Prince of Hanover (one day to be George II of Great Britain) was engaged in the mêlée and fell from his injured horse – had his squadron commander, Colonel Losecke, not helped him into his own saddle, the young prince would have been cut down by the encircling French horsemen. The dragoons were badly mauled in their withdrawal and gratefully found shelter with Sabine's British infantry with trophies and prisoners, but in very much reduced numbers. 'A noble action it was,' wrote John Deane. 'The Prince of Hanover in this action behaved himself with undaunted courage, exposing himself in the thickest of the fire.' The Earl of Stair, who was in the area with a party of quartermasters, rather prematurely looking for a good camp ground for the night, was unable to resist the chance to get into some fighting. He took his small force forward to assist Rantzau's dragoons in their scrambled withdrawal.

Vendôme now found that Biron was not pressing forward with his attack on Eyne at all. Not able to refute Puységur's confident assertion that the ground ahead was too wet for effective mounted action, Vendôme curtly counter-manded his order to advance and, leaving the cavalry of the right Wing where they stood, set off to find Burgundy, presumably to try to coordinate some kind of proper attack on the Allied bridgehead. Little further thought seems to have been given to Biron and what remained of his Swiss detachment, as the escalating battle roared away to the west. The Marquis was eventually taken prisoner, along with almost all of his surviving soldiers. The anonymous French dragoon officer wrote, 'The Regiments of Pfeiffer and Villars are quite ruined, and almost all their officers are taken, with all their baggage.'

Meanwhile, Burgundy had been steadily moving with the infantry of the right Wing of the army to take up a defensive position behind the Norken stream. He was diverted from this prudent course by the impudent way in which Rantzau's dragoons drove through the Royal la Bretache Régiment, and he took it upon himself to send forward six battalions of infantry to occupy the hamlet of Groenewald, which sat on the left of the lengthening, but still far from complete, Allied line of battle. This was a very useful move potentially, for, if the place could be held in force, it would seriously impede Cadogan's efforts to expand his bridgehead. However, as the French infantry, led by the Gardes Français and the Régiments du Roi and Royal Roussillon, came on at about 4pm (in column due to the close nature of the heavily cultivated orchards and gardens along the Ghent road) they ran straight into the four Prussian infantry battalions that Evans was leading forward from the pontoon bridges to occupy the very same hamlet.

By chance, the Prussians were first on the ground and two of their battalions had already shaken out into line, so that their fire was immeasurably more effective in the opening exchanges than that of their more numerous opponents. The Duc de St Simon described the tactical handicap suffered by the French infantry at this stage of the battle:

As soon as they arrived, they threw themselves among the hedges, nearly all in column. The columns that arrived from time to time to the relief of these were as out of breath as the others, and were at once strongly attacked by the enemy, who, being extended in lines and in good order, knew well how to profit by our disorder.

The heads of the French columns were swept away in the ferocious Prussian musketry fire, and confusion rapidly set in as the junior commanders desperately tried to form their men into some kind of line. The Colonel of the Royal Roussillon Régiment, the Marquis de Ximenes, was among those killed. The attempt to fight back was in vain: the French soldiers were at a terrible practical disadvantage, too close to the Prussians to manoeuvre properly, and they soon fell back in confusion towards the more open ground where they could rally and try to recover their formation. Burgundy had intended that the infantry would have cavalry support, but for obscure reasons he did not ensure that they moved forward at this point. However, the disorderly withdrawal of the French infantry was seen by Vendôme, who had yet to confer with Burgundy on what was the best course of action. Infuriated at the repulse, he quickly rode forward to take charge of the attack on Cadogan's flank, and immediately ordered twelve more battalions of infantry of the right Wing into a renewed assault as the pace of battle escalated. The French commander then summoned twelve more battalions forward to add their weight to the effort.

Faced with such heavy numbers, the staunch Prussian infantry fell back to cover the inn at Schaerken on the Diepenbeek stream. Cadogan was, as usual, well forward. He could plainly see that Evans's troops would not hold their ground for long, and that the left flank of his still-to-be-established line of

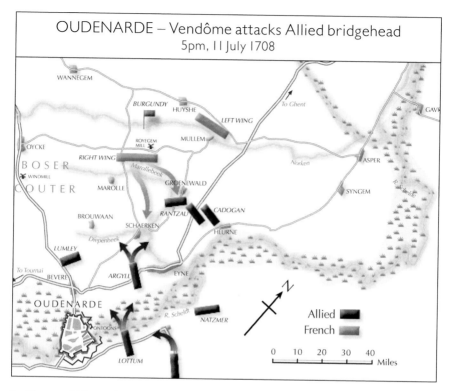

OUDENARDE – Vendôme attacks Allied bridgehead
5pm, 11 July 1708

battle would be vulnerable and 'in the air'. Leaving Rantzau's rather battered dragoon squadrons to watch the Ghent road, he began to edge Sabine's British and Plattenberg's Dutch troops to their left, and this enabled the renewed French attack on Groenewald and Schaerken to be held, for the time being. Still, sixteen Allied infantry battalions, weary from their forced march, were confronted by thirty relatively fresh French battalions. Vendôme's superior numbers soon began to tell in the smoke-filled lanes and orchards, and the moment was one of great danger for Marlborough, but the French attacks, while valiant, were poorly coordinated. Instead of overlapping the shorter Allied line, the regimental commanders allowed themselves to be drawn into the brawling battles around Groenewald and Schaerken. Meanwhile, crucially for Marlborough, his main force, covered in the dust of the road, was now beginning to arrive on the field.

'Red John' Campbell, 2nd Duke of Argyll, had now come galloping across the pontoon bridges at the head of the first of twenty more battalions of German and British infantry, hot and sweating from the line of march.

John Campbell, 2nd Duke of Argyll, 1st Duke of Greenwich (1678–1743)

The Duke of Argyll, whose grandfather, the 9th Earl, had been executed by James II on account of his rebellion for his Protestant faith, was commonly known as 'Red John' among the troops. John Campbell was an experienced soldier, having served, as Lord Lorne, in Flanders during the Williamite wars of the 1690s. At the siege of Venlo in 1702 he fought as a volunteer under 'Salamander' Cutts in the storming of the citadel, and he commanded a brigade of Scots infantry, employed in the Dutch service, during the attack on Ramillies in 1706. Although he served under Marlborough during many campaigns, and distinguished himself with his bravery, Argyll in time became an ardent critic of the Captain-General, scorning his methods and questioning his motives. He was active in stirring up trouble for the Duke in London.

In the latter stages of the Allied campaigns in Spain, Argyll was sent to command the British troops, and was appalled at the corruption and inefficiency, most notably under Queen Anne's allies, that he found there. The soldiers were many months in arrears of pay, and Argyll had to use his own credit to see that they got enough money to avert a mutiny. The task he was given at this time was, in fact, impossible, but he acquitted himself well in the circumstances.

Argyll was also a noted and astute politician, and he played an important role in the negotiations that led to the Union of England and Scotland in 1707. His antagonism towards Marlborough was shared by many, politicians and senior officers alike, as the war for Spain dragged on, but was remarkably ill-judged for such an otherwise shrewd man. His conduct was not forgotten by the Duke: during the 1715 Jacobite Rebellion, Marlborough (now reinstated by George I as Captain-General) had Argyll removed from the command of the government troops in Scotland on the rather thin grounds that he was not energetic enough, replacing him with his own good friends, first William Cadogan and then Joseph Sabine.

He hurried these troops into position on the left of Cadogan's line, which was increasingly threatened with envelopment by the more numerous French infantry. By about 4.30pm, the Allied battle-line was fanning out westwards along the Diepenbeek stream, beginning to overlap the advancing French infantry as they were sent in once again by Vendôme. Concerned at the security of their right flank, the French began to draw back, but the army commander was at hand, calling forward more and more battalions from the right Wing, loudly shouting directions and encouragement, showing the officers where to place their men in the increasingly confused musketry battle in and around the constricted lanes and hedges alongside the Diepenbeek and Marollebeek streams. Before long, thirty-six Allied infantry battalions were locked into hand-to-hand fighting with fifty French battalions, and were having a tough time holding their ground. Despite this, the French army was stumbling into an unplanned, untidy battle, for which they had not prepared. This kind of action, however, was just what Marlborough and Eugene had sought. The Allied commanders were driving ruthlessly, even recklessly, forward while the French were fumbling – Colonel de la Colonie wrote with simple understatement of the truth, 'As the time of day was somewhat advanced, it was possible, had it been wished, to have avoided giving battle.' Either way, the French commanders could still choose to draw off relatively unscathed, with Marlborough's punch meeting only thin air, or they could thrust forward with an all-out attack to drive the Allied advanced guard into the waters of the Scheldt. As the evening came on, it was unthinkable that they would do neither.

My Lord Duke Shone in the Battle

As the infantry fighting escalated along the gardens and streams outside Oudenarde, the Duke of Burgundy took up position with his lordly entourage beside the windmill at Royegem. The time was shortly after 5pm, and from the high ground there he could not really see what was going on in the enclosed country that lay between the heights and the low-lying ground along the Marollebeek and Diepenbeek streams. Furthermore, no one seems to have thought to place any scouts on the Boser Couter, the high feature off to the west, much of which was in dead ground to the French, and therefore potentially very dangerous. The powerful left Wing of their army still stood awaiting orders behind the Norken stream on the track that runs from the river crossings at Gavre up to the Ghent road and on to the higher ground. Meanwhile, the infantry of the right Wing had been allowed to drift into a brawling and confused battle for which they had neither planned nor prepared.

Much of the Allied army was still hurrying along the road leading from Lessines. Marlborough was nowhere near to deploying his full strength, and this, to a degree, counterbalanced the careless French failure so far to use their left Wing. Field deputy Sicco van Goslinga remembered, 'It was no longer a march, but a run.' Infantry and dragoons who had been detailed to watch over the baggage trains and officers' coaches abandoned this mundane task, tipping the vehicles off the road to clear the way, and were soon hurrying along to the beckoning sound of the guns. Count Lottum's twenty Prussian and Hanoverian battalions were now trotting over the pontoon bridges over the Scheldt to move into place in support of Argyll. They extended the Allied line of battle left towards the ruined Brouwaan chateau while thrusting the French back from the inn at Schaerken, which had been set alight. Marlborough's plan to confront the French army and force an open battle was coming to fruition, but the eventual outcome of the day was as yet undecided. The tactical handling of the troops on the ground, with no comfortingly neat, formally drawn lines of battle, would be critical. The French still had a good opportunity to mass their forces properly and crush the outnumbered Allied advanced guard, who were precariously fighting with a major water obstacle immediately at their back. If attacked with enough force, they would surely still be driven to destruction in the Scheldt. This, of course, would take proper coordination and cooperation between Vendôme and Burgundy, and these qualities were sadly lacking. In addition, the time available to them was critically short. In the event, it did not happen – the army commander had lost control of himself and was on foot, fighting like any junior infantry officer beside the Diepenbeek, shouting orders and oaths and thrusting soldiers into place, while Burgundy and his deferential aides remained on the higher ground at Royegem, and appeared not to know what to do for the best.

For Marlborough, this continuing French indecision was an unexpected and very welcome gift, repaying in full measure the risk he had audaciously taken. He rode to oversee the critical infantry fighting as it spread towards Brouwaan chateau on the left of Lottum's line. The Prussian Brigadier-General Grumbkow wrote, 'My Lord Duke shone in the battle, giving his orders with the greatest sang-froid, and exposing his person to danger like the commonest soldier.' Henry Lumley's seventeen squadrons of British cavalry and dragoons were now in place at the small hamlets of Bevere and Mooregem, watching the potentially vulnerable left flank of the expanding bridgehead and guarding the exits from Oudenarde town itself. The Duke asked Prince Eugene to take command on the right of his line; here, the Hanoverian dragoons had been joined by Dubislaw Natzmer's twenty Prussian squadrons, who were no longer needed to guard the road from Lessines. These provided some measure of security, but the massed ranks of the French left Wing, dimly visible across the Norken stream, might at any time stir themselves and sweep down along the line of the river past Heurne to roll up the slowly strengthening Allied army from one end to the other. Cadogan's British and Dutch infantry had been drawn into the fighting alongside the Prussians for possession of Groenewald and nearby Herlegem, but the focus of the battle continued to stretch out westwards towards Brouwaan, where the opposing battle lines lengthened as the evening came on. Marlborough had little choice but to reinforce his left to prevent the French from turning that flank with their heavy attacks, but as he did so, the right flank of his army remained exposed. The Duke was however, at about 6pm, able to send Lumley's horsemen across to Eugene on the right flank to bolster the squadrons of Natzmer and Rantzau, as Overkirk's Dutch and Danish corps were at last now pouring through the streets of Oudenarde and out towards Bevere to take up a position on the rounded mass of the Boser Couter hill.

The Allied line of battle, swaying backwards under pressure from a third set of attacks by Vendôme's infantry, was now reinforced by eighteen fresh battalions, Hessians and Hanoverians, which came doubling over the pontoon bridges and were directed by Marlborough straight into position along the Diepenbeek stream. This allowed Lottum's weary soldiers to pull back a short way, recover their dressing and be resupplied with ammunition before turning to their right and marching along behind the Allied line to reinforce the still exposed right flank of the army. The move took about thirty minutes to accomplish, and so deftly was the switch made in the smoke and noise of battle that Vendôme, on the far side of the stream, was not to know that it ever took place. He was soon made painfully aware, though, of the renewed pressure on

Oudenarde. Looking towards Oudenarde from the Boser Couter hill. The low-lying ground over which the infantry battle was fought.

his own flank in the area of Groenewald and Herlegem to his left, a pressure exerted by the sudden arrival of Lottum's infantry. The French troops had driven in the Allied line of battle there, but now they were having to give ground slowly in the face of superior numbers as their opponents' strength grew. Vendôme was bewildered by the constant pace of battle on his right between Schaerken and Brouwaan, while simultaneously, the troops on his left at Groenewald and Herlegem came under this fresh pressure.

Vendôme, holding his troops to their task with grim determination, sent one of his aides, a Captain Jenet, to find Burgundy with a demand that the rest of the army hurry forward from the approaches to the heights of Huyshe and into action. With his own, intuitively aggressive nature, he would have assumed that this reinforcement, the need for which was so obvious, was already on its way. The young prince had, it is true, already instructed the Marquis de Grimaldi to advance with the cavalry of the left Wing to support the infantry attacks and threaten the Allied right flank. Grimaldi responded readily enough, but the leading squadrons, under command of Colonel Cisterne, soon trod marshy water along the margins of the Norken and Marollebeek streams, and they halted. The earlier warnings about the impassibility of the ground for cavalry seemed to be correct, and Grimaldi (who on other occasions proved to be a very sturdy fighter) rather feebly called off the advance. The Marquis de Capistron commented, 'Some officers

insinuating *mal a propos* to the Duc de Bourgogne, that there was a quagmire, and an impracticable Morass; whereas the Duc de Vendôme and the Comte d'Evreux had passed over an hour before.' Vendôme was, in effect, left to fight on alone with the embattled infantry of the right Wing of the army, although he would never be told this as Captain Jenet, who was entrusted with the important message, was killed on the way back to the Diepenbeek stream.

The evening was coming on, heavy with drizzle and mist after the oppressive heat of the day, and visibility across the battlefield, so important for good decision-making, was increasingly difficult. Even so, Burgundy and his party, which included many experienced officers perfectly able to give good advice had they

Louis, Duke of Burgundy (Bourgogne). Nominal commander of the French army at Oudenarde.

wished, really should have got forward to a position where they could see what was going on. The view they had from the windmill simply did not reach down into the dead ground in the gardens and along the streams; perversely, though, they could see perfectly clearly the well-ordered lines of Allied cavalry under Lumley, Rantzau and Natzmer, massed along the Ghent road on the Allied right. This sight impressed Burgundy with the strength of his opponents there, and as much as anything else it may have fixed in his mind the need to keep the left Wing of the French army concentrated and ready to counter any move by these squadrons. Yet, at heart the young man knew that he was wrong and was heard to mutter, 'What will M. de Vendôme say, when he learns that, instead of attacking, I entrenched myself?'

Marlborough had directed Overkirk with his Dutch and Danish troops to move out from Oudenarde, over the Boser Couter hill, concealed from view by the French. By his doing so, Vendôme's flank would be completely turned and the right Wing of the French army facing encirclement. If time allowed,

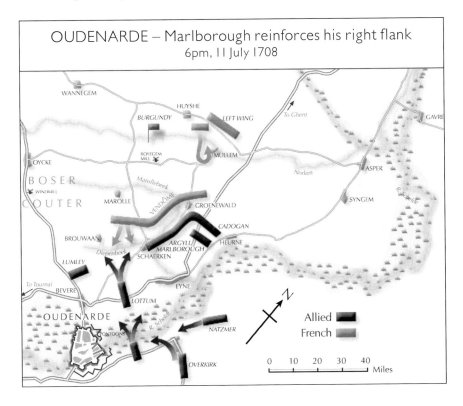

Overkirk might, perhaps, reach out far enough onto the high ground to cut across the very road by which the French would, if necessary, have to make any withdrawal. Frustratingly, the usually reliable Veldt-Marshal was slower than expected in getting into place, partly because his 20,000 troops had to share the road through the town itself with a British infantry brigade (the 1st English Foot Guards and the newly arrived 2nd English Foot Guards, the Coldstream) who were struggling to get into position near the Brouwaan chateau. Also, one of the pontoon bridges hastily erected in the town earlier in the day gave way under the weight of the marching soldiers; congestion and delay in the town's Ghent Gate resulted despite everyone's best intentions, and it was about 7pm before Overkirk's corps began to get into place, a full hour later than Marlborough had expected. On the way the Veldt-Marshal detached eight Dutch infantry battalions under Major-General Week to support the Allied infantry fighting their desperate battle with the French around Brouwaan. Week's troops joined the Hessian and Hanoverian infantry near the chateau to drive the French back from the Diepenbeek in the increasingly hard fighting. Richard Kane remembered,'Their Infantry that defended the Marshy Ground behaved very gallantly, insomuch that our Foot could not force them.' While the pounding infantry battle roared on beside the streams with unflagging violence, Count Tilly, the Dutch cavalry commander, had particular trouble getting his twelve Danish squadrons through a copse of trees on the blind side of the hill. This further delay was very unhelpful, and it took a British cavalry officer, who had scouted the area with Marlborough earlier in the afternoon, to show them the path.

During this tense period, the whole Allied line of battle along the Diepenbeek and Marollebeek gamely strove to hold back the repeated attacks of Vendôme's infantry. The close country that so hampered the French commanders in assessing the situation and arranging their dispositions with anything resembling competent skill, tactically suited the highly professional French infantrymen very well, and they pressed forward their attacks with great gallantry to recover lost ground. The simple, highly concentrated thrusting forward of the infantry of the French right Wing neatly fixed them tightly in position along the two streams, ready for Overkirk's stroke against their unguarded flank. The left Wing of the French army, standing unemployed on the track leading from Gavre to Huyshe, now had insufficient time, even if the vital order had been given, to move forward in strength and have any real impact into the battle. The moment to use them properly had passed by, and they were now no more than simple spectators of the catastrophe overtaking their comrades.

The arrival of Lottum's infantry and then Lumley's cavalry on the right of the Allied line had significantly strengthened the position against any belated

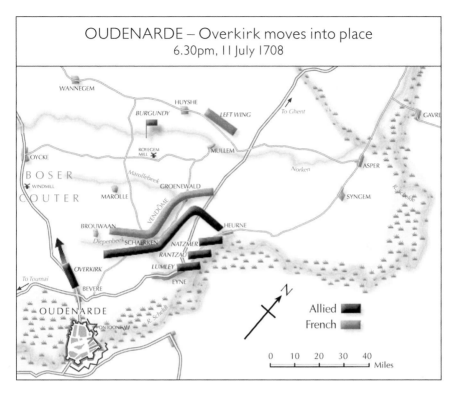

OUDENARDE – Overkirk moves into place
6.30pm, 11 July 1708

interference from the French left Wing. Prince Eugene was in command there, and was typically impatient to move the pace of the battle from defence to attack. At 7pm, Natzmer's Prussian squadrons were sent on a raid against the left of the French position near to Herlegem, Cadogan's infantry opening their ranks briefly to allow the horsemen through. This dashing effort, which plainly demonstrated how wrong the senior French officers were when they claimed that the ground in that area was unsuited to cavalry action, broke through two French infantry battalions and overran a battery. Burgundy's attention was caught by the sudden exploit and, as was probably intended, diverted from Overkirk's move across the Boser Couter at the other end of the line. He promptly sent in a strong counter-attack by the Maison du Roi cavalry of the left Wing. These fine horsemen, 'rich in scarlet with silver facings', impatient from the inaction of the afternoon and evening, came cantering forward promptly. Natzmer's troopers found themselves outnumbered and threatened with encirclement – canister raked the horsemen and every hedge flamed and spat with musket-fire at close range. The charging Prussians came to an abrupt halt, then turned about and rode hard for the protection of Lumley's British squadrons, who moved forward to cover the withdrawal. Natzmer's squadrons took heavy casualties before they got away; he was cut about the head, and only escaped with his life by desperately leaping his horse over a water-filled ditch. The gentleman troopers of the Maison du Roi did not pursue very far, daunted by the steady ranks of Lumley's still fresh British cavalry who awaited them alongside the Ghent road.

Overkirk's corps, nominally under the command of John Friso, the youthful Prince of Orange, were at last in place on the Boser Couter, staring at the raw, exposed flank of Vendôme's line of battle in the low-lying ground before them. The delay in this deployment was understandable, but the Allied infantry had been tested in the meantime, and this strike against the flank of the French army was late in coming. Count Tilly's Danish cavalry were supported by sixteen Dutch infantry battalions commanded by the Swede Count Oxenstiern. Their deployment had not been seen by Burgundy and his staff; the approach had been on the blind side of the hill, and in the poor light of a wet evening with the

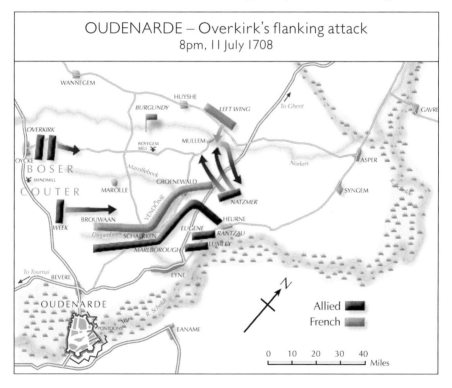

OUDENARDE – Overkirk's flanking attack
8pm, 11 July 1708

drifting smoke of the battlefield, it is not surprising that the movement around the French flank had gone unnoticed. If any of Vendôme's infantry officers had seen the Dutch and Danes on the hill, they had more pressing demands on their immediate attention, as Argyll's infantry, now supported by Week's troops – the Dutch Guards and the Nassau-Woudenberg Regiment – pressed forward across the Diepenbeek stream.

At about 8pm, Overkirk's corps, both horse and foot, received the order, and they poured down the grassy slope in a disciplined and entirely un-expected attack, cutting in cleanly behind the right of the French line of battle. Vendôme's infantrymen were suddenly looking over their right shoulders in alarm. Simultaneously, Cadogan's British, German and Dutch infantry pressed forward past Herlegem and Groenewald at the other end of the line. To the bemusement of the numerous staff officers who clustered at Burgundy's elbow near to the windmill at Royegem, the right Wing of the French army, pressed at every point, was suddenly facing encirclement. As Overkirk's attack came in, Burgundy hurriedly deployed some squadrons of cavalry and dragoons to meet the new threat, but these were dreadfully unprepared to meet the shock of the sudden move, and were of little effect. The Danish horsemen also overthrew several squadrons of the elite French Gens d'Armes in a hectic sword-swinging mêlée, and although Burgundy sent in some companies of grenadiers to their support, these were brushed aside by Oxenstiern's infantry. The anonymous French dragoon officer wrote, 'We were fallen upon by a great number of the enemy's horse, to hinder us from succouring the rest [Vendôme's troops] who were put to the rout.' What passed for command and control in the French army that day just disintegrated. To avoid capture, Burgundy and his party took themselves off towards the Ghent road in the drizzle. As they glanced down at the low-lying ground where Vendôme's infantry were still fighting for their lives, it seemed that the progress of the encircling Allied columns was marked in the darkness like glowing snakes of spitting fire. 'We drove them from ditch to ditch, from hedge to hedge, and from one scrub to another,' remembered John Millner of the Royal Irish Regiment. The Duc de St Simon wrote of the confusion that gripped the French at this point:

The troops of the right gave ground so fast that the valets of the suites of all who accompanied the princes fell back upon them with alarm, a rapidity, and a confusion which swept them along with extreme speed, and much indecency and risk.

Soon, Cadogan's men near to Royegem were exchanging shots in the failing light with the advancing Dutch, as the encircling pincers closed around the French. Marlborough called them to a halt at about 9.30pm. The rain and failing light of nightfall saved the French from a complete disaster. Had Overkirk got into position on the Boser Couter sooner, it seems likely that the whole of the right Wing of the French army would have gone into the bag. Nonetheless, hundreds of Vendôme's soldiers were taken prisoner as their regiments broke up in confusion. Many others managed to slip away into the gloom of the gathering night; they were, in reality, fleeing for their lives, not leaving the battlefield as soldiers. At the other end of the field the left Wing, which had for the most part stood inactive on the track leading from the river crossing at Gavre all afternoon and evening, began to trickle away northwards, their dispirited commanders looking only to find shelter from pursuit behind the protection of the Ghent–Bruges canal.

Vendôme met Burgundy in the rain near to Huyshe at about 10pm, as what was left of their army began to move hurriedly past on the road to Ghent. The veteran general was exhausted, smeared with blood and grime, and not surprisingly was in a foul temper at being left to fight a pitched battle without support. He angrily interrupted the prince's explanation and demanded that

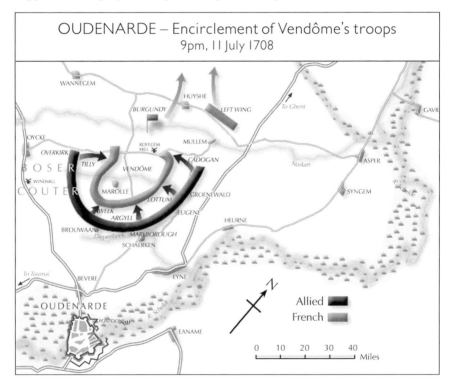

OUDENARDE – Encirclement of Vendôme's troops
9pm, 11 July 1708

Louis-Joseph de Bourbon, Duc de Vendôme (1654–1712)

The grandson of an illegitimate child of King Henry IV of France, Louis-Joseph de Bourbon, Duc de Vendôme was a skilful and energetic military commander, but he was noted for his slovenly personal style and brash contempt for what he regarded as the effete polite world of Louis XIV's court at Versailles. The courtiers, in the main, returned this sentiment, with a lively disdain for his boorish manners. Despite this, the King tolerated Vendôme and his dreadful habits, partly because of his royal lineage, but also because he was a very good soldier, whose many successes undoubtedly outweighed his occasional failures.

Wily and elusive, he foiled Marlborough in 1707, but bungled the battle at Oudenarde the following year.

Vendôme entered the French Army in 1672, and rose steadily in rank, fighting as a Lieutenant-General at Steenkirk (1692). In command of the French forces in Catalonia, he captured Barcelona in 1697. Vendôme fought Prince Eugene at Luzzara in northern Italy in 1702, and at Cassano in 1705.

It was very unfortunate for France that Louis XIV insisted that his eldest grandson, the 26-year-old Duke of Burgundy, accompany the army in Flanders, so that he should become better acquainted with the officers and soldiers on campaign. The young royal prince (who died of measles in 1712) and Vendôme despised each other, and their fractured command of the army contributed greatly to the defeat at Oudenarde. Vendôme's dishonest and misleading account to the King of that battle led to his being replaced as army commander and, temporarily, dismissed from royal service. He was soon reinstated – his military abilities were too great to be squandered – and sent to Spain, where he campaigned very successfully, most notably perhaps at Brihuega in December 1710 when a British detachment under command of Earl James Stanhope was defeated. The following day, at Villaviciosa, Vendôme's army was confronted by

> Imperial Field Marshal Stahremberg and fought to a standstill, although the Frenchman was left in command of the field with his battered force.
> Vendôme died of food poisoning at Vinaroz in Spain, in all likelihood as a result of his sordid personal habits, while still on campaign in June 1712.

the withdrawal of the left Wing and the cavalry of the right Wing, which had hardly been engaged at all, be halted – they should be made ready to stand and resume the battle in the morning. There was a dull, embarrassed silence, with only the Comte d'Evreux speaking in Vendôme's support, as there was evidently a general realisation of the terrible shock to the morale of the army that would result from the grossly mismanaged fighting that day. At last, seeing the way things stood and that he had no support, Vendôme agreed to continue the army's withdrawal, contemptuously remarking to Burgundy, 'And you, Monseigneur, have long desired it.' There was a horrified silence as the insulting accusation attached itself not only to the prince, but to all those staff officers who had clustered deferentially around him all afternoon and evening, and yet had done nothing. Burgundy let the cutting comment pass, and Vendôme scornfully turned his horse and rode off to the north, giving no orders and paying no attention to the success or failure of the army's withdrawal. His example was followed by many of the senior officers. The Marquis du Capistron, Vendôme's private secretary, wrote, 'No sooner had he given the word, for the army to retreat, but all got on horseback, and with astonishing precipitation, fled to Ghent.'

Colonel de la Colonie remembered that his own regiment, the Grenadiers Rouge, did not leave the field until well into the early hours of 12 July, so perhaps the flight northwards of the French army was not quite the haphazard, undignified scramble that is sometimes portrayed. Regimental commanders were in many cases left without proper orders and had to make the best of an appallingly confused situation. A large body of cavalry of the left Wing received no instructions at all, apparently overlooked in the confusion. 'The Chevalier de Rozel,' St Simon wrote, 'Lieutenant-General at the head of one hundred squadrons, received no orders. In the morning he found himself utterly forgotten; he at once commenced his march but to retreat in full daylight was very difficult.' Together with the Marquis de Nangis (who had once enjoyed an interesting liaison with the young Duchess de Bourgogne), de Rozel skilfully brought this immensely valuable body of cavalry away from the track leading from the Gavre river crossing, to the safety of the French camp near Ghent, without being intercepted. Kane's dismissive comment on the French flight was, 'Vendome, with his shatter'd Troops, made the best of his way to Ghent, nor did he think himself Safe till he had got through the Town.'

Marlborough ordered a pursuit of the French, but this could not properly press forward until daybreak, and the night hours were occupied with gathering in as many prisoners as possible in the rain and darkness. 'Had we been so happy,' the Duke wrote, 'as to have had but two more hours of daylight, I believe we should have put an end to the war.' With the dawn, forty squadrons of cavalry and dragoons under Lumley and von Bülow were sent splashing northwards through the mud along the Ghent road to harry the retreating French. They were supported by infantry, but soon ran into a well-posted French rearguard. Due to the narrowness of the road between stretches of rough ground, the Allied horsemen could not deploy properly, and the leading squadrons of Pentz's Hanoverian dragoons had a tough time fighting their way back out of difficulty. John Millner wrote, 'Our whole Army return'd from the Pursuit and pitch'd Camp on the same Ground where we, the Day before, had fought the Battle.'

That same morning, Marlborough rode into the town square in Oudenarde to find thousands of French prisoners gathered there. These men pressed forward in their curiosity to see this outstanding general, whose confidence and daring, which contrasted so starkly with their own commanders' lamentable perform-ance, had brought about their defeat the previous day. The Duke, unperturbed by their attention, calmly acknowledged their salutes by raising his hat and bowing slightly to left and right as he rode through the throng to be received by Brigadier-General Chanclos. Among his first tasks, as always, was to write to Duchess Sarah in London with news of the day's events. Lord Stair, who had enjoyed a busy day's fighting with his party of quartermasters, took the letter:

This being to bring the good news of a battle we had yesterday, in which it pleased God to give as at last the advantage. Our foot on both sides having been engaged has occasioned much blood; but I thank God the English have suffered less than any of the other troops; none of the English horse having been engaged. I do, and you must, give thanks to God for His goodness in protecting and making me the instrument of so much happiness to the Queen and nation, if she will please to make use of it.

This last phrase, implying that Queen Anne was inclined not to appreciate his victories, was very unfortunate. She was undoubtedly tiring of the war, and the comment touched a raw nerve when the Duchess showed her the letter. Great offence was taken as a result: 'I am sure I will never make an ill-use of so great a blessing,' the Queen wrote rather coolly to the Duke. His courteous reply just about smoothed over the Queen's ruffled feelings, but the strains in their friendship were showing ever more clearly.

Vendôme's report of the action was understandably rather more sombre. He wrote to Versailles, 'I cannot comprehend how 50 battalions and 130 squadrons could be satisfied with observing us engaged for six hours and merely look on as though watching the opera.' Undoubtedly he had a point, but Vendôme, not Burgundy, was the army commander and his was the entire responsibility for handling the army in battle; his own gross and intemperate mismanagement on the day could not long be hidden. Veldt-Marshal Overkirk's dispatch to the States-General ran:

> *I give myself, the Honour to congratulate their High Mightinesses upon this important victory. We shall endeavour, all we can, to make our Advantage of it; the Enemy will have much ado to bring their Army into the field again, this Year, in a good Condition. The loss of Slain on their side is very considerable, besides a good number of officers (some of whom of Distinction) and common soldiers, prisoners ... The bravery and wise conduct of the Duke of Marlborough and Prince Eugene cannot be enough commended, nor the zeal and courage of the other generals.*

The disparity in the tally of casualties between the two forces engaged, to say nothing of the shock to the morale of the French soldiers who had been led so ineptly, shows very clearly how great the defeat at Oudenarde was for France. Neither commander had used his whole force that afternoon by any means, Vendôme through a lack of coordination with Burgundy, and Marlborough because a large part of his army was still on the road from Lessines when darkness fell. It seems likely that no more than about 60,000 troops on either side were engaged. The French army had some 5,500 killed and wounded, with another 9,000 unwounded prisoners falling into Allied hands, while over 100 regimental colours and cavalry standards were taken and ten pairs of kettle-drums. The artillery in both armies had been little engaged: there were not many French guns deployed in the close country where Vendôme fought his lonely battle, and few, if any, seem to have been captured by the Allies. Many of the French regiments that managed to get away from the encirclement of their right Wing were dispersed in the confusion and darkness, with their soldiers now virtual fugitives looking only for sanctuary in the nearest French-held town. The sad state of morale among the French soldiers can well be imagined. By stark comparison, the Allied army had 2,972 killed and wounded, and very few prisoners taken. This quite slight loss was soon made good by desertions from the French service, particularly Walloons, Swiss and Germans, in the general dismay at the scale of the defeat beside the Scheldt and the inept handling of the battle by Vendôme and Burgundy. Marlborough's most telling comment on the effects of the day was, 'Our greatest advantage is the terror that is in their army.'

Vendôme drew his battered and dispirited army behind the comforting shelter of the Ghent–Bruges canal. 'The French generals in sullen discontent [one] with another, were gathering the broken remains of their army, and intrenching themselves.' Meanwhile, riding ahead of his troops, Marshal Berwick, with twenty squadrons of cavalry, reached Sart le Bussiere on the Sambre on 12 July and heard the dire news of the defeat at Oudenarde the previous day. He immediately sent his cavalry to Mons to cover that fortress, and directed the rest of his army towards Valenciennes. Little could be done at that moment to interrupt a determined Allied move across the French border, but Berwick began to gather together the fugitives fleeing from the debacle at Oudenarde and to try to adequately garrison the fortresses in the area. He commented in his memoirs:

I found a great number of straggling parties of the army ... Upon a review of them, the whole number at Tournai, Lille and Ypres amounted to upwards of nine thousand men; the enemy had made as many prisoners ... It has always been found that the loss of one battle was followed by the loss of all Flanders, for want of garrisons.

Marlborough held a council of war with his generals in the Governor's palace in Oudenarde on 12 July. The most obvious next course of action was to pursue the French across the water obstacle and try to bring on another general action there. However, such a bridging operation, one that Vendôme would be bound to resist actively, was fraught with potential difficulty. Marlborough wrote, 'If we could get them out of their entrenchments and from behind the canal of Ghent and Bruges, we should best them with half their numbers, especially their foot. This, is one of their reasons for their staying where they are.' The road to the French border, on the other hand, appeared to lie invitingly wide open to the Allied army.

On 13 July 1708, Marlborough sent Count Lottum with a strong force of cavalry and infantry to level the unoccupied French defensive lines between Ypres and the Lys river, and this work was begun two days later: 'We detached M. Lottum with forty squadrons and thirty battalions towards Menin, with orders to pursue this march directly towards the enemy's lines between Warneton and Ypres, and endeavour to force them.' Meanwhile, Marlborough had put forward to his commanders an ambitious plan to advance deep into northern France to the very gates of Paris. Resupply would be by the ships of the Royal Navy cruising in the English Channel, and additional British troops, originally embarked and intended for service in Spain, would be landed on the Normandy coast. The Duke argued the merits of the plan persuasively: 'We are now masters of marching where we please.' However, Prince Eugene, usually the most intrepid and aggressive commander, was not in favour. 'He thinks it impractical till we have Lille,' Marlborough wrote. The Prince was probably right, as the whole project was fraught with potential risk: there was little confidence that the Royal Navy had the capability to sustain properly a major army operating deep in hostile territory with long lines of supply and communication vulnerable to interruption. The Dutch commanders were also against the plan, arguing that the southern border of Holland would be at risk from the attentions of both Vendôme and Berwick once the Allied army marched into France. Disappointed, but not very surprised, Marlborough accepted the opinion of his generals and turned his attention instead to the great French city and fortress of Lille.

Louis XIV learned of the disastrous battle beside the Scheldt on 14 July, and quickly sent the veteran Marshal Boufflers to take command of the garrison in Lille, 'the first and fairest of all his conquests', which would be invested by the Allied army on 13 August. He also sent instructions that the recent French gains in northern Flanders were to be held, and this was astute, because the French hold on Ghent and Bruges denied the Allies the use of the valuable waterways of the region. The big guns of the siege train, and the huge amount of stores and matériel necessary for the Allied army to sustain itself deep in French territory, would have to be dragged laboriously over the rough rutted roads from Brussels. That this would be done with hardly any loss or interference indicates very well the low state of the morale and spirit among the French commanders and their troops at this time. Marlborough's army was almost immediately operating deep inside the French fortress belt, and for a time was exposed to attack from both the flank and the rear. However, on 18 July he could write, 'The Prince of Savoy has been with us nearly a fortnight ... All his troops are on this side of Brussels, where they render us essential service, by keeping the enemy in check while we are so far in advance.'

The digging of the siege trenches before Lille began on 28 August, and the bombardment of the defences, directed at first against the St Mark and St Magdalene gates on the north-eastern side, began five days later, but progress with the siege operations was disappointingly slow. The Allied engineers had underestimated the strength of the defences, the resilience of the garrison under Boufflers's inspiring leadership, and the enormous daily expenditure in shot, powder, siege materials, fodder and food required for the operation. The pace was severe, and Veldt-Marshal Overkirk, whose support was such an asset to Marlborough, died of the strain. A British officer wrote, 'Whatever way we make our approaches, notwithstanding of all our boyous [fascines], blinds and angles, we are always flanked and our men very often kild both with small and cannon shot.' Every ounce of the supplies and munitions for the operations had to be dragged forward over the roads, as Vendôme still controlled the waterways of northern Flanders, preventing their use to ferry provisions to Marlborough's increasingly hungry army. This virtual blockade of the Allied army validated Louis XIV's instructions that Ghent and Bruges were to be held, no matter what.

Vendôme and Burgundy continued to argue or ignore each other as they saw fit, and Berwick soon resigned his command in frustration at the lack of determination and cooperation in the French army in Flanders. Vendôme, having tried but failed to manoeuvre Marlborough away from Lille, posted his army at the crossing points along the Scheldt (at all but Allied-held Oudenarde) and effectively cut off Marlborough's army from resupply from Brussels, Antwerp and southern Holland. Accordingly, the Duke switched his

Wynendael. The Wynendael tapestry at Blenheim Palace. *By kind permission of His Grace The Duke of Marlborough.*

supply route northwards to Ostend, but there was a series of small but bitterly-fought actions as the French garrisons in the area tried to interrupt the daily convoys on which the besieging Allied army depended. The most notable of these took place on 28 September 1708, when Comte de la Motte tried to overwhelm a convoy escorted by a detachment under command of Lieutenant-General Webb, near to the small village of Wynendael. Webb handled the action very well, posting his men in cover and forcing the French to come through a narrow gap in the surrounding woods. De la Motte had to withdraw after some fierce fighting which cost him 3,000 casualties, while Webb's own loss was nearly 1,000 killed and wounded – it was no minor affair. Most importantly, the valuable supply convoy got through safely, but the fact that it provided only enough powder for just two weeks' sustained battery firing at the defences of Lille indicates the laborious operations that had to be undertaken, at great risk and heavy cost, to sustain the army in the siege.

At times, it really seemed that Marlborough's army was likely to starve, and his troubles multiplied when Prince Eugene was shot and wounded while in the trenches. The Duke had, for a time, to command both the siege operations and the movements of the covering army, while worrying about the daily resupply of his troops. That he successfully undertook all these tasks speaks volumes for his skill and energy, and he was able to see, for the first time, the poor state of the equipment and munitions in the siege works and the lack of progress with the operation itself. He wrote to Sidney Godolphin:

Upon the wounding of Prince Eugene, I thought it absolutely necessary to inform myself of everything of the siege; for before I did not meddle in anything but the covering of it. Upon examination I find that the engineers did not deal well with the Prince, for when I told him that there did not remain powder and ball for above four days, he was very much surprised. ... Our circumstances being thus, and the impossibility of getting a convoy from Brussels, obliged me to take the measures for getting some ammunition from Ostend, which we could never have attempted but for the good luck of [having] the eight English battalions there.

Despite all these difficulties, and the constant efforts of the French armies, the siege of Lille progressed and the city was given up on 25 October 1708, when Boufflers withdrew with his garrison into the formidable citadel to continue the struggle.

Vendôme had closed the line of the river Scheldt to interdict the Allied supply movements, but an attempt in November by the Elector of Bavaria to take Brussels failed miserably. Marlborough was able, in a very skilful operation, to force the line of the Scheldt at several points and open the Allied supply routes once more. The French, 'in a Panick, Fear and Distraction, abandon'd their Lines and Entrenchments, the Work of three months past . . . and to their eternal reproach, retired thence in Hurry, Disorder and Confusion,' remembered John Millner. The siege of Lille went on without pause, and Boufflers was forced to submit on 9 December. He was granted good terms, being allowed to withdraw from Lille citadel two days later with his surviving soldiers without giving their parole. Louis XIV wrote to the Marshal with warm congratulations on his achievement in holding out for so long: 'I cannot sufficiently praise your vigour, and the pertinacity of the troops under your command . . . You are to assure them, and the whole of the garrison, that I have every reason to be satisfied with them.' The loss of the fortress was a bitter blow, and its capture a significant military achievement for Marlborough, but the Allied army had been detained in the huge task for four precious months. The French army, so prostrate and humiliated after the debacle at Oudenarde, had obtained a reprieve.

Marlborough now moved rapidly northwards to force the line of the Ghent–Bruges canal and retake the towns of northern Flanders, lost to such dismay in the Allied camp in early July. 'Without them, we can neither be quiet in our winter quarters or open the next campaign with advantage,' the Duke wrote. Ghent was held by a good-sized garrison under Comte de la Motte, but, despite exhortations from Versailles to hold firm, and increasing cold weather which made siege operations a misery for the soldiers, he gave up the town and withdrew with his troops to French-held territory at the close of the year. As Vendôme and the French field army were making no serious effort to interrupt the Allied operations, de la Motte, although heavily criticised, could do little else. Bruges was abandoned at the same time, as was Plas Endael.

The Allied army was at last, after a long and arduous campaign, able to seek shelter in winter quarters. This was just as well, for one of the most bitterly cold winters in memory had settled over much of Europe, a period when 'not a man had a dry thread on his back, which was followed by so severe a frost,' according to Christian Davies. Wine froze in the glass at Versailles, the olive trees died of frost in Avignon, and soldiers dropped dead of the cold on the march. In much of France, ravaged and weakened by years of war, there was starvation, desperation and even riots.

Louis-François, Marshal Boufflers. Conducted epic defence of Lille, August–December 1708.

Part 4

Malplaquet, 11 September 1709

Introduction

After the extraordinary successes for Marlborough's army in 1708, both in the battle at Oudenarde and then at the siege of Lille, the campaigns in the years that followed marked a noticeable decline in the fortunes of the Duke and of the Grand Alliance. Not only was the Duke's power and influence in London waning while, correspondingly, the strength of his opponents there grew, but his health – always a little fragile with frequent dizziness and migraine headaches – continued to deteriorate. At the age of fifty-nine Marlborough was an elderly man by the standards of the day, and the physical and mental demands of almost continual campaigning were severe and unrelenting. Without a doubt, he was beginning to flag, and this can be no surprise. In addition, there was the belief, casually cultivated in the councils of the Alliance in the glorious aftermath of Ramillies, that, after the Duke's resounding victories, the French King had no option but to submit meekly to whatever was now demanded of him. When this delightful notion was proved to be false, bitter resentment was directed at Marlborough, particularly from his critics in London, at what was deemed quite wrongly to be a failure of his making in not producing a neat conclusion to what was rapidly becoming an overly burdensome and expensive war.

Perhaps the most telling factor in the relative decline in the effectiveness of Marlborough's methods lies not in the levels of his own energy, resourcefulness and daring, for these remained impressive, but in the response of his opponents – the French Marshals who faced him on campaign. They were skilled in the arts of war, but had to contend season after season with Marlborough's inventive tactics, quickness of decision-making, and keen appreciation of the relative strengths and weaknesses of position and opposing forces. These men were not fools, nor would they come like lambs to the slaughter. They watched the Duke closely and learned from him – what might have been a shock to the French in 1704, 1706 and 1708 was no real surprise in 1709, 1710 or 1711. This can be seen at all levels, from minor tactics such as the adoption of the flexible platoon firing technique by the French and their allies, in place of the more clumsy firing by rank that had been commonplace in their armies before about 1705; on a wider scale, the French commanders gradually became used to Marlborough's tactical methods – that he would invariably strike hard at each flank, and cause reinforcements to be committed to hold the ground there, then piercing the weakened centre to win the day before the opponent could rebalance his forces. This can be seen clearly at Malplaquet in 1709, where Marshal Villars's tactics, perfectly good given the ground, were designed to hold the flanks firm while catching Marlborough's thrust through the centre in a carefully laid artillery killing zone. Although the Allies were successful on that grim occasion too, the victory was more expensive and heavily qualified than on earlier fields of battle – Villars anticipated rather well what Marlborough would do, with one very significant exception, and prepared accordingly.

The French adapted their tactics in another, more subtle, way. With the sole exception of Malplaquet, when Villars tried to avert an Allied siege of Mons, they did not venture out from formidable lines of defence to challenge Marlborough in the open after Ramillies. At Oudenarde in 1708, of course, the French had not intended to fight at all until Marlborough forced an engagement while they marched comfortably along. Such sheltering behind lines of defence had been the French way before, in 1703 and 1705, while Vendôme had exerted himself rather well to evade the Duke throughout 1707. In the later campaigns, Marshal Villars, an aggressive commander by temperament, also stayed carefully behind his lines. This cannot be regarded as timidity or craven conduct, as his army was severely reduced in numbers and military capability by the dire shortages in France. Louis XIV was aware that there was more than one way to win a war; he was astute enough to see that, in the early years, his armies might triumph in Spain, Italy or southern Germany, while Marlborough was tied down unproductively in the southern Netherlands. In later campaigns, as peace negotiations to bring the tired war to an end rambled on, the French King could play for time – he was well aware of the Duke's failing influence. Marlborough needed a resounding victory in open battle to cow the French, to silence his critics, and to force a peace that would suit the Allies; Louis XIV's generals, on the other hand, simply had to endure, to outlast the Duke's tenure in command of the Allied armies, and to wait for a negotiated settlement to come in time.

The field on which the huge, grinding battle at Malplaquet was fought is, strangely, rather smaller than that of Marlborough's other great victories. It is attractive and relatively little changed by modern development, the woods on either side of the Gap of Aulnois have been rather thinned over the years, but their outline is unmistakeable. It is right on the border between France and Belgium, but the customs post is now abandoned and may be demolished. The wide plain to the south around the small village of Malplaquet, the scene of a huge cavalry battle in 1709, is still open and laid to crops. The battlefield among the woods is an attractive place to visit, and it is not at all difficult to make out how the opposing generals arranged their armies for battle that dangerous autumn day in 1709.

The Infernal Labyrinth

Early in 1709, Louis XIV earnestly sought peace to save his country from what appeared to be certain ruin; negotiations to end the war for Spain had been going on for some years, sometimes with sincerity, sometimes just as a ploy to delay and confuse the other side. Now, it seemed that the Grand Alliance could dictate the terms of the peace to their heart's content. After the disasters to his armies in 1708, surely the French King could do little but accept whatever was put before him. In the end, the peace terms that were laid out gave the Grand Alliance the victory in the war – everything they sought was conceded to them – 'A Good, firm and lasting Peace, Confederacy and perpetual Alliance,' the grandiose Peace Preliminaries rather optimistically trumpeted. The claim of the Duc d'Anjou to the Spanish throne was to be abandoned, and the empire would go almost undivided to the Habsburg claimant; Alsace and the fortresses east of the Rhine would be given up by France, as would Lille, Menin and Mauberge to augment the enlarged Dutch Barrier; the port and fortifications of Dunkirk would be demolished; and Gibraltar, Minorca, Newfoundland and Hudson's Bay would be handed to Great Britain.

There was a deep flaw in all this, and the Allies were too taken up with their own success to realise it; they might have won the war with Louis XIV, but they had manifestly failed to beat his grandson, who had proved to be very popular with the Spanish people in general. The young French prince, who spoke no Spanish at first, had become their King, and he was well aware of their generous affection for him. Philip V could be just as obstinate as his grand-father in Versailles, and would not lightly leave Madrid just so that France could have peace. The military efforts of the Grand Alliance had repeatedly faltered in Spain. They could not remove the French claimant by force of arms, but this glaring lack of success where it mattered most led the Allies into a foolish and arrogant blunder.

A quite unnecessary provision was entered into the peace treaty terms by the Allies at a late stage. It would bind Louis XIV to ensure total compliance and even to use French troops to remove his grandson from the throne in Madrid if Philip V refused to go voluntarily. More than that, a number of other important towns were to be handed over to the Allies as security for Louis XIV's meeting the terms of the peace. Should he fail to ensure that his grandson was removed from Madrid within a strictly limited timescale – only two months – hostilities would resume and, in the meantime, valuable strategic fortresses and territory would have been given up by France. This demand was absurd – Marlborough certainly thought so, at least in retrospect – but given the poor state of the country and his threadbare armies, the King felt he must accept even this humiliation. He underestimated his own people. 'The news,' one of the ladies at the French court wrote, 'fills everyone with indignation', while his own grand council in Versailles reacted angrily to the proposal: 'A French King,' the Dauphin declared, speaking for his own son, 'should make war on his enemies, but may not do so on his grandchildren.' Louis XIV was moved to tears by his son's frank speech and the simple, brave and unqualified support of his advisers. Marshal Villars heard of the terms being demanded and wrote to assure the King that he could rely on the army whatever came. 'The French Ministers absolutely refused an amendment which might, they sayd, possibly engage their master for a condition so un-natural as to make war with his grandson.' The peace treaty terms, apparently agreed but now rejected entirely on that one point, were returned to the astounded Allied plenipotentiaries who had been gleefully awaiting their acceptance. Whether or not it meant disaster, France would fight on. 'Let us show our enemies,' the King wrote to his provincial governors, 'that we are still not sunk so low, but that we can force on them such a peace consistent with our honour.'

Ironically, although few observers seemed to recognise it at the time, Louis XIV would never have had to fulfil the ignoble condition to remove his grandson by force, even if he had ignored the advice of his own council and agreed to it. Once the Dutch were in possession of their considerably enlarged Barrier, they would not go to war again just to put an Austrian prince on the Spanish throne. Francis Hare saw this and was presumably not alone; he wrote, 'A Spanish war may prove very troublesome as well as expensive, and the load will lie entirely upon England, when other Allies have got all they want.' Eminent men on both sides misread the signs at this crucial time, with significant consequences. The Grand Alliance had arrogantly assumed too much, and a stiff price would be paid as a result.

While the ultimately unsuccessful negotiations for peace continued, the preparations for a new campaign lagged, as it was generally thought military action would not have to be undertaken at all. Marlborough was careful to keep his army at short notice to move, but at one point he wrote to the Duchess, 'Everything goes so well here that there is no doubt of its ending in a good peace.' The overall effect of the failure of the negotiations in early June 1709 was that the armies took the field later in the year than would have been usual. Preparations were also hampered by the poor spring weather, coming soon after the very cold winter months, which made the roads unusable in many cases and prevented the armies from easily finding forage for their horses. At this time Marlborough expressed more concern at the inability to feed the army's horses than anything else. The French troops in Flanders were also in a poor state after the terrible campaign of late 1708 and the effects of the cold weather. Vendôme had been replaced and the new commander, Claude-Louis-Hector, Marshal Villars – 'a gallant, enterprising man, intolerably vain and full of himself,' according to Captain Robert Parker – had boundless energy. His irrepressible enthusiasm was infectious. Steadily, the ranks were refilled with recruits – there was hunger in much of France and soldiers must be fed – and the morale of the troops revived. They were heavily outnumbered by the Allied army, though, and Villars was obliged to maintain a largely defensive posture, using the security of a well-prepared defence known as the Lines of La Bassée, behind which he could manoeuvre to foil his opponents.

The successes of the previous year had proved to be something of a mirage for Marlborough. After his extraordinary victory at Oudenarde in July 1708, the French army had been prostrate and dispirited, and he had laid siege to and taken Lille, the second city in France. But that immense effort had eaten up the season of good campaigning weather and beyond. The French army had not only survived, but had regained its self-respect to a degree that, after the defeat in July, had not seemed possible. The Duke's troubles in London continued to mount, partly because of his fiery wife's quarrels with Queen Anne, but also as his political opponents grew in influence and confidence; increasingly they had the ear of the Queen. At a time when it seemed obvious that the war had been won, fewer people were inclined to value the Captain-General and his efforts. Time was not on Marlborough's side. Absolute victory in the field over the French army remained a pressing need; with that every-thing, perhaps, could be put right for the Duke.

'This was a very wet Spring,' Richard Kane wrote, but by mid-June Marlborough's army began to move forward from across the plain of Lille, 110,000 men strong. With a relatively short campaign season ahead, there was little likelihood of success in trying to breach the French lines. Daniel Dopff and William Cadogan carried out their own close reconnaissance of the works that

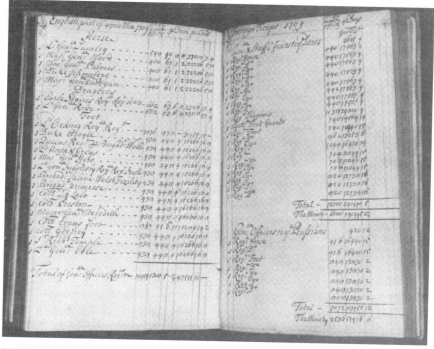

Marlborough's order book for 1709, showing clearly the regimental strengths for the Tournai and Malplaquet campaigns.

ran from St Venant on the Lys river through Béthune to Douai on the Scarpe. They declared any attack likely to fail: 'Prince Eugene, myself and all the generals did not think it adviseable,' Marlborough wrote to his wife. Still, the capture of a major fortress might well force Villars to come out into the open, or the way might be laid bare for an advance into northern France in the following year. Tournai on the Scheldt was the selected objective, relatively isolated between Allied-held Lille and Ath, and the Duke employed a subtle ruse, at first sending Prince Eugene marching towards La Bassée with his Imperial troops. Villars took the bait and reinforced his lines of defence between La Bassée and Douai. He also drew troops out of other places, even including Tournai, to confront the Allied advance. Suddenly, the Prince turned his marching columns aside, and before Villars understood what was happening, Tournai, with its recently reduced garrison, was invested by the Allies on 27 June. To screen these operations, the minor fortresses of St Armand and Mortagne were occupied by the Prince of Orange, although not held permanently as yet. Louis

The siege of Tournai, 1709.

XIV tried to make the best of things, sending congratulations to the Marshal that the Allies had been reduced to merely pursuing a single siege after all their successes of the previous year, but this had a hollow ring, as the French commander had very plainly been tricked about Marlborough's intentions. However, there was a limit to what the French commander could attempt, with fewer than 90,000 troops and struggling to feed even those that he had. 'We must ask you for bread,' one French officer wrote to the Marshal, 'as we need it to live ... we can do without coats and shirts.' In such circumstances, it was no simple matter to mount a vigorous campaign with any real prospect of success away from the protection of his defences.

The French armies might be in a poor state, but they carried by assault an Allied post at Warneton on 4 July, and the siege of Tournai soon proved to be a grim affair. The fortress was well provisioned, 'the strongest and most regularly laid out in the kingdom', and the commander, the Marquis de Surville, was an accomplished and valiant soldier. The 6,000-strong garrison may have lacked the right numbers to hold the place properly, but they put up a tough fight, and the siege operations were prolonged and bloody, with extensive mining and countermining and hand-to-hand fighting in the trenches. 'Not a foot of ground,' a British officer declared, 'that was not undermined.' When the town was given up on 30 July, de Surville withdrew his garrison into the immensely strong citadel, in itself a five-bastion masterpiece of Vauban's school of military engineering. He continued the bitter struggle from there.

Villars was hampered in attempts to lift the siege by his relative lack of numbers, but he did come forward several times to try to interrupt the Allied operations. He could not risk a battle at that point, even though 'The King had sent M. de Villars permission to attack the enemy', and he had to pull back each time without achieving a great deal, apart from harassing some Allied foraging parties. Also, it had to be acknowledged that the French aims in the campaign were to be achieved as much by delay as by saving fortresses dotted here and there. By 5 August, de Surville's troops were reaching the end of their endurance: 'Our men and the enemy frequently met and fought it out with sword and pistol,' Robert Parker wrote. The Marquis obtained permission from Marlborough to send an officer to consult his army commander on the terms he might request for a capitulation. Both the King and Villars preferred to see the Allies tied down to the siege while the season for campaigning sped by, and refused that permission, unless it was as part of a general suspension of hostilities. 'There is still talk of peace being negotiated in secret.' This was not acceptable to Marlborough and Eugene, and de Surville was not prepared to expose his men to a storm and sack. He went ahead and agreed terms to capitulate the citadel on 5 September if Villars had not raised the siege by then. The French army commander would almost certainly do no such thing, and de Surville was, in effect, agreeing to give up the fortress after a decent interval to save appearances. So it proved. Marlborough was willing to avoid unnecessary casualties when he could be sure of having the place within a reasonable time: 'It will save the lives of a great many men, and we can't hope to take it much sooner.' On 3 September, the gate of the citadel was given up as a sign of submission. The garrison marched out two days later and was permitted to go to Condé to await exchange. The cost to Marlborough's army of this limited success was more than 5,000 men killed and wounded, and the campaign season for the year was now well advanced; de Surville had discharged his duty rather well in the 69-day siege at the cost of 3,500 of his own troops killed or wounded.

For some time Marlborough had been looking farther afield to the next steps in the campaign. Villars was fairly well placed to cover fortresses such as Béthune, Arras and Valenciennes, using his strongly constructed lines of defence. By comparison, Ypres to the west and Mons and Condé to the south-east were all exposed to attack. Although the occupation of Ypres might lead the Allies to a campaign against St Omer and the Channel ports, Mons was known to be comparatively poorly garrisoned and was therefore a tempting target. In addition, operations against the place would cover Brabant against the chance of French raids. No less importantly, its capture would give the Dutch the last of the Barrier Towns that they had been promised. Given all this, it is no surprise that Marlborough turned towards Mons and the dark woods at Malplaquet as the arrangements for his troops to occupy the Tournai citadel were concluded.

The Cost is Not to be Considered

On 31 August 1709, as soon as Marlborough knew that Tournai would have to capitulate, he sent Earl Orkney and Major-General van Pallandt, with twenty squadrons of cavalry and dragoons and the grenadier companies of the army, past Mortagne to isolate the small fortress of St Ghislain on the Haine river. This was achieved in the early hours of 3 September, and the Haine was forded near to Obourg late on 5 September by Prince Frederick of Hesse-Cassell (to become King of Sweden one day, by marriage) with a strong force of cavalry. He expected to be attacked by the French at any hour. In the event, a screen of French dragoons pulled back without offering resistance, and the Prince swept around Mons, cutting the garrison off from support from outside. The Chevalier de Luxembourg approached from the south with twenty French cavalry squadrons, but drew off when he found Hesse-Cassell's troops already

moving into place. Luxembourg did, though, manage to slip some reinforcements into Mons while there was time. That same day the main Allied army
was set on the march to combine with their advanced guard, although
Lieutenant-General Henry Withers remained in Tournai with a powerful mixed
force of cavalry and infantry to level the siege works and cover the move of the
army's supply trains from French interference.

It was known that Marshal Villars was moving forward with his army
from the defensive lines, which now extended to Valenciennes on the Escaut
(Scheldt). After the loss of Tournai, Louis XIV had given firm instructions that
Mons was to be saved, whatever the price to be paid. 'The cost,' he wrote,
'is not to be considered.' Accordingly, the French army had been put on the
march towards Quiévrain by 3 September, but the fast marching pace of
Marlborough's advanced guard apparently took Villars by surprise, and he
could not prevent the garrison in St Ghislain from being cut off or Mons from
being invested. Two days later, his cavalry patrols were probing the gaps in the
dense belt of woodland that ran to the south-west of the town. These copses
of the Bois de Bossu, the Bois de Sars and the Bois de Lanières shielded both
armies from easy observation, and provided the commanders with an element

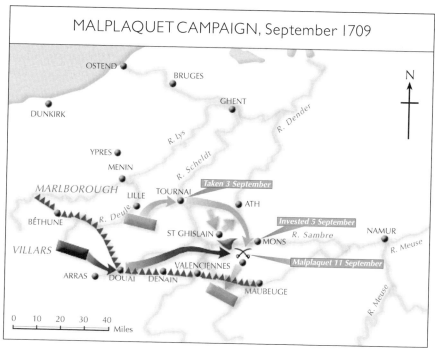

of tactical protection – any move to confront an opponent would entail forcing a way through one gap or the other. On the other hand, both Villars and Marlborough were groping rather blindly for a while, unsure quite what their opponents would do next. However, the French commander knew that a siege of Mons was intended, that much was plain, while the Allied cavalry had captured a French officer, the Marquis de Cheldon, who was inclined to gossip and promptly confirmed that Villars had crossed the Hogenau stream and intended to give battle to save the fortress.

Marlborough began to deploy his Wing of the Allied army on 8 September opposite the small village of Malplaquet near to the Gap of Aulnois, between the Bois de Sars and the Bois de Lanières. Prince Eugene was to cover the Gap of Bossu, about 6 miles to the north, with his Wing. From there he could also keep watch on the French garrison in St Ghislain and provide some element of protection for the supply trains that came lumbering along the rough roads from Tournai. The Duke was unable to concentrate his army fully until he was more sure of French intentions, but the opposing forces were steadily edging towards each other. The Chevalier de Luxembourg came forward with his squadrons to scout the Allied dispositions that afternoon. Villars might well have attempted to force a passage through the woodland belt at any of several convenient points, or try to decoy his opponent in one direction and, having drawn them off, push reinforcements and supplies into Mons. If Marlborough moved to the south too soon, Villars might cross the Haine to the north with the local support of the garrison in St Ghislain and intercept the Allied line of communication with Tournai. For all his apparently healthy superiority in numbers, the Duke might find himself temporarily out of position and off-balance, with his main strength on the left but his opponent trying to turn his right and get between the Allied army and Tournai. In that event, Marlborough's trains would be exposed to French cavalry attack; he would be able to recover his position certainly, but a great deal of damage to the closing weeks of the Allied campaign might have been done by Villars in the meantime.

However, on the morning of 9 September, as the Duke and a small party rode into the Gap of Aulnois to reconnoitre, they could see the French army approaching in full force in four grand columns of march led by the artillery. They were moving between the Rhonelle and Hogneau streams that led north-westwards from the watershed at the Gap of Aulnois. The Marshal was committing to fighting on the plain of Malplaquet, although it seemed for a time that he might pass right through the Gap and try to engage Marlborough's advanced guard before the Duke could be supported by Eugene. This possibility would pose no immediate threat to the Duke; he had no heavy equipment or guns in the immediate area, and could withdraw with his troops northwards to the hamlet of Framieres, concentrating his rather strung-out Wing while

Marshal Villars (1653–1734)

Claude-Louis-Hector, Duc de Villars, Marshal of France, served as a junior officer under the great Marshals Luxembourg and Condé, establishing a good reputation as a dashing, flamboyant and rather headstrong leader. He was employed on diplomatic duties in Germany for ten years following the Treaty of Nijmegen in 1678, and was influential in securing the allegiance of Maximilien-Wittelsbach, the Elector of Bavaria, to French interests. Villars commanded a Bavarian contingent in the campaigns against the Turks in Hungary, and was appointed French ambassador to Vienna in 1699.

Claude-Louis-Hector, Marshal Villars. Gravely wounded at Malplaquet, 1709.

In 1701, Villars served in northern Italy under Marshal Catinat, and with the Elector in Bavaria in the Tyrol in 1702, although the two men very soon found it impossible to work harmoniously together. Made a Marshal of France after a rather spurious victory at Speyerbach (where both armies ran away, but the French rallied and returned to the field with most conviction), Villars efficiently suppressed a revolt in the Cevennes in southern France in 1703–04. He commanded French forces on the Rhine in 1707 and conducted a very effective grand raid into central Germany to divert Allied resources and disrupt their campaign in the southern Netherlands that year. After the defeat at Oudenarde and the loss of Lille in 1708, Villars was appointed to command the French army on France's northern border. His energy and ebullient personality did much to revive French morale. The hard-fought battle at Malplaquet, when the Marshal was gravely wounded, is regarded by some commentators as a rare French victory against the Duke of Marlborough, albeit one that is heavily qualified. Villars proved able to foil his opponent, but could neither outwit nor beat him. In 1712, he did defeat the Dutch under Earl Albemarle at Denain, and recovered much ground that had been lost to Marlborough in the preceding three years of gruelling siege warfare.

> Villars never really recovered from his disabling Malplaquet wound, although his aides on one occasion held him flat to the table while doctors probed in vain to try to extract the fragments of musket-ball in the knee joint. The mangled leg was held in an iron brace to enable him to ride a horse. Despite this disability, the Marshal continued to campaign well into old age.
>
> Villars was appointed Marshal-General of France in 1732, and he commanded the French forces in Italy against the Austrians until his death in Turin on 17 June 1734.

closing the distance with Eugene. Simultaneously, the Marshal would be drawn out into the open to the east of the woods and nearer to the Rhonelle stream, ready for a counterstroke. Villars was not so easily caught, and by that evening it was clear he was entrenching a position in the Gap and in the woods on either side of the opening; if Marlborough was going to fight him, it was going to be at Malplaquet.

Marlborough had the option not to fight a general action at this time. Villars had failed to save Tournai, arguably a more valuable fortress to the French, because he would not risk a battle, so Mons could be expected to fall in much the same way, given time. With his numerically superior army – even after the losses at Tournai some 105,000 Allied troops with 100 guns would confront the weakened French army with only about 85,000 men and 80 guns on the position – the Duke could simply block Villars in the Gap of Aulnois with a strong force, and devote the rest of the army to reducing Mons. This might force the French commander to try to manoeuvre to lift the siege, perhaps swinging to the south towards Mauberge on the Sambre river to turn the left flank of the Allied position. In that eventuality, the chance might offer to bring on a battle in more open country. However, such a passive approach was quite at variance with the Duke's campaign aims, which were not centred at all on seizing fortresses – that was just a means to an end – but on destroying the French field army in battle. The close proximity of his opponents, digging in across the marshy fields between the woods and obviously willing to fight, was irresistible.

The French were busily fortifying their 2-mile-wide position, half the army standing to in case of attack while the others were cutting down trees to build breastworks, emplacing their artillery, and fortifying the farms around the Gap. Colonel de la Colonie wrote, 'As soon as we realised that we were not going to be attacked that day, the whole of the infantry set to work to entrench themselves in the best way possible.' Fields of fire were cleared in the woods, and dense hedges of sharpened stakes and branches, known as *abattis*, were laid across the whole French front – the trunks of the felled trees were roped and chained together to prevent their being easily dragged aside. In the open ground of the Gap of Aulnois nine strong earthen redans were constructed and manned with artillery. Near to the Bleiron Farm, slightly to one side of the Gap, a battery of twenty guns was skilfully sited in a concealing fold in the ground formed by a stream, the Rau de Bleiron. They were to fire across the front of the right flank of the position in the Bois de Lanières. On the left, in the Bois de Sars, three lines of defence were constructed, including a rather odd-shaped position conforming to a corner of the woods that, projecting into the open ground in the centre, would become notoriously known in the testing days to come as 'the Triangle'. In the open ground immediately behind the woods another line of breastworks was begun, although these were not completed before the battle.

The centre of the French position was held by seventeen battalions of the Gardes Français and the Gardes Suisse. Another thirteen battalions, including Colonel de la Colonie's Grenadiers Rouge and the exiled Irish regiments, were in support, linking the nine redans to the Bois de Sars on the left. In those woods were forty infantry battalions, among whom were the Royal La Marine Régiment and the Le Roi and La Reine Régiments, all under the capable command of the Marquis d'Albergotti. The most exposed part at the apex of the Triangle was held by the Régiment de Charost. To the French right, on the other side of the Gap of Aulnois, were thirty-seven battalions commanded by

Malplaquet. The plain of Malplaquet, looking south from the French monument.

the Comte d'Artagnan, including the Régiments de Navarre and Lorraine, the German La Marck Régiment and the Royal Italians, while a small Swiss brigade, the Régiment de May, the Régiment de Brendle and a battalion of the Greder Suisse held the fortified post at the Bleiron Farm. Eight more battalions stood nearby in support.

On the plain of Malplaquet, to the rear of the French line, were 260 rather understrength squadrons of cavalry, about 18,000 strong, commanded by the Marquis de la Vallière – even the elite squadrons of the Maison du Roi cavalry were ill-equipped and poorly mounted. The Marquis de St Hilaire, skilled exponent of aggressive artillery tactics, oversaw the sighting of the batteries, although opportunities for good fields of fire in the copses were understandably rather limited. To cover his frontage in enough strength, Villars was putting everything into the line in a very forward position – apart from the cavalry, there was not a lot in reserve. He did have the option to deploy his army into a defensive position on the plain of Malplaquet, where the lie of the land would serve to shield his dispositions from close observation by his opponents. In the more open ground the cavalry and infantry could perhaps support each other to better effect. However, there was no obvious commanding feature or strong river line on which to anchor his position there, and the woods on either side of the Gap at least provided this support to a limited degree. Given this, and the restrictions that the close country would place on the deployment of the powerful Allied cavalry, Villars accepted the disadvantages of the forward position, with his army exposed both to observation and bombardment.

Marlborough was faced with an obvious dilemma on 9 September. Every hour that he waited gave Villars and his army more time to strengthen what was already a good defensive position. However, it was really not possible to mount an attack immediately, as the ground was unknown to many of the Allied officers, and the artillery of the army had still not all arrived. The terrain in front of the woods, on the left of the French position in particular, was marshy and cut through with small streams, gullies and stagnant pools. 'Since we do not know the ground,' Prince Eugene wrote, 'we dare even less take any risks. The terrain is very uneven.' Getting the guns into position so that they could give the all-important support to an assault would plainly take some time. Marlborough held a council of war on 9 September and all agreed that the attack should wait for the artillery to get into place. This would not be complete the next day, so the effort would have to be made on 11 September. Marlborough was the army commander, his was the responsibility, and the reasons for delay were good, but Villars was allowed time to turn the Gap of Aulnois into something resembling a fortress. The French commander had, however, detached his reserve cavalry – thirty squadrons commanded by the

Chevalier de Luxembourg – southwards to cover Mauberge on the Sambre. In doing so he significantly weakened his ability to strike back at the Allies once the force of their first attack was spent. Why Villars did this remains a mystery, as Mauberge was not under any immediate threat, and if the Duke had reached out his left towards the town, he would have exposed the flank of his own army to French attack.

Marlborough had another good reason for delay. Henry Withers had finished his clearing up operations at Tournai and was now marching with his troops to join the Allied army. This powerful detachment, nineteen infantry battalions and ten squadrons of cavalry (perhaps 11,000 strong), would not arrive until 11 September, and could be let loose upon the flank of the French army after the battle had begun. Villars would probably not anticipate such an ambitious and novel move, quite contrary to the accepted conventions for fighting a battle at the time, and would be caught at a serious disadvantage, thrown off balance when his army was already committed to fighting Marlborough's main force.

The woods on either side of the mile-wide Gap of Aulnois strictly limited the frontage on which an attack could be made, and Marshal Villars's plan

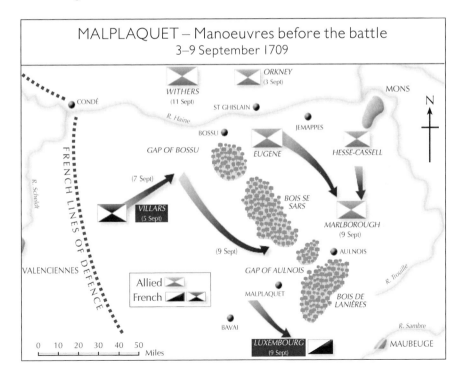

MALPLAQUET – Manoeuvres before the battle
3–9 September 1709

for the coming battle was quite simple. He was inviting the Allied infantry to attack his fortified army while being enfiladed to left and right with artillery fire from the strong French positions in the copses; when the Allies fell back, exhausted from the futile struggle at the barricades, the massed French cavalry would sweep through the centre and drive them in confusion before retiring to the plain of Malplaquet, sheltered by their own infantry and guns from any immediate response by the Allied cavalry. As the attack was renewed, so would the French counter-attack follow, and so it would go on, until Marlborough's army had exhausted itself, broken on the French defences. John Deane of the 1st English Foot Guards described the situation:

> *They had thrown up a breastwork and fasheened it very strong, just leaving passages open between brigade and brigade for the squadrons to march through and fall upon our men as they came up over the moross [marsh] ... Then when they had defeated our men and drove them back again over the moross, then they would retreat back again behind the works, still keeping the mayn body there under cover.*

The numerical advantage enjoyed by Marlborough's fine army would in this way be cancelled out as it dashed itself to pieces on the strong French position. Also, given the crucial part that the artillery would play in such an action, the apparent imbalance of forces (100 guns opposed to 80) was less obviously marked than in respective bayonet strengths.

In the circumstances this aggressive defence was a perfectly valid plan, for the French commander had little choice other than to take a defensive stance from the outset. However, he had limited his capability by letting Luxembourg move to the south with the reserve cavalry. The success of the whole plan depended to a high degree on his generals being able to hold the breastworks at every point along the line, for the whole French position could be turned if either flank gave way, or split apart if the defence of the centre failed. Villars had little in reserve with which to mount a powerful local counter-attack to restore any point of his line that was in peril; his opponents could match him man for man and still have plenty in reserve, when the detached corps under Withers was counted – as yet unknown to the Marshal, Marlborough intended to move these men in against the French flank once battle was begun. Villars's flank on the left, in the Bois de Sars, was 'short' and did not extend very far into the woods. It was, as a result, exposed to just the sort of attack that Marlborough intended Withers should make. The French commander appears to have felt that the woods themselves would provide the necessary measure of protection, inhibiting the easy passage of large numbers of troops through the copses, but this proved to be only partly true.

Marlborough's plan was also simple, and rather in his preferred style. It involved exerting extreme pressure on both of the French flanks to fix their men in place there, and to force Villars to weaken the troops holding the redans in the centre so that his flanks would not give way. When this was achieved, the Allied army would burst through the redans in the open ground of the Gap and their massed cavalry would move on to engage and destroy the French cavalry on the plain of Malplaquet. The left Wing of the army (rather confusingly, this was in place on the right) was commanded by Prince Eugene, and would force its way through the Bois de Sars with sixty-two Imperial, German and British battalions to assault the French defences at the Triangle. Simultaneously, the right Wing (on the left) composed of thirty-one Dutch, Danish and Scots-Dutch battalions under the command of John Friso, Prince of Orange, would attack the French left in the Bois de Lanières and smaller Bois de Thiery near to Bleiron Farm. Orange had the twenty-one Dutch and Saxon cavalry squadrons commanded by the Prince of Hesse-Cassell in support. George Hamilton, Earl Orkney, had command of fifteen British battalions and two Prussian battalions in the centre; Jorgen Rantzau was nearby with a strong Hanoverian brigade of four battalions. Temple's British brigade had been detached to support Lottum's attack on the Bois de Sars. Two great batteries were set up, one of forty guns to engage the French defences in the Gap of Aulnois and the edge of the Bois de Sars, and another of twenty-eight guns to support the Dutch attack on the Bois de Lanières. In reserve, behind the infantry, were the 176 massed squadrons of Allied cavalry, Imperial, Walloons, German, Dutch, British and Danes, all ready to move forward when the way through the French centre was cleared. Henry Withers and his troops were still on the road from Tournai, but he was drawing near and could be let loose at will when he arrived. Plainly, the weight of the Allied attack, both direct and indirect, would fall on the most exposed part of the French position. The woods appeared to offer protection, but in fact they offered none.

It seems that Marlborough's original intention was that Withers's nineteen infantry battalions, and possibly also his cavalry, should pass right around the rear of the Allied army to reinforce

George Hamilton, 1st Earl Orkney. Marlborough's commander of British infantry.

Orange's Dutch corps in the attack on the French right in the Bois de Lanières. The likely delay and difficulty in getting into place in good time, and the tempting opportunity for Withers to fall on the exposed left flank of the French army when it was already engaged in a battle, may have caused the Duke to change his plan. This would go some way to explain the relative lack of numbers that Orange could deploy on the Allied left when compared with Eugene's forces in their own assault on the other flank. But for Withers to have to move right around the rear of the Allied army, with all the wagons, baggage and camp impedimenta in the way, to deploy on the left would inevitably be a lengthy process, and probably mean that his troops would not get into action at all. Instead, he would move in hard against the exposed, unprotected left flank of Villars's army, when it was already engaged with the Allied attack. With this innovation, the fact that Marlborough was employing what might be regarded as his usual tactics (tactics with which the French had become familiar over time) should not matter; it was not unreasonable to believe that this method would prove equally effective at Malplaquet, especially with the added ingredient of Henry Withers' surprise flank attack.

The evening before the battle some Allied officers, recognising acquaintances at the French breastworks across the fields, strolled over to chat with them and an unofficial kind of truce held sway for a while as the soldiers stood up and walked around at their ease. It was even rumoured that the peace negotiations had been resumed and agreement reached, and that no battle would be fought the next day, but this was not so. The French soon noticed that some Allied officers were taking careful note of their arrangements and the truce was brought to an abrupt end. 'Some of them had been busy examining our position and taking sketches of different parts of our entrenchments ... they profited too well by the knowledge thus acquired.' As darkness fell, the woods around the Gap at Aulnois came alive with the mutter of musketry as patrols from the opposing armies reached out cautiously to grapple with one another. Jean-Martin de la Colonie remembered, 'Our patrols, and those of the enemy, kept up a constant fire whenever they came across each other.' That same evening, Colonel Haxhusien's German brigade stormed St Ghislain, taking 200 prisoners and a battery of guns, removing any obstacle to Henry Withers in marching straight onto the battlefield the next day. Veteran campaigner Matthew Bishop wrote with grim humour of the French gunners, who were firing shots to bed their guns into the soft ground around the Gap of Aulnois: 'Hark, don't you hear the singing birds over your head? ... One flew into a man's face not two yards from me, and took his head clean off his shoulders.'

As dawn approached on 11 September 1709, the Allied soldiers were raised from their rough bivouacs, each man was given a tot of rum or Genever gin (the French thought the Allied soldiers were drunk), and they fell into line in the emerging misty light. Squads of volunteers and pioneers equipped with axes and iron-tipped staves, backed by the grenadier companies of the army, crept forward to hack and tear at the dense lines of *abattis* that ran across the front of the French position, clearing lanes for the assault troops to use. At about 7am (accounts of the precise time understandably vary a little) the Allied bombardment began. De la Colonie wrote, 'Next morning at break of day, the battery of thirty cannon [the Allied great battery] opened fire, and by its continuous volleys succeeded in breaching the entrenchments in the woods on our left.'

The Most Obstinate and Bloody Battle

The Allied bombardment was heavy and well directed, and the French breast-works shook and splintered under the weight of shot, the defenders crouching low to avoid the storm of fire. As the morning mist gradually lifted, Prince Eugene's massed German and Imperial infantry, forty battalions commanded by Count Schulemberg and twenty-two battalions under Count Lottum, together with Temple's British brigade moved steadily forward into the Bois de Sars. Earl Orkney, who watched the advance from Marlborough's side at the great battery in the open ground, wrote, 'Really it was a noble sight to see so many units marching over the plain to attack,' but he added, 'It seemed that they must make war on moles this time.' In the woods, movement was found to be relatively easy at first, despite the wet ground, for the French had cleared much of the underbrush to improve their own fields of fire. As Eugene's soldiers clustered to get through the gaps that had been torn in the dense hedges of *abattis*, the French defenders in the first line of breastworks, the battalions of the Régiment de Charost, the Régiment de Provence and the Régiment de Poitou, came to their feet. Steadying their muskets on the parapet of their breastworks, they unleashed a storm of fire at close range – 'only pistol-shot' – into the attackers' bunched ranks. 'It is impossible,' John Millner wrote, 'to express the violence of either side's fire.' Scores of soldiers went down, including many of the regimental officers in the leading units, and those coming on behind tripped and stumbled over the heaps of dead and wounded. Smoke from both artillery and muskets rapidly accumulated, hanging low in the enclosing copses. This certainly impeded visibility for the defenders who were firing blindly into the smoke, but it also seriously hampered both orientation and command and control for Eugene's officers as they tried to encourage their men to move on in some sort of order.

The French artillery was in action now, and Colonel de la Colonie, standing with his veteran grenadiers at one of the redans in the centre of the Gap of

Aulnois, remembered seeing scores of Allied infantry going down with the salvoes: 'The cannon-shot plunged into the enemy's infantry and carried off whole ranks at a time.' The guns were taking some of Lottum's troops in enfilade as they moved to attack the side of the Triangle facing the open ground where the Allied great battery stood. 'I remember when a cannon ball took my shirt sleeve off,' wrote Matthew Bishop. The assault on the Bois de Sars shuddered to a halt, and the troops were soon milling around in confusion in the smoke and noise, while those officers still on their feet tried to get them back into their ranks. It could not be done, and the soldiers began streaming back out of the woods, looking for some open space in which to reform for another effort. Eugene was there, revelling in the anniversary of his victory

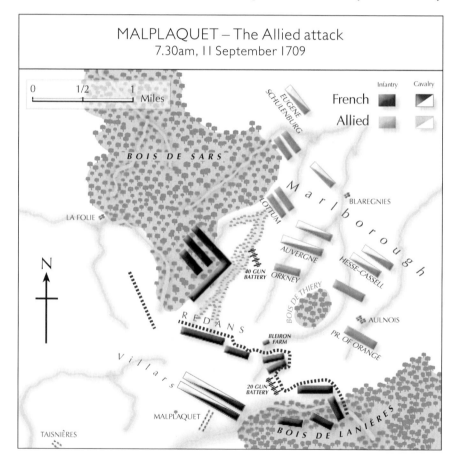

MALPLAQUET – The Allied attack
7.30am, 11 September 1709

over the Turks at Zenta, encouraging the men, and calming the officers with words of praise for their efforts.

The Allied gunners redoubled their efforts and a prominent French battery in the Triangle was completely overwhelmed by the weight of shot. As Eugene's second attack went in, the troops ignored the deadly gaps in the *abattis*, choked already with the shrieking debris of their first attack, and clambered over the obstacles instead, an undoubtedly untidy, but crudely effective, way of getting forward. A small German brigade, drawn away from the troops investing Mons, added their weight to the effort, working their way through the copses on the right of the Allied line. The French fire was still heavy, but noticeably less deadly. Visibility was made worse because the smoke hanging heavily among the trees did not blow away, and the Imperial troops were soon exchanging bayonet thrusts and musket butt blows across the splintered breastworks. The French soldiers in the apex of the Triangle, the Régiment de Charost, found that their flank was turned, and they fell back from their first-line breastworks to the second line deeper in the wood; their commander, Louis-Joseph de Charost, was among those who were shot down before they regained cover. The attackers now had the advantage of using the first-line breastworks, with a convenient parapet on which to steady their muskets, as some element of protection. So hard was the fighting that Count Lottum sent an appeal to Marlborough for more support in the assault on the Triangle. The Duke ordered that a second British brigade, comprising the 2nd English Foot Guards and a battalion of Orkney's Regiment, be detached from the centre to add their weight to the attack in the woods. As these soldiers moved into the shattered tree-line they found French second-line troops hurrying forward to bolster the effort to hold the forward breastworks and, firing low through the smoke, the British stopped the attempt in its tracks.

Steadily, and at great cost, the first line of defences was secured by the Allied infantry. The infuriated troops, without the slightest thought of mercy, bayoneted and clubbed the wounded lying on the ground, and even struck out at the dead as they moved forward to the second obstacle. A French officer wrote, 'Few of those [defenders] that sustained it escaped, for the enemy were too Fierce and Bloodthirsty, that they hack'd in pieces whatever came in their way, and even Dead Bodies when their Fury found no more living.' One of the soldiers in the woods that day with Orkney's Regiment was Donald McBane, a tough member of the grenadier company who, rather strangely, carried his infant son in his knapsack throughout the whole of the fighting. The child was so quiet that McBane thought that he must have been killed by one of the musket balls, French or Allied, that he felt pass through his coat and accoutrements, but by the end of the battle the boy had only suffered a graze to his elbow.

Despite the determination of the French infantry, by about 9am Marshal Villars's grip on the left of his position was being prised loose. He had to send troops from the redans in the centre to add their weight to the effort to hold the Bois de Sars. This was dangerous, unbalancing his carefully laid defensive arrangements, but Villars was faced with hard choices, and he was taking a calculated gamble. If he could build up a good local reserve on the left, a smart counter-attack against Eugene's battered infantry might pay a handsome dividend, restore the French hold on the position, and exert a potent threat to the right flank of the Allied centre, pinning it there, preventing any significant move towards the redans. Orkney, commanding the infantry facing the redans in the centre of the field, was concerned that a brigade had already been taken away at this early stage to reinforce the effort on the right: 'I fronted quite another way [from Eugene] to the high ground where the mouth of the defile was.'

Shortly after Eugene's attacks began on the Bois de Sars, the Prince of Orange's corps moved into their assault in five dense columns of attack on the French right in the Bois de Lanières. 'The woods there were neither as thick nor as high as those on the left,' de la Colonie remembered, 'but as the ground was much more cut up by hedges, it was on this account more advantageous to our troops.' Here d'Artagnan was supported by the veteran Marshal Boufflers, hero of the siege of Lille, who had ridden from Paris to take his part in the battle as a volunteer. Supported by the fire of twenty-eight artillery pieces, Baron Fagel's twenty-two Dutch and eight Swiss battalions, under the

Malplaquet. View from the French monument towards Bois de Thiery and Bois de Lanières. The Prince of Orange's Dutch troops attacked over this ground.

immediate command of Generals Dohna, Vehlen and Spaar, together with seven Danish battalions under van Pallandt, came on in good order, moving around the small Bois de Thiery copse in their approach. Hamilton's Scots-Dutch brigade swung to the left to try to turn the flank of the French position. As the range closed, the attacking troops were struck by a heavy cannonade from the French artillery; it devastated their leading ranks and tumbled the soldiers down in their hundreds. The concealed battery of twenty guns, sited in a slight fold in the ground near to Bleiron Farm and shielded from the attention of the Dutch gunners, did terrible damage: it fired across the front of the French breastworks and shot down the length of the advancing Dutch ranks with the most awful results.

The valour of the Dutch infantry, in the face of such a sudden weight of artillery fire, was impressive, 'Nor were Discharges of Twenty pieces of Cannon, that fired directly at once into their Battalions, able to break them, altho' they carried off whole Ranks.' Quite a number of Orange's soldiers got as far as the breastworks and pushed back the French Grenadiers and the Chateauneuf Régiment a short distance, but those who did so were promptly shot down or bayoneted by the defenders as they scrambled over the obstacle. The valiant Swede Count Oxenstiern was among those killed. As the Dutch infantry ground to a bloody halt, a smart French counter-attack, launched by the veterans of the Navarre Régiment – 'Short men, in rags ... who behaved marvellously well,' de la Colonie remembered – drove them back in disorder towards the Bois de Thiery. The twenty-one Dutch and Saxon cavalry squadrons under command of the Prince of Hesse-Cassell were already moving steadily forward. The French infantry were in some disarray after their vehement charge to clear their breastworks, and they were in no position to challenge the Allied horsemen; they fell back to resume their places at the breastworks and await the next attack. What had, fleetingly, been a chance for a smart French counter-attack on the Dutch came to nothing.

Orange gathered his infantry into formation again in the shelter of the Bois de Thiery, and they went into the attack a second time. The Scots-Dutch brigade on the extreme left – Tullibardine's and Hepburn's Regiments – took advantage of some broken ground to close with the defenders, 'skirmishing pice by pice' through the trees, as one soldier remembered. However, the Marquis of Tullibardine was mortally wounded, shot through the thigh and bleeding to death, and his men were driven back. On the right of the Dutch attack, van Pallandt's Danish troops broke into the fortified Bleiron Farm before being driven out by Christian Birkenfeld's Swiss brigade in a bloody battle at bayonet point around the farmhouse and barns, which changed hands more than once. The Danes were assisted in their attack by two Hanoverian battalions sent by Jorgen Rantzau from the open ground in the Gap, but these troops were also thrown back with heavy losses. Rantzau, quite correctly, refused to commit his other two battalions without specific orders from Marlborough, as his brigade linked the Dutch with Orkney's British and Prussian infantry, and to leave his allotted post might expose the centre of the Allied line to a damaging French attack.

The Dutch infantry struggled forward once again into a storm of canister and musket fire, taking dreadful casualties. The Prince of Orange's horse was killed, but he went ahead on foot, 'exposed to an infernal fire which covered the earth with the dead'. His staff officers were quickly shot down to his left and right as he did so. Baron Spaar was killed, as was Lieutenant-General Week, and the 2nd and 3rd battalions of the Dutch Blue Guards, so cherished

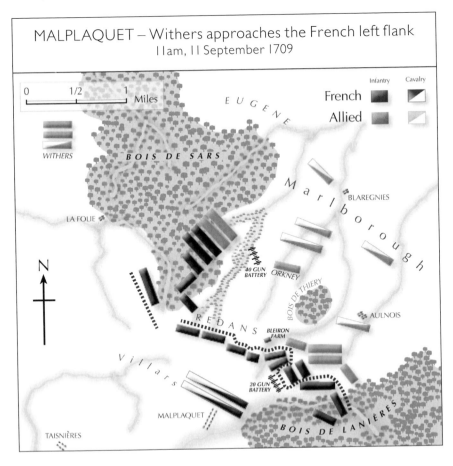

MALPLAQUET – Withers approaches the French left flank
11am, 11 September 1709

by the late King William III, piled their dead up in heaps in front of the French defences. The field deputy Sicco van Goslinga wrote after the battle that this was the most awful sight he had ever seen: 'The ditch was so thick with corpses that no inch could be seen, add to such sights the shrieks and groans of the badly wounded, and one can get some idea of the horror.' A 130-strong company of Huguenot cadets, all sons of émigré noble families, simply ceased to exist after the attack. It was all in vain. The broken Dutch regiments fell away from the murderous French fire to try to recover their order near the Bois de Thiery. Marlborough, whose attention had until then been on the bitter fighting in the Bois de Sars, rode over to speak to Orange after the failure of the second attack. He commended the Prince for the valour of his troops, but instructed him not to make a third attempt for it would plainly be a wasted effort, and the battle had to be won elsewhere. Instead, the Dutch infantry were to reform their line and manoeuvre to keep the French fixed on this flank to prevent them sending troops to other parts of the field. This task Orange performed admirably, restoring his shattered battalions into something approaching good order, but keeping just out of effective artillery range, ready to move forward once again when required.

Malplaquet. Hand to hand fighting in the Bois de Sars.

In the Bois de Sars, meanwhile, Eugene's infantry, led by a brigade of Württemberg Guard Grenadiers, were fighting their way forward one step at a time, clearing the second line of breastworks and driving towards the last line of defences at the rear of the woods. Colonel de la Colonie remembered:

The fighting which now went on in the woods was extremely stubborn and murderous, and victory hung in the balance ... The tangled nature of the ground intersected by woods on which the principal fighting took place had this advantage about it, that it was impossible to spread a panic; each brigade fought as it were independently.

Eugene was struck on the neck by a musket ball, but refused to have the wound dressed, declaring that if he did not survive the day it would not matter, and if he did the wound could be dressed in the evening. Officers of all ranks were prominent in the thickest fighting; John, Duke of Argyll, was hit three times by spent musket balls, and fearing that his men would suspect him of wearing a hidden breastplate under his clothes, stripped off his laced coat and went into the attack again in his waistcoat. 'You see,' Christian Davies heard him shout. 'I have no hidden armour. I am equally exposed with you.' Argyll's own regiment, the Buffs, were undoubtedly in some difficulties and lost their Union (third) Colour to the French in the bitter and confused fighting. Davies then went looking in vain for her husband in the firing line, but was reduced to turning over the heaps of the dead, many being her friends of long campaigns, before she found the body of her man.

Marshal Villars was aware of the growing threat to his left flank, and of necessity had been pulling infantry out of the redans in the centre. The Marquis de Chemerault, commanding the far left-hand redans, had managed to form a force of twelve battalions in this way with which to thrust between Eugene's infantry in the woods and Orkney's British and Prussian troops in the centre. 'I saw that our infantry was losing ground,' Villars remembered, 'and I posted there twelve battalions to receive them.' With so many troops already committed to Eugene's attacks and embroiled with the French in the woods, this move could pose a real threat to the Allied plans. As de Chemerault's infantry moved into position on the edge of the Bois de Sars, however, Marlborough brought forward a strong detachment of Lieutenant-General Auvergne's Dutch cavalry. The Marquis had little option but to halt and prepare to receive them; despite the wet ground underfoot, the advance could not be ignored. As it was, a more pressing threat was now becoming clear, for Withers' detached column had arrived on the edge of the battlefield and his troops could be clearly seen to the north and west. The infantry were working their way, with some difficulty, through the woods at the rear of the Bois de Sars. The time was about 11.30am and Villars's left flank was now, effectively, very dangerously turned; the French army was facing defeat.

Villars reacted quickly to the new threat; those troops still in the redans were redeployed to hold the left flank of the army. De la Colonie, who had already noticed the poor performance of the Gardes Français under the prolonged Allied bombardment, now protested at this denuding of the French centre, but was told to comply with the orders given or hand his regiment over to an officer who would do so. 'Had the Bavarian brigade not left its position, we should not have been obliged to leave the field of battle.' In this coldly ruthless way, taking an enormous risk with the security of the centre of his army, the French commander gathered a more or less respectably sized force with which to confront Withers' advance. The Chevalier du Rozel bought some valuable time for the Marshal by charging with eight squadrons of his carabiniers and dispersing the ten squadrons of Major-General Miklau's Hessian cavalry who were leading Withers' troops into position. However, the French-recruited Royal Régiment d'Irlandaise met their own countrymen of the Royal Irish Regiment in the woods and came off badly in the close-range musketry contest that ensued. A bitter struggle began along the low, gently rolling ridge that runs from La Folie Farm southwards to La Louvière Farm, almost a separate battle in itself. It was mostly an infantry affair, no cavalry or guns, out in the open with the opposing lines exchanging furious volleys of musketry at close range. In the end, in an hour or so of heavy fighting, Withers' attack was held and then thrown back by the French. 'They returned our volley with great success,' wrote Matthew Bishop. 'My right and my left hand man were shot dead ... one time I remember it wounded my Captain and took my left hand man, and almost swept off those that were on my right.'

Villars was on this flank, anxiously watching the ebb and flow of the fighting around La Folie Farm and along the edge of the Bois de Sars where Eugene's troops were, just about, being held back by de Chemerault and d'Albergotti. At about 1pm, Armand de St Hilaire, the French artillery commander, rode over with news that the British and Prussian infantry were flooding through the almost deserted redans in the centre of the Gap of Aulnois. Colonel de la Colonie wrote, 'They caused their infantry to advance, who in turn protected the passage of many squadrons through the gaps in the parapet.' This was the risk that Villars had run and was the price paid for the security of his army's left flank under the extreme pressure that had been exerted by the Allied attacks. Before he could give fresh orders, at about 1.30pm, his mounted party was swept with musketry fire from some of Eugene's troops who had approached through the edge of the woods. Jean-Noel de Chemerault was killed, d'Albergotti fell from his rearing horse and fractured his leg, and Villars

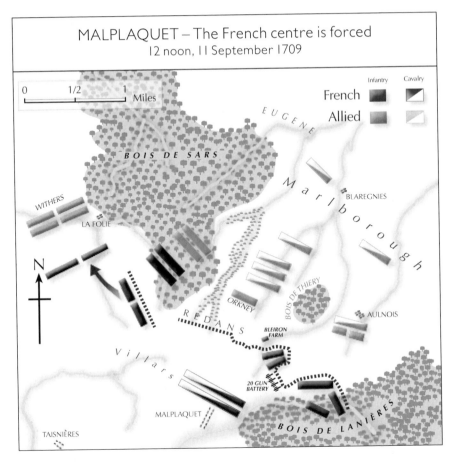

MALPLAQUET – The French centre is forced
12 noon, 11 September 1709

was shot in the knee. In agonising pain, the French commander was lifted from his horse and, after attempting and failing to continue to give orders, was carried off the field, fainting from loss of blood. 'We heard that the Marshal de Villars had been dangerously wounded, and was incapacitated with a bullet through the knee,' de la Colonie wrote.

The crisis for the French army this day had come: they were held on the right by the Dutch, driven back and heavily engaged around La Folie and La Louvière Farms on the left, their centre was pierced, and the army commander gravely wounded. The Marquis de Puységur was at hand, and he gave the order for the French infantry on the left to break contact. A staff officer was sent to the right to summon Marshal Boufflers to take over the command.

The veteran defender of Lille, the only man on the field with the unquestion-able authority to assume that command at such a perilous moment, rose to the occasion, and hurried to the group of staff officers on the left flank. As he rode he could see the Allied infantry pouring through the centre of the position – d'Artagnan's infantry on the right could well be enveloped by the Dutch to their front and the British and Prussians to their left. The French army would be split into two, and disaster threatened unless swift action was taken. As a holding measure, at Puységur's direction the French infantry on the left advanced towards the edge of the Bois de Sars where Eugene had managed to drag some guns through the copses to fire on the French cavalry on the plain of Malplaquet. The Imperial troops drew back under the renewed French musketry, and the Saxon infantry commander, Lieutenant-General August Wackerbath, was gravely wounded. In the breathing space that was achieved the French were able to disengage and fall back away from the wood-line in fairly good order, although an officer in Orkney's Regiment wrote that twenty-two French guns were abandoned among the trees. Eugene's soldiers, so weary and reduced in numbers after their terrible battle in the Bois de Sars, did not pursue for the time being. At this point, it could fairly be said that the two armies had fought each other to a standstill, but the French were dreadfully exposed, while Marlborough retained the ability to strike hard. Now, Boufflers ordered the massed French squadrons to move forward to engage the Allied cavalry, which were beginning to pick their way through the captured redans in the centre of the field. If these men could be held and driven back, the French army might be able to withdraw more or less intact from the field, mauled but ready to fight another day.

D'Auvergne's Dutch squadrons led the renewed Allied advance, together with Henry Lumley and Cornelius Wood's British cavalry and dragoons. Von Bülow's Hanoverian and Prussian cavalry followed, with the Imperial cavalry in support. The Dutch troopers were not yet clear of the redans – only the leading squadrons had made their way across the boggy

Jean-François de Chastenet, Marshal de Puységur.
Fought at both Oudenarde and Malplaquet. Author
of influential military theories.

Malplaquet. The Allied cavalry move through the French centre. Afternoon 11 September 1709.

ground of the Gap of Aulnois and on through the defences – when the first line of de la Vallière's French cavalry came charging forward to engage them. The Dutch were in some disarray and not able to receive properly the charge of the Garde du Corps and the Grenadiers à Cheval, but two squadrons of Stair's Dragoons were already in place and drew the sting out of the French charge. Orkney remembered that James Campbell, one of the squadron commanders, took off the head of an officer in the Garde du Corps with a neat backhanded stroke of his sword and 'behaved like an angell'. The Allied squadrons were narrowly able to get clear of the redans and form up to receive the second French charge. A huge swirling cavalry battle now sprawled out across the plain of Malplaquet.

The French squadrons had suffered all morning long from the Allied bombardment of the redans and breastworks as the 'overs', the roundshot that missed the mark, skipped on across the plain of Malplaquet, ploughing through the ranks of horsemen with deadly effect. This had been endured stoically, but now the French came vigorously forward, and the first-line Allied cavalry were thrown back in confusion. Had Orkney's infantry not been at hand, adding their musketry volleys to the contest, dragging round some abandoned French guns in the redans to use, and even bringing forward some of the guns from the great battery, the Allied attack might have stalled badly. 'The Cavalry battle was joined,' Marlborough wrote, 'and went on with great fury.' Six times the French charged and six times they were thrown back. 'There was such a pelting at each other,' Orkney recalled. The son of the exiled Jacobite Pretender, the Chevalier de St George, was wounded by a sabre slash in one of the furious mêlées. It could not last, and by about 3pm Boufflers could see that, for all their vigour and valour, his cavalry commanders were being worn down – as so often the lack of proper infantry support for the French cavalry was fatal; their opponents, because of better arrangements, had that vital asset. Peter Drake, serving with the French Gens d'Armes, wrote of 'the fire of Colonel Prendergast's Regiment, who lay unseen by us at the reverse of

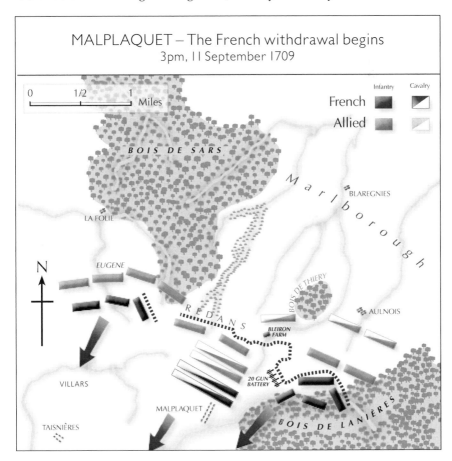

MALPLAQUET – The French withdrawal begins
3pm, 11 September 1709

the entrenchments, and poured their shot among us and some other French squadrons that had penetrated so far, which made a great slaughter.' The Irish soldier of fortune recalled being set on by German dragoons after mistakenly riding into their ranks, and having his jacket set alight by the wadding of a carbine shot that was discharged close to his chest.

The Cornette Blanche, the treasured standard of the Gardes du Corps, was lost to an Allied trooper; every time the French squadrons recovered from a charge, they lost ground, and were gradually being pushed off the plain, with the very real danger that they would be split away from the infantry on either flank. Then the French army could be defeated in detail. The Allied infantry on both left and right were pressing forward once again, the cheers of Orange's Dutch troops could be plainly heard, and the Prince of Hesse-Cassell's squadrons had moved past the Bois de Thiery, threatening the flank of d'Artganan's infantry in the Bois de Lanières – the French really had to go or be destroyed. 'They broke our Centre, at the very same time that our Right began to yield to the Efforts of the Enemy's left ... Victory was declared against us, and we were forced to yield.'

The order was given by Boufflers, and d'Artagnan got his infantry away on the right, marching towards Bavai as the Dutch approached for a third time – even the guns at Bleiron Farm, which had done so much damage, were saved. The Marquis de Goesbriand disengaged the infantry from the Bois de Sars on the left with equal skill. The weary French cavalry covered their withdrawal across the plain of Malplaquet towards Quiévrain, and the reserve cavalry under the Chevalier de Luxembourg reappeared and helped screen the movement. The slippery banks of the marshy Hogneau stream caused some delay, and a number of Henry Withers's squadrons attempted a pursuit but pulled back as soon as they were challenged by Luxembourg's comparatively fresh troopers. However, Colonel de la Colonie remembered more than a trace of confusion and a lack of coordination among the French commanders at this time, which, but for the weariness of the Allied army, would have had serious consequences: 'I met the Chevalier de Rozel, who was asking for infantry, which by this time was a considerable distance off; for as soon as each regiment had passed over [the Hogneau stream] it marched away without waiting for the rest.'

The full, dreadful scale of the losses to both armies could not yet be known, but it had been a severe contest, and the French could claim to have held their own on the field. 'The Marshal de Villars has, this Day, receiv'd a considerable wound, but Surgeons say there is no danger,' Marshal Boufflers wrote to Louis XIV in Versailles. 'Never was misfortune attended with greater glory.' Perhaps so, but Marlborough's army, with scarcely a pause, was able to press on with the siege of Mons. 'The Enemy's army marched yesterday in the Afternoon

Malplaquet. The monument on the spot where Marshal Villars was wounded.

nearer Mons, which they are going to besiege,' wrote Boufflers in his second dispatch to the King. The French, for all their undoubted valour, would soon fail in their task to save the fortress, and that is the true measure of success and failure at Malplaquet. The Duke to his wife:

I am so tired that I have but strength enough to tel you that we have had this day a very bloody Battaile, the first part of the day we beat their foot, and afterwards, their horse. God almighty be prais'd it is now in our power to have what peace we please, and I may be pretty well assur'd of never being in another Battel.

Without any doubt, the price that the Allied army paid for success was shocking. With nearly 105,000 troops on the field of battle, they suffered about 21,000 casualties in the fighting between 7am and 4pm. By contrast, the French army, fielding only 85,000 men, had some 13,000 casualties, of whom

The Casualties at Malplaquet

That Malplaquet was a very expensive battle is beyond question, but estimates of the actual number of casualties varied widely at the time and continue to do so to this day. The French, in particular, wished to exaggerate the scale of the Allied losses while minimising their own in order to hearten their troops after what had been, by common consent, an awful period for them. However, Marshal Villars's absurd claim that his army had taken only some 6,000 casualties that day rightly attracted wide derision at the time and, was, in fact, a very poor compliment to his soldiers, implying that they could be driven from a massively strong position with comparatively light losses. In any case, Marshal Boufflers wrote some weeks after the battle that, even then, 6,000 wounded men were still receiving medical attention.

What is not in doubt is that Marlborough and Eugene's army suffered significantly more heavily than the French. A list published in Holland soon after the battle, gave the Allied losses as 17,732, a very precise, and on the face of things, authoritative figure, but a report in the National Archives at Kew lists the Allied infantry losses alone as 18,353. If that was so, it would certainly put the total Allied loss at over 20,000, a figure often given by commentators on the battle. Given the scale of the task, and the manner in which the French had dug-in and fortified the position, this is not surprising.

It is apparently impossible to be precise, but the actual casualty totals mask the achievements of the opposing commanders. Villars had fought to save Mons and in this he failed, even though he inflicted the greater punishment in the battle. Mons fell to Marlborough and Eugene soon afterwards, and the Allied commanders in that sense could be said to have been successful – with such losses it is perhaps inappropriate to use the word 'victorious' – although their aim had been to destroy Villars's army and this had not happened. Also, Marlborough's opponents in London were quick to heap blame on him for the handling of the battle, while the Dutch, whose infantry had suffered the most, made hardly any criticism. M. Andre Corvisier, in his most useful book *La Bataille de Malplaquet* (1997), discusses the extent of the casualties suffered by both armies in some detail and his conclusions are certainly of interest.

The Fortress of Mons, captured by Marlborough, October 1709.

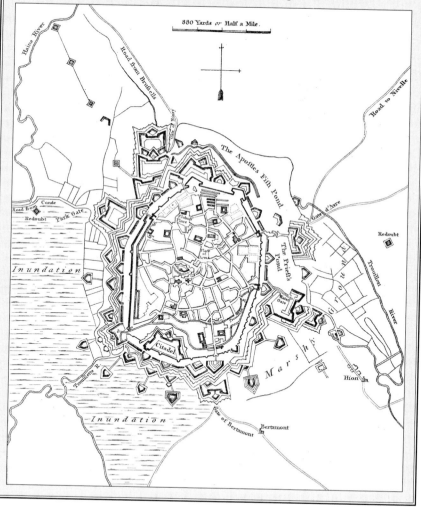

only 500 or so were taken as unwounded prisoners – a measure of the good order in which they got off the field. They did, however, lose most of their artillery in the woods on their left and in the redans in the centre. The Allied army had succeeded on the field of battle, but they really had been fought to a standstill and had to draw their collective breath. The French were left to march away, battered, but with pride intact. Boufflers described the losses to his King:

I could not get an Account of the Number of the Killed and Wounded on our side; I only know that it is very considerable, which is very difficult to avoid, in such Terrible, Long and Obstinate Actions. It cost us a great deal; and we canot but with Concern lament the loss of So many Brave Men of Merit.

The woods on either side of the Gap of Aulnois were choked with thousands of the dead and wounded. Peter Drake, who had fought with the French cavalry, was sitting forlornly on the ground, wounded by several sabre cuts, when he saw the Duke of Marlborough and his staff riding by. The Irish soldier of fortune called out and offered his parole, and the Duke ordered that his wounds be tended to. There was no chance, though, that the Allies could deal with all the French casualties who were still alive, and so Marlborough sent a messenger after Boufflers asking that carts and wagons be sent back under a truce to collect them. Although the actual number of casualties was always open to dispute, with the French playing down their own losses (Villars ludicrously admitting to only 6,000 killed and wounded), there was a wide sense of shock at the cost of the battle, which would not be equalled in Europe until Borodino in 1812.

'I have every minute an account of the killed and wounded which grieves my heart, the numbers being considerable,' Marlborough wrote. 'In the battle the French were more obstinate than in any other war. I hope and believe it will be the last I see.' There was widely expressed surprise that so accomplished a commander as the Duke should have brought his army to suffer in this way – the neat, elegant and hardly painful victories at Ramillies and Oudenarde appeared to be a thing of the past. Well, it was conveniently forgotten that the glittering triumph at Blenheim in 1704 had for much of the day been in doubt and had cost the Allied army a grinding 13,000 casualties, even though the victories in 1706 and 1708 had, without question, been comparatively cheap to obtain. Perhaps the Allied army, for all the gallantry and ability of its middle-ranking commanders, was now just too big to be managed effectively with the command and control procedures of the day.

A French officer wrote soon afterwards with witty irony about the battle, of the claims of success made on both sides, and about the unsatisfactory outcome for both commanders. Villars had fought to save Mons and had failed, while Marlborough had fought to destroy the French army and he too had failed:

The Eugenes and Marlboroughs ought to be well satisfied with us during that day, since, till then they had not met with resistance worthy of them. They may now say with justice that nothing can stand before them; and indeed what shall be able to stay the rapid progress of these heroes, if an army of one hundred thousand men of the best troops, strongly posted between two woods, trebly intrenched, were not able to stop them one day? Will you not own with me that they surpass the heroes of former ages?

For all the efforts of the French, within a few days Marlborough's army had reimposed the investment of Mons, although a small number of reinforcements and supplies were slipped into the garrison before this could be done. As so often before, the pace of operations was slowed by the lack of speed with which the big guns of the Allied siege train could be brought forward. The Duke wrote on 26 September, 'After a great deal of trouble we have at last got some part of our Artillerie from Brussels, so that we open'd last night the Trenches where poor Cadogan was wounded in the neck. I hope he will do well.'

The Governor of Mons, the very able Marquis de Grimaldi, and his troops fought well, and they put in several sharp sorties against the siege operations, but it was soon evident that Boufflers was in no position to challenge the Allies seriously. Prince Eugene, who commanded in the trenches, did not even put his soldiers to the labour of constructing lines of circumvallation and contravallation, as was customary to protect a besieging force from interruption. Marlborough commanded the covering army, took up a position near to the Haine river, and had no real difficulty in keeping the French at a distance. The Chevalier de Luxembourg did manoeuvre with his cavalry against the Allied supply lines, but he drew off when challenged. Boufflers was hampered not only by the losses sustained at Malplaquet, which could not readily be made good, unlike the Allied casualties which were replaced quickly, but by a continued chronic lack of supplies. De la Colonie wrote:

All the corn magazines were empty, the hard frost had prevented their replenishment, and as it was imperative that provision should be made of at least a four days' supply of bread before beginning an advance, the project became impossible. M. Dangeat, Intendant of Mauberge, who controlled these stores, when threatened with being hanged at the gate of the town if he did not find some means of providing some bread for these four days, declared that he was ready for the hanging!

Mons fell on 20 October, and Grimaldi and his garrison were permitted to withdraw to Mauberge and Namur. Marlborough hoped to go on to attack Mauberge, but the weather was turning foul, his generals were reluctant to do more, and the army was tired. Operations came to a close and the troops went off to their winter quarters a week later. The campaign had been a stern one, expensive in men and effort, with results that were heavily qualified. Without doubt the Duke of Marlborough's enemies in London, men who were envious and suspicious of his motives, had been given strong ammunition with which to attack him afresh. In Holland, by contrast, whose infantry had suffered so heavily in their attacks on the Bois de Lanières, there was relatively little criticism. However, field deputy Sicco van Goslinga was stung by comments attributed to Anthonius Hiensius, the Grand Pensionary of Holland, that only Tournai and Mons, together with an expensive battle at Malplaquet, were the meagre results of the 1709 campaign. Goslinga had often been a remarkably ill-informed critic of Marlborough and his methods, but he was brave and energetic enough, and Hiensius's comments stung him into protest:

Is it, in fact, a small thing to take two of the strongest places in Europe, and win one of the most obstinate and bloody battles ever fought? You appear, however, to suppose that we can march straight onto Paris. In truth, let me tell you; an army does not march like a traveller, finding bed and board at every stage.

It could be said that Marlborough and Eugene had allowed themselves to be tied down to a rather static campaign centred around two major sieges, with a bloody battle in between, when they might have done better to employ their greater resources in striking at one or other flank of the ill-equipped and over-extended French army. The Allied commanders' liking and aptitude for manoeuvre had certainly not been in evidence. However, their numerical advantage could be exaggerated, particularly as their opponents had, of necessity, to hold to the defensive, yet to move against either flank would inevitably expose territory elsewhere to French raids. Also, with the campaign starting so late in the year, there was a limit to what could be achieved, even in the best circumstances.

The plain fact was that the French had again proved to be incapable, literally incapable, of defeating Marlborough. On the other hand, competent French commanders like Marshal Villars could probably make any major advance into northern France drawn-out and prohibitively expensive for the Allies. What the French could not win on the field of battle, they might win by delay, putting off the decision point in the war while the Grand Alliance grew weary and lost its sense of unified purpose. At this point in 1709, the outcome of the war was rapidly being decided anyway – Philip V was increasingly popular with the Spanish people and Archduke Charles could not be forced on them – this had been tried and failed. The Austrians, meanwhile, made themselves secure in northern Italy and, courtesy of the Duke of Marlborough's victories, in the southern Netherlands. The war had run its course, but no one seemed able to bring it to a close.

Part 5

Marlborough's Final Campaigns, 1710–11

Introduction

In four astonishing battles between 1704 and 1709 – Blenheim, Ramillies, Oudenarde and Malplaquet – the 1st Duke of Marlborough firmly established his reputation as a great Captain, widely regarded as the finest military commander of his generation. It can be argued that his achievements on the battlefield have never been equalled by a British commander, and at the same time, he conducted the foreign policy of Great Britain almost on his own. The Marshals of France, once regarded as invincible in the arts of war, and their gallant soldiers were beaten and driven to despair by his calm and ruthlessly efficient methods. The Duke's soldiers, not only Queen Anne's troops but also those drawn from all across north and western Europe, trusted his abilities and they repaid his concern for their welfare – evidenced as much as anything else by his ardent desire to seek outright battle and therefore bring a speedy end to the war for Spain – with loyalty and affection.

Despite all this, and the Duke's undoubted victories over the French and their allies, the war, expensive in men, reputations and money, dragged on, largely because the Grand Alliance had no plan, and proved unable to devise one, to conclude a satisfactory and acceptable peace. Louis XIV's fortitude in the face of adversity and the resilience of his field commanders and their long-suffering soldiers, when combined with the perverse inability of the parties to the Grand Alliance to offer terms that would be acceptable both to the French King and to his people, ensured that there could be no peace. Holland was exhausted financially by the costs of the war, but a new treaty agreed with Great Britain promised the Dutch a considerably enlarged Barrier, to the degree that the Austrians, who were not consulted, were almost excluded from the government and possession of the southern (Spanish) Netherlands. The States-General, despite the exhaustion of their treasury, found all this impossible to resist and fought on. The death of Emperor Joseph, which would soon bring his younger brother, Archduke Charles, to the Imperial throne, neatly answered the thorny question of who should be the King of Spain.

To add to the very real difficulties of bringing Louis XIV to an abject acceptance of the terms laid before him, Marlborough's influence in London was gradually eroded. His political allies were in decline, and a newly elected Tory government, averse to the risks and high costs involved in foreign entanglements (unless very real trade advantages could be shown), began rapidly to undermine the Duke's position. Rumours circulated that he had no wish to bring hostilities to an end and to leave his post as commander of the Anglo-Dutch armies, with all the prestige and financial advantages that came with the position. Marlborough disdained to reply to such malicious talk, and probably did not do enough to refute the allegations properly. But, then, he was actively pursuing the military campaigns of the Grand Alliance in the Low Countries. He could not safeguard his own position in London where others, most notably his wife, the fiery Duchess Sarah, instead made a point of pursuing a bitter and unnecessary quarrel with Queen Anne. Partly in consequence, although she had already tired of what seemed to have become a pointless and endless war, the Queen's support, for so long the bedrock of Marlborough's position, ebbed quickly away. The Duke, usually so astute, made matters worse with a very ill-advised request that he be appointed Captain-General for Life, so that his position at home and on the Continent could be assured. The post had previously been held by General Monck, a Cromwellian soldier, and the irony seemed to be missed by Marlborough when he asked for the appointment from a Stuart monarch. The request was first made in 1709, and Queen Anne had no hesitation in refusing the Duke over the matter. When he asked again, she refused him again. This was common knowledge, and Marlborough's position and prestige were inevitably further weakened. The Duke made matters worse by writing a letter to the Queen, full of bitter complaint at the treatment he had received. It, too, failed to make her change her mind.

During this whole period of exhausting campaigning, with the sure knowledge that he was losing ground to his opponents and critics in London, ground that could, probably, only be recovered by achieving a major victory in open field in the style of Blenheim or Ramillies, Marlborough suffered worsening health. 'Sensible of the inconvenience of old-age', he had for some years been tormented with migraine headaches, as in the hectic summer days before Oudenarde in 1708. Now he began to have persistent ear-ache on the left side, a truly debilitating affliction when attempting to control huge and complex military operations. The Duke's continued, if expensive, successes against the French fortress belt throughout 1710 and 1711 are all the more remarkable as a result.

Marshal Vauban's Fortress Belt

In the late 1670s, King Louis XIV, having by conquest considerably extended the borders of France, sought to protect his newly acquired domains with a massive and complex belt of modern fortresses. These were designed by Sébastien le Prestre Vauban, the King's master military engineer, who had developed, along with others such as the Dutchman Meinheer van Coehorn, an intricate theory of dense and precise layered defence. These fortresses were of particular importance along France's northern border in Artois, Picardy and Flanders, where there were few natural defences apart from river lines. Vauban foresaw that one day an invading army would come through the southern Netherlands to attack northern France and planned accordingly. The often dilapidated defences of such towns such as Lille, St Omer, Béthune, Arras, Douai, Aire and Valenciennes were extensively improved and enlarged, each one becoming an example of the military engineer's art.

When the time came, many of the fortresses that Vauban had designed and constructed at huge effort and expense fell to Marlborough's ruthlessly efficient methods, whenever he attacked them. However, this all took time, and Vauban's wider aim was achieved – Marlborough might take his fortresses, one by one, but he would have insufficient time to break through and get out into the open fields of northern France.

Vauban was made a Marshal of France in 1703, but fell from favour with Louis XIV when he advocated sweeping social reform. He died in 1707, not living to see Marlborough's troops exhausting themselves in fighting their way through his fortress belt.

That We Must Part from Such a Man

'I am so sensible of the necessity of the Duke of Marlborough's presence in Holland at this critical juncture, that I have already given the necessary directions for his immediate departure.' In this way Queen Anne, writing to the House of Commons, underscored the Duke's importance in the forthcoming campaign in 1710. Despite such overt support, her tone was cool – Marlborough's influence was faltering, and time was becoming short in which he could hope to bring the French army to battle, drive it to destruction, and so win the war for Spain.

Marshal Villars was still recovering from the wound received at Malplaquet, and in the meantime, the Marquis de Montesquiou (formerly the Comte d'Artagnan) was in command in Flanders. Both he and Villars, who only joined the army once the campaign was under way, proved unable to prevent the fall of Douai on the river Scarpe in June. Many French units were understrength, and their army still lacked adequate provisions. Marlborough then moved quickly to lay siege to Béthune on the Lys, but the fortress held out until late in August. The season for campaigning was speeding by, and the French fortress belt was fulfilling its primary purpose – to delay any invader. Marlborough was being denied the victory he sought. Meanwhile, his faltering position in London can be seen in a letter he wrote to James Brydges, the Paymaster-General, on 7 July. He was:

much obliged to you for the kind part you take in our successes here; we should be very happy if they could contribute towards quieting and calming the ferment at home, which otherwise may unravel whatever it is possible for us to do on this side.

Much as Villars regretted the loss of the important fortresses of Douai and Béthune, he was too wily to allow his weakened army to be cornered and made to stand and fight. From time to time he did advance, with due caution, and manoeuvred to catch part of the Allied army at a disadvantage. Villars appreciated that time was more on his side than on his opponent's. The fortresses of St Venant and Aire on the Lys river were the next objects of Marlborough's attention, and their capture might lay open such important places as Calais and Dunkirk to attack. St Venant fell without too much trouble – its defences were obsolete and inadequate, and the garrison wisely did not choose to sacrifice themselves in a hopeless task. Aire was a very different matter; the defences were well laid out and the French troops under command of the tough Marquis de Goesbriand resisted fiercely. The weather was terrible, the conditions in the trenches utterly miserable, and casualties among both besiegers and garrison were heavy. 'This defence was the best,' Marlborough wrote with heartfelt, grudging admiration. At last, on 8 November 1710, to general relief on both sides, de Goesbriand submitted on good terms, and the weary troops could go off to their winter quarters. Marlborough returned to London to find little credit for his arduous efforts and few friends at Court. The Duchess had now lost all her posts and appointments, and Marlborough's pleas to the Queen failed to get her reinstated.

The Duke took the field for the 1711 campaign with an army almost 120,000 strong – a formidable force once again. Marshal Villars, aware not only that his own army was virtually all that stood between the Duke and Versailles, but that peace negotiations were in progress – some in public, some privately – was cautious and once again held firmly to the defensive. Although the French fortress belt had, to a considerable degree, been compromised by Marlborough's successes in previous campaigns (the loss of Arras or Cambrai might lead the Allies out into open country at last) time increasingly appeared to be on France's side. The Grand Alliance was growing weary and its unity of purpose, never very strong, slowly fractured as the Allies looked to their own interests. Accordingly, the French commander concentrated his army behind the defensive Lines of Non (Ne) Plus Ultra which stretched from the Channel coast to Valenciennes, behind which he could reasonably expect to defy Marlborough to do his worst.

In April, the Emperor Joseph died of smallpox in Vienna and his younger brother, Archduke Charles, who might have been Carlos III in Madrid in other circumstances, was elected to the Imperial throne. Now, unless the old Habsburg empire of Charles V was to be recreated, no one expected the Austrian Emperor also to be King of Spain. The ostensible main cause of the war was, in effect, settled, and the only thing that remained was quite how the Spanish empire was to be divided. This complication in Vienna unavoidably delayed preparations for the new campaign, and Prince Eugene and his troops were soon called away to watch the Rhine frontier and to safeguard the Imperial Diet at Frankfurt during this period of anxiety and uncertainty for the Empire. With a reduced army now about 95,000 strong, Marlborough's options were limited, particularly as British regiments were also being diverted to an irrelevant campaign in north America. Marshal Villars could deploy superior numbers of troops, but the Duke still hoped to draw the French out of their defences and into a battle. He undertook an imaginative campaign to besiege the important fortress of Bouchain at the confluence of the Scheldt and the Sensée rivers. The threatened loss of this place might induce Villars to fight after all as Cambrai, Le Quesnoy and Valenciennes would also be exposed to attack. By first decoying the Marshal away to the west, and then rapidly countermarching the 36 miles to get across the Sensée at Arleux in a celebrated operation that became known as 'the passage of the Lines of Non Plus Ultra', Marlborough was able to invest Bouchain with the loss of hardly a soldier. Villars closed up to the south side of the fortress. Though he was able to deploy a larger army, he proved unable to interrupt the complex Allied siege operations, becoming instead something of an irritation to Marlborough, but little more. Bouchain and its strong garrison fell to Marlborough on 13 September 1711 while the French field army looked impotently on.

This neat operation was Marlborough's last major military success, as plans for an immediate follow-up attack on Le Quesnoy came to nothing. Little remained now between the Allied armies, soon to be rejoined by Prince Eugene and his Imperial troops, and the plains beyond the French fortress belt. An enticing possibility for the next campaign beckoned, but it required continued resolve and a determination to press forward. The Duke would not be there with the troops whom he had led so well: he was dismissed by the Queen from all his posts at the end of 1711. The poor excuse for this dramatic step was that he could then answer, impartially, the spurious charges being made against him of peculation and corruption while in command of the Allied armies. Louis XIV was naturally delighted at the news, declaring, 'This will do everything for us that we desire.' The opinion of the soldiers in Marlborough's army, who never lost their respect and trust for him for all that he demanded of them, may be summed up by the disgusted comment of Matthew Bishop: 'That we must part from such a man, who conquered all the generals of France.' In fact, the war for Spain had now run its course, for Philip V was comfortably settled in Madrid while Emperor Charles was perfectly content to be in Vienna. Military operations dragged on without much conviction or definable aim and Britain withdrew from hostilities in 1712 to the loud protests of the other parties to the Grand Alliance. The Dutch and Imperial forces under Prince Eugene were badly over-extended in operations against Le Quesnoy and Valenciennes, and Marshal Villars soundly defeated Earl Albemarle and his detachment at Denain in July that same year. The French subsequently recovered much ground that had been lost since their defeat at Malplaquet three years earlier.

A tired peace came to Europe with the Treaty of Utrecht in 1713 and the subsequent Treaties of Rastadt and Baden, by which the Spanish empire was divided; the principal aim of the Grand Alliance, as originally conceived in 1701, had been achieved. Austria received the southern Netherlands and much of northern Italy, while Holland recovered in modified form its Barrier against French aggression, although this was noticeably smaller than had been agreed in 1709. Great Britain retained such territories as Gibraltar, Minorca and Newfoundland and gained significant preferential trading rights with Spain's colonies. Perhaps most significantly for domestic affairs in London, overt French support for the Jacobite cause was withdrawn, and the eventual Protestant succession of George, Elector of Hanover, was confirmed. What had been widely regarded as the overbearing power of France was hobbled for generations to come, but Louis XIV retained his territorial gains in Alsace,

The Treaty of Utrecht

The War of the Spanish Succession came to a close with the Treaties of Utrecht (1713), Baden (1714) and Rastadt (1715), although these are generally known collectively as the Treaty of Utrecht. The main treaty provisions were:

- Philip V (the French claimant) was recognised as King of Spain, as long as the crowns of France and Spain were kept separate.
- Naples, the Milanese, Sardinia and the Spanish Netherlands (now to be the Austrian Netherlands) came under Imperial Austrian rule. The States-General of Holland regained their Barrier Towns in revised form.
- France retained Alsace and Strasbourg, but relinquished her fortresses on the eastern bank of the Rhine – Kehl, Briesach and Freibourg.
- Louis XIV's allies, the Elector of Cologne and the Elector of Bavaria, were restored to their estates.
- The Hanoverian, Protestant succession to the throne of Great Britain was guaranteed. James III (the 'Old Pretender') was expelled from France.
- Great Britain retained Gibraltar, Minorca, Newfoundland, Hudson's Bay, Arcadia and St Kitts, and was guaranteed access to certain Spanish ports. Less preferential trade terms were also given to Holland. The fortifications of Dunkirk were to be demolished (which they were, after much procrastination by the French).
- The Kingdom of Prussia was recognised, and given overlordship of Upper Guelderland.
- Victor Amadeus, the Duke of Savoy, received Sicily and part of the Milanese.

Languedoc, Franche-Comté and Artois, something which in the despair of the spring of 1709 had seemed unthinkable.

The Duke and Duchess of Marlborough went to live abroad in 1712 to avoid the malicious and politically motivated charges of corruption and peculation. On the death of Queen Anne in 1714 and the accession of George I, the Duke regained all his posts. He did not resume his former pre-eminent influence at court though; the German King, while appreciating his abilities, appeared not to wish to have the Duke too close. During the 1715 Jacobite Rising Marlborough remained in London, and the suppression of rebellion was entrusted first to John Campbell, Duke of Argyll, then to William Cadogan and Joseph Sabine.

Marlborough was able to manage the reduction of the British Army to peace-time levels without too much harm being inflicted. Among his innovations was the creation of the Royal Regiment of Artillery as a distinct corps. In increasing ill-health, the Duke suffered several strokes and gradually retired from public life. He died in June 1722 and was succeeded as Master-General of the Ordnance by his old comrade Cadogan.

Marlborough was arguably Britain's greatest ever soldier, and was almost certainly shown to be her best tactician. He could not, however, win the war for Spain; time just did not permit. The Duke dominated the European military scene for nine tempestuous years, humbling the vaunted Marshals of France and the armies of the Sun King. At the same time, almost in the same breath, he conducted, single-handedly it seems, the foreign policy of Queen Anne and her government, having to deal, very successfully, with such awkward characters as Charles XII of Sweden and 'Their High Mightinesses' the States-General of Holland. Two resounding victories – Blenheim and Ramillies – established for ever Marlborough's renown. To these he added the breathtakingly skilful, almost casually off-hand, tactical triumph over the French army at Oudenarde. Then the dark day at Malplaquet saw Marlborough at his most resolute, overcoming the French who were spoiling for a fight and had established an extremely strong defensive position. There the cost was arguably too high for the comparatively limited reward. The Duke was running out of two valuable commodities – time, and faith in his ability to bring the war for Spain to a glorious conclusion. He may be excused: as has been seen, this was a prize that could not be won. If Marlborough ever failed at all, it was in that he undertook a task which, having grown in scope over time, was beyond achieving.

A Guide to Marlborough's Battlefields

1. Blenheim, 13 August 1704: Walking Blenheim Battlefield

The wide Bavarian cornfields of the Danube valley afford a magnificent setting for one of the greatest and most spectacular battles in history. Bounded on the southern side by the great river and to the north by the wooded hills stretching to Swabia and Franconia, the battlefield at Blenheim is a delight to visit. Modern development has been quite limited and the small villages and hamlets, while rather larger than in 1704, are still distinct and have lost little of their charm and character. The houses today are unsurprisingly more prosperous in appearance than would have been the case 300 years ago, with the result that the villages are almost certainly more attractive now than when the armies of the Duke of Marlborough and Marshal Tallard met there.

The visitor to this beautiful area may wish to begin their tour at the small town of Donauwörth at the confluence of the Danube and Wörnitz rivers, only about fifteen minutes drive from the plain of Höchstädt itself. Looming over the old town is the Schellenberg hill, scene of the desperate assault on the entrenched French and Bavarian corps by Marlborough's advance guard on 2 July 1704. The actual scene of the action is separated from the fringes of the town by a modern bypass and there is a public swimming pool in the trees near the crest of the hill, but much of the slope over which the troops fought with such ferocity is untouched. The rear of the hill, leading down towards the Danube, is occupied by a German army base and is not open to the public. The wooded heights, however, give a wonderful view over the surrounding country, northwards to Ebermörgen where the Allied armies crossed the Wörnitz on their march to the Schellenberg, and westwards up the line of the valley of the Danube towards the plain of Höchstädt, the Nebel stream and Blindheim itself.

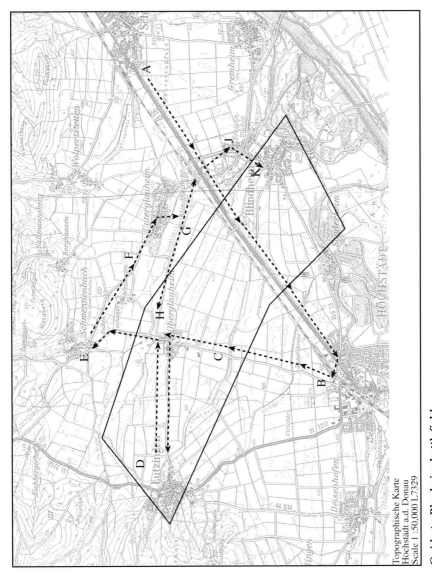

Topographische Karte
Höchstädt a.d. Donau
Scale 1 :50,000 L7329

Guide to Blenheim battlefield.

221

It is also well worth driving the 30 kilometres northwards to Nordlingen, the last completely walled town in Germany. The Allied wounded were brought here after both the Schellenberg fight and Blenheim; the Evangelische church contains a number of attractive and elaborate memorials to those senior officers who died. Among them is Marlborough's great friend Johan Wigand van Goor, General of Dutch infantry, who fell in the assault on the Schellenberg. There were a number of battles around Nordlingen during the Thirty Years' War and their locations are also worth exploring.

Taking the main road westwards, the B16 from Donauwörth towards Ü, the villages of Münster and Tapfheim are soon reached. This was the route used by Marlborough and Eugene, and it is where the Allied army combined on 11 August 1704 in the face of the threat of the advancing French and Bavarian forces. The distance between the Danube on the one hand and the wooded hills to the north on the other makes this a vital narrow corridor for east–west movement, and it offered a good position for defence, had the Duke and Eugene not had something more adventurous in mind. In the village of Tapfheim, the two commanders climbed to the belfry of the ornate church tower to view 'through their perspective glasses' the growing encampment of the Elector of Bavaria and the French Marshals on the plain of Höchstädt.

Just to the west of Tapfheim is the small village of Schwenningen, on the main B16 road, and nearby is the hamlet of Wolperstetten at the foot of the Fuchsberg hill. Marlborough and Eugene rode into this area on 12 August 1704 to complete their reconnaissance, and their cavalry escort clashed with French foragers as they did so. The Marquis de Silly sent his own cavalry to hamper the Allied pioneers as they laboured to clear paths for the army across the many small streams in the vicinity. The wooded hills beside the road sheltered the sleeping Allied army on the night before the battle.

At the scene of the great action itself, the B16 roads runs straight across the battlefield. It follows the ancient route, and does not detract from the scene in any serious way. In the mid-nineteenth century, a railway line was constructed next to the road but it still follows the same route closely, although an embankment is visible in a few places. In addition, a new road was built a few years ago to bypass from north to south the village of Lutzingen, taking traffic from Höchstädt to Nordlingen, but it is not very obtrusive. More noticeable is a new barn that has been built on the edge of the plain close to Unterglau, where Marlborough's troops crossed the Nebel stream, but then, this is working farmland and such gradual change is to be expected. On the southern and eastern edge of the battlefield, the Danube has been channelled and straightened over the years, and no longer meanders through marshy meadows. These meadows have been largely drained, but are still wet underfoot in places, and the original course of the river, rather like a shallow cutting, can be made out with careful observation.

The Nebel stream (shown on modern maps as the Nebel Bach) is an obvious feature, splitting the battlefield in two as it crosses the plain from the hills to the north-west and running to its confluence with the Danube near to Blindheim. In most places the stream is about 2 or 3 metres broad (narrower near to Lutzingen) and although the ground is more drained than in the past, it is still a very obvious obstacle to easy movement. It is possible to scramble across, at the risk of a wetting, but this is neither easy nor recommended, and there are several road and farm-track bridges which give easy passage.

The ground between the Schwenningen defile and the Nebel stream, over which the Allied troops moved into position that morning, is firm and obviously easy going. However, as the visitor moves past Unterglau towards Weilheim Farm and Schwennenbach, the area allotted to Prince Eugene in which to draw up his troops, the ground is less satisfactory and quite broken up in places. It is easy to see why, before modern drainage and land management took effect, the Prince had such trouble getting into place in good time. Also, the topography of the area means that the ground close to the hills is inevitably slightly higher than that towards the Danube. Eugene's troops were, in fact, climbing a long, if quite gentle, incline to get into position.

After crossing the Nebel in the vicinity of Unterglau, a short and easy slope, rising in all only from 415 metres elevation to 429 metres, leads after 150 metres or so onto the plain of Höchstädt. This was the site of the encampment of the French and Bavarian armies. The open fields, dotted with a few small copses of trees, provide wide and attractive views in all directions. As Captain Robert Parker said, 'Here was a fine plain for the cavalry on both sides to show their bravery.' There is hardly an obstacle to be seen once the Nebel is crossed, and the whole area of the vast conflict is laid open to the observer. The great distances involved – the battlefield stretches for about 6 kilometres from Lutzingen to Blindheim – can be disconcerting at first, and a few moments of orientation with map and compass are advisable. The hills of the Swabian Jura to the north are obvious, and the visitor will do well to pick out and identify the distinctive church towers in the villages – Höchstädt, Blindheim, Schwenningen, Unterglau, Oberglau and Lutzingen. Identifying these and finding their location on the map provide orientation and illustrate very well the scale of the task facing Tallard and his colleagues when fighting a pitched battle under the hot August sun against an active and dangerous enemy. The failure of Tallard to appreciate sooner what Clerambault was doing with the French infantry away on the right flank becomes a little more understandable once the vastness of the terrain is seen.

When visiting the Blenheim battlefield, it is best to take a modern map (Topographische Karte – Höchstädt a. d. Donau 1:50,000 L7329), compass and binoculars. A well-drawn battle plan to compare with the modern map will also be useful. Generally, the ground is firm, but stout shoes are advisable. Trespassing should obviously be avoided, and the gardens around the villages are plainly private, but the author has found no difficulty in 'walking' the farmed parts of the battlefield. The Country Code should be observed and common sense employed where livestock and standing crops are concerned, and a polite manner shown at all times. The sight of a stranger walking, and with a map, usually attracts a tolerant smile and greeting from local people. The tercentenary commemorations of the battle in 2004 certainly increased awareness in the villages around the plain of Höchstädt of the momentous events that took place there.

The visitor might start the tour from the roadside at Schwenningen (Point A on the adjoining map). Look south-west across the open ground of the Oberstrassfeld towards Blindheim, the houses of which are partly hidden by trees; this is the scene which greeted Marlborough as his soldiers marched out onto the plain early in the morning of 13 August 1704. It is easy to appreciate just how narrow the gap is at Schwenningen and what a chance Tallard missed in not holding the place. It can also be seen what a difficult manoeuvre it was to thread the eight marching columns (nine if Cutts's troops are counted) through the gap in good time and good order before gaining the wider ground on which to form ready for battle.

From Schwenningen, a short drive down the B16 past Blindheim soon brings the visitor to Höchstädt. Turning sharp right at the entrance to the town on side road ST2383 leading to SR2212 towards Lutzingen (Point B), the road leads gently upwards towards the plain of Höchstädt. Almost immediately after crossing the railway line turn right again onto a byroad, the DLG36 Glauheimstrasse towards Oberglau. Within a kilometre or so, after crossing a small junction known as the Xavierkreuz, the visitor is among wide open fields (Point C). Lutzingen is to the left; Oberglau is straight ahead; Unterglau is ahead and to the right beyond the line of small trees which marks the course of the Nebel stream. Blindheim is off to the right. This is the site of the French and Bavarian encampment, and halting here and facing east, it is possible to see what the Comte de Merode-Westerloo saw that daybreak as the Allied armies poured forward through the Schwenningen defile into the open country. Marlborough's troops formed up on either side of Unterglau, in full view of their opponents. When standing on the plain, though, it is immediately apparent what an advantage the French cavalry had in being able to use the slope leading downwards to the Nebel, gradual though it is, when engaging Marlborough's advancing squadrons.

A short drive further along DLG36 leads to Oberglau, which the Marquis de Blainville defended with such tenacity. There is not a lot to see in the village, so it is best to take the turning left along DLG38 to Lutzingen. On the forward edge of the village, near to the junction with route ST2212 which leads northwards through the hills to Nordlingen, is the site of the Bavarian great battery (Point D). There is little left of the gun emplacement, but it is easy to visualise the Bavarian gunners at their deadly work, decimating the Prussian infantry as they pressed forward across the Nebel. Retracing steps to Oberglau, turn left across the Nebel to Schwennenbach (Point E). From the edge of the village an excellent view is had back towards the plain of Höchstädt. This is where Eugene struggled to get his soldiers into position. From Schwennenbach, drive along DLG32 to Weilheim Farm (Point F). This group of buildings occupies a slight rise above the local fields, and there is a fine field of view westwards to Oberglau, Höchstädt and Lutzingen. Here Eugene placed his batteries, rather late in the day, and it was across the wide cornfields ahead, beyond the Nebel, that his cavalry and infantry attacked with such devotion and at heavy cost to fix the troops of Marsin and the Elector, and prevent either commander from going to the assistance of Tallard near to Blindheim. The course of the Nebel stream can be made out by the thin line of trees (partly demolished by local beavers) which crosses the entire frontage. There is little cover or dead ground to aid an attacker, as Eugene's troops found to their cost,

Blenheim. The plain of Höchstädt, looking towards Lutzingen from Weilheim Farm.

Unterglau village seen from the plain of Höchstädt.

and the French and Bavarian gunners had excellent fields of fire. It will, however, readily be seen that the villages are set too far apart for the batteries sited there to support each other properly with overlapping fire.

Driving on to Unterglau, it is easy to park at the roadside, and a short walk along one of the lanes between the houses soon brings the visitor to the Nebel stream. There is a small bridge opposite the church in Unterglau, and from here a good view westwards is gained of what the Allied soldiers saw as they crossed the stream (Point G). Höchstädt church tower is straight ahead, almost concealed by the brow of the plain, while that of Blindheim is to the left, partly hidden by trees. It will be seen that the slope, while gradual, puts part of the stream almost in dead ground to troops on the higher parts of the plain. This posed a real problem for the French gunners, whose field of observation cannot have been very good (the slope is less pronounced towards Lutzingen where the Bavarian artillery were placed). The wheat was unharvested on the day of battle, and crops in the eighteenth century grew taller than they do today, so this would have obscured the line of sight. Firing along the slope, rather than downwards to the stream, would have overcome the difficulty, and this may explain why accounts of the French artillery effort to hamper Marlborough often mention the battery near to Blindheim.

A few moments' walk from the bridge takes the visitor up the short slope onto the plain of Höchstädt, where the Allied cavalry and infantry deployed after crossing the Nebel. Höchstädt church tower is more easily visible, dead ahead. Again, it will immediately be noticed how the French artillery in Oberglau, to the right, had no chance to achieve overlapping fire with the batteries around Blindheim to the left. From the bridge near Unterglau, a short walk northwards along the Nebel brings the visitor to the strip of land between Oberglau and the stream (Point H), where the Marquis de Blainville's French and Irish troops put in their counter-attack on the Dutch infantry under the Prince of Holstein-Beck. The ground is still quite wet underfoot in places, and it is easy to imagine the Dutch soldiers floundering about in the mud, caught under de Blainville's musketry while Marshal Marsin's French cavalry came sweeping forward. To the north-west, Weilheim Farm can be clearly seen, and here Count Fugger's armoured cuirassiers stood, refusing to move to the aid of the Dutch until they were called forward by Marlborough.

Finally, it is worth walking along the bank of the Nebel stream (an underpass gives the pedestrian a way across the railway line, but care must be taken getting over the B16 Donauwörth–Ü road), or driving the short distance along the DLG32 past the small railway station into Blindheim village itself. Here the climax to the day took place. Near to the village the Nebel is divided in two by a small tree-covered islet, and the banks of the stream, fringed with willows, are wet underfoot (Point J). The two watermills set alight by the French were sited here, by the road-bridge that takes the DLG22 into the centre of the village. It is not difficult to make out where Cutts's infantry lay while waiting for the order to assault the French barricades. Looking down the main street towards the church, the first turning on the right, a small residential road, leads to an easy slope coming down from the plain of Höchstädt. Across this field swept von Zurlauben's Gens d'Armes to scatter Rowe's Regiment in the opening moments of the battle. The lower-lying ground along the bank of the stream sheltered Wilkes's Hessians until they moved forward to recover Rowe's colours from the French cavalry.

The village contains a number of houses and barns which are contemporary to the battle, and it is evident that these are smaller than the more modern houses of Blindheim. Large parts of the place were devastated by fire during the fighting, but the character of the village has not been lost over the years. Several of the old buildings stand just across the road from the church, and, on close inspection, it is possible to make out the marks of musket balls on the walls. In the village square is the Baroque-style church (Point K), the interior of which is very attractive, but the battlefield visitor will find the walled churchyard of most interest. This was prepared for defence and held in strength by French infantry in 1704, and a costly battle was fought here in the closing moments of daylight. Earl Orkney's infantry, deployed from the plain of Höchstädt to finish things, fought their bloody way along the street leading at right-angles alongside the churchyard to the square. Here the Marquis de Blanzac gave the order to the French to lay down their arms and surrender their colours. Here, too, James Abercrombie tried to seize the regimental colour of the Régiment du Roi, and got cut across the forearm for his trouble. Set into the churchyard wall is a small commemorative plaque, recording the great conflict here so many years ago.

On leaving Blindheim village, take the road signposted to Höchstädt. Within about 2 kilometres the small hamlet of Sonderheim is reached, close to the original course of the Danube. The river is now straightened and the water meadows drained, but in this area the fleeing French cavalry fell down the steep bank while Hessian dragoons confronted Marshal Tallard as he attempted to escape the rout of his army.

Finally, Höchstädt is a pleasant small town, with a number of excellent restaurants in which weary battlefield travellers can refresh themselves with local beverages and cuisine. By the roadside at the entrance to the town there is a stone memorial to the conflict, erected in 1954. In the town square is the Heimat Museum, which contains a large and very interesting diorama to the battle of Blenheim and is well worth a visit. The address of the museum is: Alten Rathaus, Marktplatz, 7, Höchstädt a. d. Donau.

2. Ramillies, 23 May 1706: Walking Ramillies Battlefield

Ramillies is really too far away for the visitor from the UK to get to comfortably and return home in a single day. When driving straight to the battlefield from the Channel Tunnel or ferry, the journey takes a good two or three hours, depending on the traffic. It *can* all be done in a single day, of course, but insufficient time is then available to explore the large battlefield and do it justice. So, the visitor should allow two days – time that will be well rewarded on this wonderful site. The most convenient route is that past Tournai and Lille (both the scene of major Marlburian sieges) and on to the Brussels area. Strangely enough, Waterloo, just to the south of Brussels, is a good place to use as a base for a visit to Ramillies. By doing so, the battlefield visitor has a variety of decent hotels from which to choose. In the spirit of killing two birds with one stone, the scene of Wellington's famous victory can also be taken in, as well as the more unspoilt pleasures of Ramillies, which is only about half an hour's drive to the south and east.

There is little opportunity in Ramillies or neighbouring villages to get refreshments, but the small town of Egheze only five minutes' drive to the south, has a good selection of bars and cafes – the Cheval Blanc is the author's favourite hostelry for prompt and friendly service at lunchtime. Belgian weather being what it is, a visit between the months of May and September is likely to be most promising; May is particularly good as, if the visit is well-timed, the anniversary of the battle can be celebrated on the field itself.

In addition to Ramillies, the visitor might also like to head a few kilometres to the north to seek out the 1693 Williamite battlefield of Landen/Neerwinden and the site of Marlborough's triumph in 1705 at Elixheim (they are only a few hundred metres apart and are both pleasantly unspoiled). The great citadel fortress of Namur (sieges in 1692 and 1695) is about half an hour's drive to the

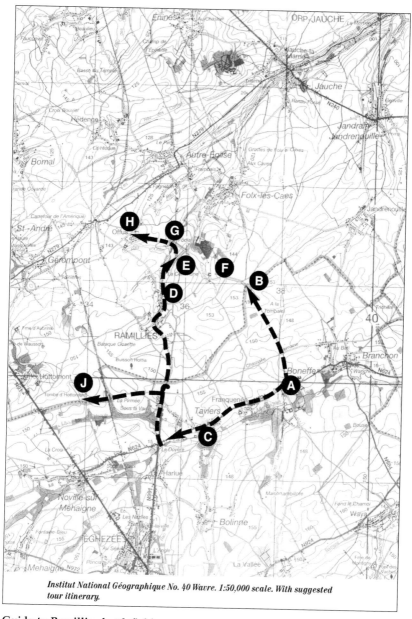

Institut National Géographique No. 40 Wavre. 1:50,000 scale. With suggested tour itinerary.

Guide to Ramillies battlefield.

south, and only slightly further afield are Mons (1709 and 1914), Malplaquet (1709), Jemappes (1792), Ligny (1815) and Le Cateau (1914). It can truly be said that the battlefield visitor has an embarrassment of riches from which to choose in this fascinating area.

Standing beside the curious tumulus known as the Tomb of Ottomonde, slightly to the rear of the wide plain between the villages of Ramillies and Taviers, the visitor to this beautiful spot is treated to one of the great battlefield vistas in the world, hardly changed over the years. The terrain, when looked at across the intervening, slightly undulating fields around the Tomb, can be seen to be quite flat, although rising gently to the north. On this marvellous wide stage, the tactically important watershed feature between the Mehaigne and Petite Gheete streams, a great cavalry battle was fought on Whit Sunday, 23 May 1706, perhaps involving 25,000 horsemen in all. That battle was lost by the French, leading immediately to the collapse of Marshal Villeroi's fine army and the rapid conquest of present-day Belgium by the Duke of Marlborough's victorious forces.

The view from the foot of the Tomb is deceptive, however, for the more broken ground beyond Ramillies to the north is hidden from sight; it is in dead ground, that oh-so dangerous space that should concern all commanders when choosing a spot from which to fight. In that dead ground, leading along the valley of the Petite Gheete stream and its minor tributaries to Offuz (Offus in modern usage) and Autre-Eglise, Marlborough chose to throw in his main infantry effort early in the battle. By doing so, he induced his less alert opponent to send infantry reinforcements northwards, away from the support of the French cavalry in the crucial battle on the plain to the south. These cavalry were the centre of gravity for the French and Bavarian army, and became exposed to the Duke's schemes. At the masterful height of his tactical powers, Marlborough adroitly switched his own main effort from the north to the south and commenced the ruthless destruction of the French squadrons from their weakened, and glaringly exposed, right flank.

The Ramillies battlefield is unencumbered with much of the modern debris – regimental markers, tourist trails and interpretative boards – that litters and spoils so many other battlefield sites. A small number of the now inevitable wind-farm-type windmills on the far horizon do not intrude on the scene very much. The villages of Taviers and Franquenée (Franquenay) in the south, and Ramillies, Offus and Autre-Eglise lying just to the north of the watershed between the Mehaigne and Petite Gheete, are, as can be expected, larger and more prosperous than in the early eighteenth century. Also, although the countryside is generally quite open and rolling, the scattered woods and copses are probably rather more numerous these days. The villages retain their individual characters, and many of the cottages and farms date back to the time of the battle; the visitor can get a good idea of the atmosphere of the area as it might have been in 1706 without too great an effort of imagination. Noticeably, in the south the vast big sky and big horizon expanse of the plain between Ramillies and Taviers has an air of quiet grandeur. The more broken country to the north of Ramillies has, by comparison, a rather closed in, almost constricted feel with deep sunken lanes and hedges, well suited to the visitor who wishes to picture the brutal infantry battles that raged for possession of the villages there.

The lie of the land of the Ramillies battlefield is not particularly complex, but there are some deceptive twists and hidden corners, and so a few moments' study of the map is recommended at the start (Institut National Geographique, No. 40, Wavre, 1:50,000 scale). This time and effort is well repaid. The only reason that Marlborough and Villeroi fought here at all was that the passage from east to west, or vice versa, was made difficult, if not actually impossible, by the many small, marshy rivers and streams in the area. The 2-kilometres-wide plain between the headwaters of the Petite Gheete around Ramillies and the bogs of the Mehaigne at Taviers to the south offered the firm ground and easy going so valuable to and eagerly sought by army commanders. The eminent British military historian Sir John Fortescue described the ground:

From the stream [the Mehaigne] the ground rises northwards in a steady wave for about half a mile, sinks gradually, and [then] rises into a higher wave at Ramillies, sinks once more to the northwards of that village and rolls downward in a gentler undulation to Autre-Eglise.

So, much of the southern part of the battlefield is well-drained ground, firm underfoot and ideal for horses and the passage of guns and wagons, an asset not easily found elsewhere in the region. Both the opposing commanders knew this; they had each scouted the area the previous year during the campaign that led to the forcing of the Lines of Brabant. This knowledge, inevitably it might seem, led them to Ramillies that Sunday in May; that was how the battle came to be fought there.

Looking at the topography from the map, it can be seen that the battlefield is situated at the highest point on the plains of Brabant. The fall in the ground towards the streams in the area, to both north and south, is quite pronounced, albeit gently shelving in places (particularly on the open ground to the south of Ramillies, which is, in effect, a plateau between the Petite Gheete and the Mehaigne) – hence the existence of the geographical watershed feature. The 'high' ground around Ramillies village is at about 150 to 155 metres above sea level, while the plateau of Jandrenouille to the east is only slightly lower, with just one elevated place on which to site guns. The ground to the west of the

Petite Gheete, the plateau of Mont St André, is undulating and rather higher in many places. So the expression 'ridge-line', which is often applied to accounts of the battle when describing the terrain between Ramillies, Offus and Autre-Eglise, can be a little misleading. It only ranks as such (and quite a modest feature it really is) by being made steep to the visitor who descends into the valley of the Petite Gheete stream when approaching the villages from the east. The stream valley drops in the north to less than 120 metres above sea level, while the Mehaigne at Taviers far to the south is about 140 metres above sea level.

A good starting place for the visitor to the Ramillies battlefield, whether travelling on foot or by car, is at the small hamlet of Boneffe on the N264 road (Point A on the adjoining map), just to the east of the plain on which the cavalry battle was fought. Colonel Wertmüller and his Dutch Guards formed up and stepped off from here in the opening clash of the afternoon. By looking to the north and the east, it is possible to get a good idea of the wide extent of the plateau of Jandrenouille, across which the Allied army came on its approach to battle. Open and fairly level, devoid of any major natural obstacles, this afforded an excellent forming-up area for the Duke of Marlborough when making his arrangements, the troops shaking out rapidly from line of march to column of attack in response to his urgent messages. The speed with which the Duke could do this left the French commander with little chance to change his mind and draw off to avoid battle (although, in fact, he showed no sign of actually intending to do so). A few kilometres to the east, just out of sight, the Allied troops had marched over the demolished Lines of Brabant, along which many of the soldiers would have remembered the fight at Elixheim the previous year.

From Boneffe, a few hundred metres along the farm track in a northerly direction is the Chausée Romaine (Roman Road), crossing from east to west. The church spire in Ramillies village can be clearly made out to the west (care is needed as Taviers, Ramillies, Offus and Autre-Eglise church spires and tower can all be seen at various points, and a compass is very handy to maintain true direction-finding on the wide plain). A glance to the left, back towards the N624 road will show the small hamlets of Franquenée and Taviers, where the Swiss and Wertmüller's Dutch fought such a desperate action – 'almost as bloody as the rest of the battle put together,' according to Colonel de la Colonie. Going onwards onto the plateau of Jandrenouille, to the 153-metre elevation feature (Point B) the visitor gets a fine view to the west of the Ramillies–Offus ridge-line, which was occupied by Villeroi's army. In this immediate area, making use of the relatively high ground on the otherwise gently rolling plateau, Marlborough established his great battery of 24-pounder guns with which to engage the French artillery around Ramillies.

By retracing the route to Boneffe, and going westwards along the N624, Franquenée is soon reached. The hamlet is still separated from Taviers by the water meadows of the Mehaigne stream and its tributary the Visoule (which rises near to the Tomb of Ottomonde), although these are largely drained now, but the reedy grass, the damp ground and a few willow trees give the game away. Go on to Taviers itself, pausing to consider the desperate battle at bayonet point that the Dutch Guards won there. Looking to the north (from Point C) towards Ramillies, it can be seen that artillery placed there could not support the Swiss garrison in Taviers and vice versa, although, if sited properly, a cross-fire of a kind might have been achieved to hamper the Allied cavalry as it advanced. In the event, with their lack of numbers in the opening exchanges and only a botched counter-attack to help them, the Swiss had little chance of holding the place. The determined attack put in by the Dutch veterans, backed up by light artillery, completely unhinged the right of the French line of battle at the very outset of the action and they never really recovered their tactical poise.

The visitor should then go from Taviers along to the crossroads junction of the N264 and the N991, turning to the north along the N991 towards the village of Ramillies itself. Within a few hundred metres the old Roman Road is crossed again. On the left is the wide rolling plain, still laid to arable crops as in 1706, over which de Guiscard's French cavalry were deployed to meet Overkirk's Dutch and Württemberg's Danish squadrons. It is so obviously perfect country for mounted action, a great open arena on which the commanders on both sides could exercise their troopers' skill to the utmost. The ground rises very gently from 148 metres above sea level to 155 metres on the plateau between the area around Ottomonde and Ramillies. Despite their lack of numbers and proper infantry support, the French cavalry put in a fine performance. It took a hard struggle before the Danes could slip past their right flank to the Tomb of Ottomonde (seen with its crown of trees in the distance) and turn to face the raw open flank of the French and Bavarian army, which was by then entirely off balance.

Going further northwards along the N991 (passing the Chemin de Marlborough on the way), the visitor soon comes to the centre of Ramillies itself. Alessandro Maffei's headquarters, La Haute Censée Farm (where the barn still shows signs of the musket-shot from the battle), is on the left-hand side, and soon the church is reached on the right (Point D). This rather plain building has a churchyard littered with some decrepit relics of the First World War. There is little obvious sign of the field of rye in which the Scots and French fought with such ferocity and where James Gardiner was shot and left for dead alongside the churchyard wall after losing the regimental colour. The walled graveyard now occupies that site, and is a good spot from which to consider the dispositions of the French and Bavarian armies, the arrangements they made for the defence of Ramillies, and to see the view that Villeroi's commanders had of the Allied army as it came on to battle in the morning sunshine across the plateau of Jandrenouille. It will be noticed from this spot, by reference to the map, that Autre-Eglise to the north (the left of Villeroi's line of battle) and Taviers to the south (the right of his line) both curl around the observer: the French line was an enormous arched formation, inconvenient for moving troops quickly from one flank to the other.

The houses in Ramillies village itself are larger than the mean cottages of the early eighteenth century would have been, but the general feel of the place makes it easy to imagine the desperate struggle as the Allied infantry tried and failed several times to break their way in, being repulsed on each occasion by the French garrison, aided by their Irish and German allies. Almost opposite the church is a lane that leads upwards to Offus and the plateau of Mont St André, and here Maffei made his stand with the German brigade before being taken prisoner by the Dutch cavalry.

Just on the northern edge of Ramillies there is a slight crest where the N991 bends to the right (Point E). Standing on that noticeably elevated verge gazing westwards, the visitor is looking across the valley of the Petite Gheete stream itself towards Offus – the church spire is plainly to be seen ahead – and the plateau of Mont St André. Slightly to the north it is just possible to see among the trees the tower (not a spire, unlike its neighbours) of the church in Autre-Eglise at the very end of Villeroi's line of battle. This is the area where the Elector of Bavaria massed his cavalry and infantry, and to which the French Marshal hurried his vital infantry reserves in response to the growing, but illusory, threat to his flank, a decision taken to the detriment of the cavalry battle on his right.

Before leaving the viewing point on the edge of the plateau of Jandrenouille, to the east the visitor can make out the slight re-entrant, partly screened by trees, formed by the headwaters of the small La Quivelette stream, which flows away to the north and its confluence with the Petite Gheete near to Autre-Eglise. This small fold in the ground, a very slight depression to the casual observer, was enough to hide from the view of Villeroi and his officers Marlborough's reinforcement of his strength in the centre and south of the battlefield, as he subtly shifted the weight of his attack from right to left. The farm by the stream (Point F) is reputedly the place where the Duke of Marlborough established his headquarters, although he spent most of the day on horseback supervising his commanders.

By walking down the slope into the valley on the other side of the N991 road, heading towards Fodia and the Petite Gheete itself, the visitor is following the route taken by Tom Kitcher and his red-coated comrades as they drove de la Guiche's brigade of Walloons away from the marshy stream (now a culverted watercourse lined with trees, and with little obvious sign of the marshes through which the Allied troops had to wade). A glance at the map will show that the valley drops quite markedly from 143 metres in elevation to about 125 metres in the space of only about 400 metres walked (Point G). So, the Petite Gheete stream valley, especially in the marshy conditions of the day, presented quite an obstacle, to infantry as well as to their mounted comrades. Tom Kitcher noted that the British cavalry and dragoons appeared to hang back in the opening attacks, and it is easy to see why, although they managed the passage of the stream in the end.

Leaving Fodia and walking up the sunken lane leading to Offus, within a few hundred metres the visitor arrives at a walled farmyard (typical of the region) on the edge of the village (Point H). Here, beside the farmhouse, it is possible to get a good view back across the Petite Gheete valley towards the Allied forming-up point, taking in the view that so fascinated the French Marshal and the Elector of Bavaria when they should have been attending to their increasingly fragile right flank. This is the ground held with such tenacity by the Walloon and French infantry under de la Guiche in the face of the ferocious British attacks sent in by Earl Orkney, who eventually managed to

Ramillies. Petite Gheete stream valley seen from Offus.

Ramillies. Looking northwards from Offus to Autre-Eglise. Orkney's British infantry attacked across this slope from right to left. Photograph taken 23 May 2006, the 300th anniversary of the battle.

force his way into Offus itself. Had he gone on, and not heeded Marlborough's command to return to the edge of the plateau of Jandrenouille, the Earl and his infantry would have been unsupported and under attack by the Elector's cavalry, who were massed on the ridge-line leading to Autre-Eglise in the north and the fields behind Ramillies to the south, following the general route of the modern N229 road.

At the end of the tour, go back south through Ramillies village, along the N991 to the Chausée Romaine. Turn right and head along this old Roman road across the plain to the Tomb of Ottomonde (Point J). It is probably not worth the effort to climb the feature, as the many trees on the summit obscure the view. However, the view from the base over the adjacent fields is terrific – looking to the north and east across the intervening shallow depressions towards the scene of the cavalry battle where de Guiscard's troopers fought all afternoon in their desperate, doomed action against the overwhelming Dutch and Danish squadrons of Overkirk and Württemberg. Away across those fields can be seen the cottages of Ramillies, with the church spire of Offus just discernible beyond. There Marlborough's subtle but devastating deceit was played on his opponent, obliging the French commander to reinforce the secondary operations in the north at the very moment that the more vital sector, on the edge of which the more fortunate present-day visitor now stands, came under most critical threat.

3. Oudenarde, 11 July 1709: Walking Oudenarde Battlefield

The scene of the Duke of Marlborough's most intuitive tactical achievement sits close alongside the much-enlarged and bustling town of Oudenarde. Modern development, residential estates, a no doubt greatly needed bypass and light industrial estates have covered over parts of the area of the deployment of the rival armies of 1708. The river Scheldt is now a channelled and straightened waterway rather than a meandering river making its gentle way between marshy water-meadows, while the once distinct villages of Eyne and Heurne, where the opening shots in the battle were fired, are now rather anonymous suburbs of Oudenarde itself, and show few, if any, marks of the battle.

However, despite this modern development, the battlefield of Oudenarde is still very rewarding and well worth the effort of a visit. It is possible to travel there from the UK in a single day, just about, but an early start is needed. The main features of this site of extraordinary action are still very evident. The wide Scheldt, one of the main waterways of western Europe, may have changed in character, but it is unmistakably a major obstacle to easy movement. To stand at the water's edge, near to Eyne, and to gaze at the willows fringing the river, it is not at all difficult to picture the scene as William Cadogan's engineers and pioneers laboured to lay their 'tin-boat' pontoon bridges that critical Wednesday morning in July. The confident, reckless audacity of Marlborough and his able Quartermaster-General – throwing their advanced guard across

Oudenarde. The Scheldt river crossing at Eyne, looking towards Oudenarde.

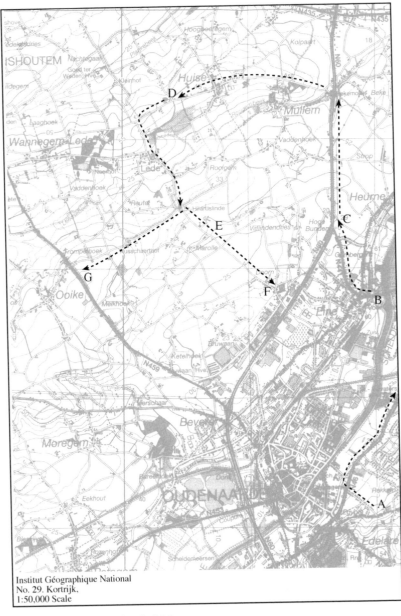

Institut Géographique National
No. 29. Kortrijk,
1:50,000 Scale

Guide to Oudenarde battlefield.

the wide river in this way, confronting the vastly more numerous French army, dragging it to a halt from the line of march, and forcing their unwilling opponents into a confusing battle that they neither sought or were prepared for – must command the greatest admiration.

Happily, the scene of most of the infantry fighting, the low-lying and heavily cultivated ground between the Ghent Road (roughly on the line of the modern bypass – the N60 road) and the higher ground at Huyshe to the north and near the village of Oycke to the west, is largely untouched by modern building. The nature of this area, neat houses and gardens, small copses of trees and quiet hedged lanes, seems to be very much as described by contemporary observers of the battle, good infantry country, no real room here for effective mounted action or the employment of massed artillery. The Marollebeek and Diepenbeek streams, along which much of the desperate struggle took place, are quite easy to identify. Even though both watercourses are more drained and less marshy than in 1708, they are in many places still quite an obstacle, requiring some modestly athletic leaping to get across with dry feet. They are, of course, just the sort of features that harassed infantry commanders might use as ready reference points for their troops to align themselves on in the dust and smoke of a rapidly unfolding battle. That the opposing battle-lines should form on these streams, with the troops hurrying breathlessly into position, was almost inevitable.

Standing on the very northern edge of the battlefield, on the high ground at Huyshe, the visitor gets a good view southwards, back across the undulating but generally low-lying ground towards Oudenarde. The steep slopes overlooking the Scheldt from the far bank at Eename, at an elevation above sea-level of about 75 metres, can be clearly seen on the horizon. The attractive tower of Oudenarde town hall is plainly visible, as are the spires of the several churches. It will immediately be noticed that much of the area over which the actual fighting took place is in dead ground to the observer. Always dangerous, this terrain is hidden from easy view by the several folds that lead gently, but progressively, down from the high ground to the banks of the Scheldt. Huyshe is at 50 metres elevation, nearby Lede is at 55 metres, while Rooigem (Royegem), slightly forward of the highest ground and actually where the Duke of Burgundy took up a position with his entourage and was able to see very little, is only at 35 metres. The Boser Couter to the west, near the village of Oycke, is at nearly 50 metres, while the site of Brouwaan chateau, on the right flank of the French battle-line, is at 25 metres. The lines of the Marollebeek and Diepenbeek streams drop to well below 20 metres along much of their length, while Oudenarde and the Scheldt riverbank, by comparison, are only 10 metres in elevation. This indicates very clearly the amphitheatre profile of the low ground, bounded on three sides by higher ground, and the 'rolling' nature of the battlefield, gentle but quite pronounced in places – anyone standing on the higher ground, as Burgundy and his entourage did, would have found it very difficult to see with any clarity what was going on while the Duc de Vendôme fought his lonely battle in the low-lying orchards and fields. A commander must get to where he can see what is happening, and Burgundy neglected to do so – his staff officers, who did not lack experience, were guilty of that same neglect.

The visitor to the Oudenarde battlefield is probably best to start the tour on the heights at Edelare-Eename (Point A on the accompanying map) which overlook the town, the river Scheldt and the battlefield beyond. Despite recent quite lush tree growth, it is relatively easy to pick a vantage point from where the salient features, Oudenarde town with its towers and spires, the wide river and, in the distance, the commanding high ground at Huyshe straight ahead and the rounded Boser Couter off to the left, can all be made out. Also, the crossing points over the Scheldt used by the French army, in the distance downstream at Gavre, can also be seen on a clear day by using binoculars.

After getting bearings with the aid of a map (Institut Geographique National No. 29, Kortrijk, 1:50,000 scale) and compass, the visitor should take one of several available roads down to the foot of the hill. Join the N46 road, which skirts the southern edge of Oudenarde, and turn to the right to go along the line of the river for a few hundred metres, before turning left onto the N441, signposted to Eine (Eyne), and the approaches to the road-bridge over the Scheldt. Turn onto the slip road on the right-hand side just before going onto the bridge itself to find a convenient open space in which to park (Point B). From here a very short walk leads to the river's edge, and by crossing underneath the bridge on the towpath, it is possible to get a very good view through the trees of Oudenarde to the west and the line of the river as it curves around towards the suburb of Heurne to the east. It was at about this point that William Cadogan and his advanced guard got across the Scheldt to drive Biron's Swiss infantry back, and established their bridgehead early in the afternoon of 11 July 1708. The character of the river has changed, of course, but the feel of the place seems just right, a good spot in which to get an understanding of the task that faced Cadogan that day and that would surely have daunted lesser men. An interesting feature of the bridge here at Eine is that it is dedicated (possibly when being rebuilt after the Second World War) to the American GIs who lost their lives fighting to secure the river crossing in 1944. The British 4th Armoured Brigade was also engaged just to the north of the town, but there is no commemorative marker.

There is not a great deal to see now in Eine or Heurne, so take the N441 northwards to the junction with the N60 (main road to Ghent), which is soon reached (Point C). By turning to the right, towards Ghent, the visitor can see the quite flat meadows between the road and the houses, across which Jorgen Rantzau's Hanoverian dragoons charged with such gusto to drive in the French cavalry flank guard. This action provoked Burgundy into his rash infantry attack without consulting Vendôme. However, modern development has covered enough of the area leading back to the river for it probably not to need further examination. After continuing to drive along the N60 for about 1 kilometre, take a turning to the left towards Huise (Huyshe) – do not go further on the N60 to the crossroads with the N435, as that is just a long way round to the same destination. It was, however, the track leading from Gavre to the higher ground on which the left Wing of the French army stood immobile all afternoon, without direction or orders while the battle was fought and lost.

Along the minor road, which gradually rises in elevation through a stand of trees, the village of Huise (Huyshe) is soon reached. Go straight through the small chicane in the village square (there are several pleasant cafés here in which the traveller can obtain refreshment), and move out onto the high ground of the ridge, which forms the northern rim of the amphitheatre in which the battle was fought. Beyond the houses of the village, a prominent windmill will soon be seen on the right (Point D), and from this point a fine view can be had across the battlefield to the Scheldt and the heights of Eename at which the tour started. This was the area that the French army had originally intended to occupy, from which to stand and defy Marlborough to attack, before they were drawn into an unplanned battle along the streams close to Oudenarde. Even with a pair of binoculars, a good modern map and a compass, and the customary advantages of an elevated viewpoint, it will immediately be found that it is not easy to make out the precise features of the area – how much more difficult, then, it must have been for the French, with the smoke of battle drifting across the low-lying country before them, and the hampering drizzle that came with the evening. Recently a row of Leylandii has been planted on the slope a few hundred metres ahead, which does not help observation at all.

Driving further towards Wannegem-Lede, noticing that the ground rises gently all the time, the visitor should turn to the left through the small hamlet of Lede and down into the more low-lying country between Huise and Oudenarde. The terrain is quite flat, if sloping, and the cottages and gardens give a good idea of the enclosed nature of the field over which the opposing infantry fought their battle. The Marollebeek stream, now a culverted water-course, will soon be crossed (Point E) as it runs away to the east to then swing southwards before its confluence with the Diepenbeek near to the Ghent road. Soon Doorn is reached, and just before the modern light industrial estates on the edge of Oudenarde, a small bridge takes the country road over the Diepenbeek stream itself (Point F). This was the area known in 1708 as Schaerken, an inn or public house (possibly a brothel), where the infantry fighting was at its most fierce. It is also a good spot to pause, as there is a very pleasant small restaurant here, where an excellent lunch can be had at the very edge of the stream. The visitor will notice that at this point the Diepenbeek is actually quite deep and represents quite an obstacle.

By retracing steps through Doorn to the country crossroads just beyond the Marollebeek, at a small roadside Calvary memorial (marked on the map as St Hilaruslinde), and turning to the left, the visitor will within a few minutes reach the N459 road which runs north to south (Point G). The village of Ooike (Oycke) is nearby, and this is the high ground of the Boser Couter, which forms the western rim of the battlefield. Across this low, rounded hill came Veldt-Marshal Overkirk with his corps of Dutch and Danish troops, after struggling free of the congestion in Oudenarde itself, to turn the right flank of Vendôme's Wing of the French army as it fought to hold the line of the Diepenbeek stream against the surging Allied attacks. From here it is possible to get a very good view across the low-lying battlefield, and by not glancing too much to the right towards the modern suburbs of Oudenarde, it is not that difficult to visualise the frantic scene and desperate fighting of that July day.

Finally, it is well worth the effort to drive into Oudenarde itself, despite the inevitable traffic congestion. The town hall and main square are both very picturesque and full of historic interest, and there are a number of attractive churches. There is also a good selection of shops, as well as plenty of bars and restaurants where the weary traveller can relax and enjoy a meal after a hard day marching over this fascinating battlefield.

Oudenarde. Looking from the Boser Couter hill towards the Diepenbeek and Marollebeek streams. Vendôme's infantry were trapped in this area.

4. Malplaquet, 11 September 1709: Walking Malplaquet Battlefield

The battlefield of Malplaquet is only about 15 kilometres to the south of Mons, and sits squarely on the border between France and Belgium. Malplaquet village itself is actually in the municipality of Taisnières-sur-Hon in northern France. The area is a watershed, with the ground running gently away to both north and south, and cut through with many small streams and gullies. This character is particularly pronounced on the Belgian side, where numerous small streams run northwards to the Trouille river, and the terrain there is rather lower than on the plateau on the French side. Even now, when modern drainage techniques have had their effect, a lot of the ground is wet and rather marshy in many places, and it is easy to see why so many contemporary accounts of the battle mention this difficulty in relation to both the movement of troops and the siting of the batteries of heavy guns. There has been relatively little modern development, and although the woods, which played such a prominent part in the battle, have been thinned out in places, the general outline of the copses today conforms fairly well with that of the early eighteenth century.

The names of the woods around Malplaquet have also changed somewhat, so care has to be taken when comparing modern maps with more contemporary documents and accounts. The gap between the Bois de Sars and the Bois de Lanières where much of the action took place is clearly marked though. The Triangle, scene of dreadful fighting, can easily be made out where the trees jut out into the open ground in distinctive fashion, and the Bois de Thiery, around which the Dutch infantry attack surged, is still quite prominent but has also been thinned out in part. Le Bleiron Farm, near which the French sited their deadly hidden batteries to fire along the small Bleiron stream, is an attractive group of buildings with a small commemorative plaque on a wall proclaiming that Marlborough stayed there the night after the battle. Also of particular interest are La Folie Farm and La Louvière Farm (where Marshal Villars slept before the action) on the French left, from where Villars conducted his desperate defence of that flank as Henry Withers's surprise attack came pounding in across the fields from the north-west.

Malplaquet is not a particularly complex battlefield; at about 5 kilometres across it is the smallest of the sites of Marlborough's great victories. It is, unfortunately no longer possible, as Winston Churchill did in the 1930s, to stroll about and find roundshot lying in the long grass, although the bit-boss of a horse bridle, possibly from one of Marlborough's troopers, was picked up by the author a few years ago at the side of a track on the Allied side of the battlefield.

The nature of the terrain means that an observer on one side of the watershed has no easy view of his counterpart in the dead ground on the other side. This

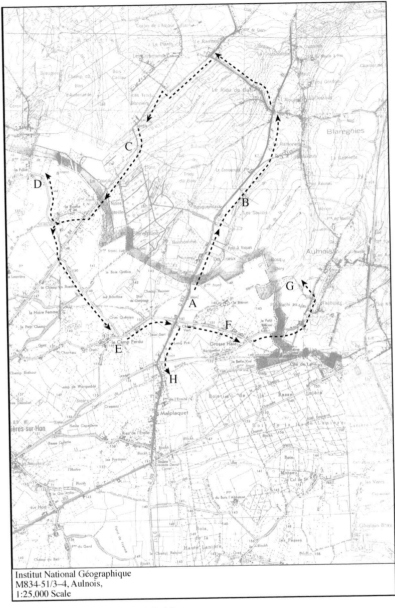

Institut National Géographique
M834-51/3–4, Aulnois,
1:25,000 Scale

Guide to Malplaquet battlefield.

lack of observation caused Villars to site his defensive redans well forward and squarely in the centre of the Gap of Aulnois, where they were exposed to a terrific artillery bombardment in the opening phase of Marlborough's attack. In addition, the 'overs', the roundshot that missed their target (as some inevitably did), then went skipping on across the open ground beyond the watershed and had a damaging effect on the massed French cavalry on the plain of Malplaquet to the south, who had no means to respond but had to endure throughout the long hours of the morning infantry battle.

As always, a good map is indispensable, and Institute National Geographique, M834-51/3-4 Aulnois, 1:25,000 scale gives all the detail required. The woods provide fairly useful reference points for orientation. In 1909, a monument was erected by the French beside the main road (now the D932) that runs north to south through the battlefield, to commemorate the 200th anniversary of Malplaquet. There is a well-known and rather charming photograph of tired but cheerful British soldiers of the BEF trudging past the monument during their withdrawal from Mons in 1914. The French like to think of Malplaquet as a victory, on the overly simple basis that their casualties were fewer than those of Marlborough and his allies. They are, of course, quite mistaken, and the monument is now slightly dilapidated. However, it does provide a very convenient and slightly elevated starting point for the visitor to this attractive battlefield to compare map and compass to ground and get proper bearings (Point A on the accompanying map). The monument is at about 150 metres elevation above sea-level. From this spot the open ground of the Gap of Aulnois is plainly visible to the north, just beyond the now disused customs post, and the flanking woods of the Bois de Sars and Bois de Lanières are plain to see. The smaller Bois de Thiery and Bleiron Farm are also visible to the north and east, while the slight ridge curving from the La Louvière Farm to La Folie Farm can be made out by looking to the north and north-west. This feature is at about 147 metres elevation, although further to the west it drops away to 140 metres or less. The open plain of Malplaquet, on which the great cavalry battle of the afternoon was fought, lies immediately to the south, rising gradually to about 154 metres, with the houses of the village itself in the distance. It will be noticed that the nearest house, at the crossroads beside the D932 road, near to Le Château Vert, has a rather naive but charming mural painted on the wall, depicting French soldiers in action circa 1709.

By driving north from the French monument, after a moment the Belgian border is crossed (no passport problems these days) and the battlefield visitor comes to a long straight stretch of road within a couple of hundred metres. Parking at the verge, with care – the traffic tends to be light but quite fast here (Point B), it is possible to get a good view of the woods to the west, which form the Triangle feature, part of the Bois de Sars. In this area, Marlborough

Malplaquet. Looking into the Bois de Sars triangle from the Allied side. Marlborough's great battery was sited near here.

established his great battery of forty heavy guns, and the view across the rather marshy ground to the tree-line can be seen to be open with good fields of fire. Looking southwards from here, back towards the customs-post, it is immediately apparent that the area around the French monument, and the plain of Malplaquet itself, is in dead ground to the observer. There is no obvious sign now of the French redans, as years of ploughing has obliterated any real trace of them. Before moving on, the visitor should look closely at the ground on either side of the road. The fields are quite marshy with many small gullies and ditches, which are much more pronounced here than on the rather firmer ground to the south where the French army deployed. It is easy to see why the Allied commanders had trouble getting their heavy and cumbersome artillery pieces into position.

By driving further north, within a kilometre or so a crossroads is reached. Turn left here and follow the small paved road to a T-junction, turning left again towards the village of Sar le Bruyère (from which the wood takes its name). This road takes the visitor alongside the Bois de Sars (marked on some maps as the Bois du Temple). At the entrance to the woods (Point C) there is almost immediately a sharp left turn, near to which is a poignant memorial to a young French officer who was killed in the First World War. Park near to here, and take the opportunity to walk a little way into the woods. (These are mostly privately owned, and care must be taken not to trespass.) The atmosphere is closed in, quite claustrophobic, and even though the defenders in 1709 had cleared fields of fire, there would have been little visibility beyond a few dozen metres. This gives a very good idea of what the conditions must have been like for Eugene's infantry as they forced their way at such heavy cost through the three lines of French defences in these copses.

Going further on, the battlefield visitor soon comes clear of the woods on the very straight D84 road, travelling in the general area of La Ruelle Farm. The first turning on the right soon leads to La Folie Farm, close to where Withers's troops emerged from the western edge of the tree-line of the Bois de Sars to turn the left flank of the French army, which was still struggling to hold back Eugene's attacks (Point D). The low ridge-line, stretching along the 145-metre contour-line, takes a long curve to the west towards La Louvière Farm, and is the position held by Villars's troops, who had been hastily redeployed from the centre to hold back this surprise attack. Head back towards La Ruelle and then turn to the right; within a few hundred metres a left turning leads to Le Camp Perdu (Point E). By following the road round to the left, past a commemorative marker near to the spot where Villars was shot and wounded, the crossroads is soon reached at Le Château Vert on the main D932 road just to the south of the French monument.

Malplaquet. Looking towards the Bois de Thiery from the French positions in the Bois de Lanières.

In this way the visitor will have covered the entire area of the Allied right and the French left in the battle, and by going straight over the crossroads on the D932 will have traversed the general line of Villars's defences. Soon a black marble monument on the left-hand side of the road will be seen (Point F). This was erected quite recently, and commemorates the Swiss soldiers, of both armies, who fought in the battle. At the T-junction turn to the left towards Le Petite Bleiron, and a belt of woods stretching on both sides of the road will soon be reached – this is the most northerly part of the remaining Bois de Lanières, some of which has been felled over the years (the bulk of the woodland is now to the south), where d'Artagnan's infantry held back the Dutch attacks. The small but distinctive copse of the Bois de Thiery can be clearly seen to the north, as can Le Bleiron Farm to the left. By going on a little further towards Aulnois, and taking the first turning on the left, the visitor soon reaches a small stream known as the Rau de Bleiron (Point G). Le Bleiron Farm can be seen to the left, and it was along this re-entrant, dropping from 150 to 145 metres elevation along its length, that the French gunners sited their pieces so well and did such damage to Orange's attacking Dutch and Danish infantry as they moved towards the French breastworks in the Bois de Lanières.

The battlefield visitor should then retrace their steps to the Le Château Vert on the D932 road, and by turning to the left, drive southwards for a few hundred metres or so (Point H). This area is the 2,000-metres-wide plain of Malplaquet, where the French squadrons were massed, and where they suffered all morning from the effects of the Allied bombardment. Here, too, the great cavalry battle swirled around that September afternoon as the French tried repeatedly, but ultimately in vain, to throw the Allies back through the Gap of Aulnois. The wide, open terrain is still under cultivation and obviously well suited to cavalry action; like the rest of the battlefield, it has been little affected by modern development. To the south and west, beyond the villages of Tasnières sur Hon, and Hon-Hergies, is the small Hogneau stream, which the French army had some difficulty in crossing in their withdrawal from the field of battle, as was described by Jean-Martin de la Colonie. Had the Allied army not been so exhausted by the struggle that day, they might have turned this movement across the marshy water obstacle into a rout.

Finally, the battlefield visitor looking for refreshment may choose either Mons to the north or Bavay to the south, both only a few kilometres away and well supplied with bars and restaurants. The author has found the Le Bourgogne restaurant in Bavay a very pleasant place to get refreshment after a day on the battlefield. In addition, there is an interesting small museum in the town, dedicated to the '11th September Battle', which is well worth a visit. The address is Rue des Juifs, 6, 59570, Bavay, and opening times during April to November are 9am to 6pm. There is a small entrance fee for adults.

Bibliography

The distinguished military career of the 1st Duke of Marlborough has often been recounted, not least by his eminent descendant Sir Winston Churchill, whose monumental work, *Marlborough His Life and Times* was published in the 1930s. All the richness of Churchill's use of language is brought fully into play in this fine work, but it is well to remember that he had a distinct tendency to admire Marlborough's good qualities no matter what, and was sometimes wilfully blind to his occasional failings. The immensely valuable, voluminous *Letters and Dispatches of the Duke of Marlborough*, found by chance in the 1840s, and collected and edited by General Sir George Murray, are an indispensable contemporary resource. They do not often include the correspondence that the Duke was replying to, so only one half of the picture is seen, but it is a vivid picture. Copies are scarce, but are well worth the effort to find.

It seems rather odd that so significant a battle as Ramillies, in particular, should have received such little attention by authors, to the degree that until very recently only one published work, listed below, had so far been devoted to it. The astonishing events of the day and the immediate consequences of the battle were so far-reaching that it appears they almost have to speak for themselves, without any evident parallel in military history. Such eminent authors as Churchill, Frank Taylor and David Chandler had, of course, devoted extensive chapters to the action in their valuable works on the campaigns of the Duke of Marlborough. Now, the impishly named Bringfield's Head Press has published a very attractive and readable commemorative anthology of essays, poems and prose to mark the 300th anniversary of the battle, and this is also listed below.

JSAHR – Journal of the Society of Army Historical Research.

Alison, A., *The Military Life of John, Duke of Marlborough*, 1848
Atkinson, C.T., *Marlborough and the Rise of the British Army*, 1921
Atkinson, C.T., (ed.), 'Gleanings from the Cathcart Mss', *JSAHR*, 1951
Atkinson, C.T., 'Wynendael', *JSAHR*, 1956
Atkinson, C.T., 'Ramillies Battlefield', *JSAHR*, 1960
Barnett, C., *Marlborough*, 1974
Belfield, E., *Oudenarde, 1708*, 1972
Belloc, H., *The Strategy and Tactics of the Great Duke of Marlborough*, 1933
Bishop, M., *Life and Adventures, 1701–1711*, 1744
Bowen, H., 'The Dutch at Malplaquet', *JSAHR*, 1962
Burn, W., 'A Scots Fusilier and Dragoon under Marlborough', *JSAHR*, 1936
Burns, A., 'The Malplaquet Battlefield', *Royal Artillery Journal*, 1933
Burrell, S., (ed.), *Amiable Renegade, Memoirs of Captain Peter Drake*, 1960
Chandler, D., (ed.), *Captain Robert Parker and Comte de Merode-Westerloo*, 1968
Chandler, D., *Marlborough as Military Commander*, 1973
Chandler, D., *The Art of Warfare in the Age of Marlborough*, 1976
Chandler, D., (ed.), 'Journal of John Deane', *JSAHR*, 1984
Churchill, W.S., *Marlborough, His Life and Times*, (two book reprint edition) 1947
Corvisier, A., *La Bataille de Malplaquet*, 1997
Coxe, W., *Memoirs of John, Duke of Marlborough*, 1848
Cronin, V., *Louis XIV*, 1964
Dalton, C., *The Blenheim Roll*, 2006 (reprint edition)
Dickson, P., *Red John of the Battles*, 1973
Falkner, J., *Great and Glorious Days*, 2002
Falkner, J., *Blenheim, 1704, Marlborough's Greatest Victory*, 2004
Falkner, J., *Marlborough's Wars: Eye Witness Accounts*, 2005
Falkner, J., *Ramillies 1706, Year of Miracles*, 2006
Falkner, J., *Marlborough's Sieges, 1702–1711*, 2007
Falkner, J., *Oxford Dictionary of National Biography*, 2004, entries for: Arnold
    Joost van Keppel, 1st Earl Albemarle; William, 1st Earl Cadogan; Colonel
    James Gardiner; Captain Robert Parker
Fortescue, J., *History of the British Army*, vol. I, 1899
Fortescue, J., (ed.), *Life and Adventures of Mrs Christian Davies (Mother Ross)*, 1929
Hamilton, G., (Orkney), 'Letters of 1st Earl Orkney', *English Historical Review*,
    1904
Hatton, R., *Louis XIV*, 1972
Henderson, N., *Prince Eugen of Savoy*, 1964
Horsley, W., (ed.), *Chronicles of an Old Campaigner*, 1904
Johnston, S., (ed.), 'Letters of Samuel Noyes, 1702–1704', *JSAHR*, 1959

Kane, R., *Campaigns of King William and Queen Anne*, 1745
Langallerie, M., *Memoires*, 1710
Lediard, T., *Life of John, Duke of Marlborough*, 1736
Mcbane, D., *The Expert Swordsman's Companion*, 1728
Millner, J., *A Compendious Journal, 1702–1711*, 1733
Money, D., (ed.), *Ramillies, 1706, A Commemoration in Prose and Verse*, 2006
Murray, G., (ed.), *Letters and Dispatches of the Duke of Marlborough*, 1845
Nosworthy, B., *The Anatomy of Victory*, 1992
Petrie, C., *The Marshal, Duke of Berwick*, 1953
Sautai, M., *La Bataille de Malplaquet*, 1910
Scouller, R., *The Armies of Queen Anne*, 1966
St John, B., (ed.), *Memoirs of the Duc de St Simon*, 1876
Sturgill, C., *Marshal Villars and the Spanish Succession War*, 1965
Swift, J., *The Conduct of the Allies*, 1711
Taylor, F., *The Wars of Marlborough, 1702–1709*, 1921
Tindal, N., *Continuation of Rapin's History of England*, 1738
Trevelyan, G., *Select Documents for Queen Anne's Reign*, 1929
Trevelyan, G., *Blenheim*, 1930
Trevelyan, G., *Ramillies and the Union with Scotland*, 1932
Trevelyan, G., *Peace, and the Protestant Succession*, 1934
Verney, P., *The Battle of Blenheim*, 1976
Weygand, M., *Histoire de l'Armée Française*, 1938

Index